Finding Utopia

Finding Utopia

Another Journey into Lost Ohio

Randy McNutt

Black Squirrel Books™
Kent, Ohio

For John Lowery Jr.

© 2012 by The Kent State University Press, Kent, Ohio 44242

ALL RIGHTS RESERVED
ISBN 978-1-60635-131-4
Manufactured in the United States of America

 BLACK SQUIRREL BOOKS™
Frisky, industrious black squirrels are a familiar sight on the Kent State University campus and the inspiration for Black Squirrel Books™, a trade imprint of The Kent State University Press.
www.kentstateuniversitypress.com

Cataloging information for this title is available at the Library of Congress.

16 15 14 13 12   5 4 3 2 1

Contents

Introduction: Moving On   1

Part One: Big Dreams, Small Places
  1   Finding Utopia   11
  2   The Pull of Magnetic Springs   24
  3   In Search of the Believers   35
  4   Autumn at SunWatch   47
  5   Knights of Shawnee   53

Part Two: Lost Legends
  6   Army of the Damned   69
  7   A Village of Bones   84
  8   The Road to Fort Laurens   100

Part Three: Back Roads
  9   Freedom's Towns   109
  10 Colors of Tranquility   124
  11 The Legacy of Edward McClain   136
  12 Ghosts of Rogues' Hollow   141
  13 Confederates on the Island   148

Part Four: Ghosts of the Stage Lines
  14 The Wickerham Secret   161
  15 Riding the Line   174
  16 Major Buxton, I Presume   188

Part Five: Vanishing Places
17 Ammo Towns   199
18 Phoneton Calling   205
19 Freezing on the Underground   210
20 Above the Fruited Bog   218
21 Camp Sherman of the Mounds   224

Ghost Town: The Naming of Ohio   232
Bibliography   245
Index   250

Introduction: Moving On

> A place belongs forever to whoever claims it hardest, remembers it most obsessively, wrenches it from itself, shapes it, renders it, loves it so radically that he remembers it in his image.
> —*Joan Didion*, "In the Islands"

One steamy August morning I returned to the house where I grew up to clean out the garage. Knowing it would be a backbreaking, heartbreaking job, I had postponed it—once, twice, even three times. It was the final step in preparing the little yellow Cape Cod for sale.

I would have preferred to hire a junk removal company, but the place—the contents—meant too much to just turn it over to strangers. When I said this to a friend who also grew up in the neighborhood but now lives out of town, he said, "Really now, who cares?"

I did. That was the problem.

While I worked at sorting through things and packing up boxes, images of my family's past rolled and flickered in my head, much like a surreal film. I saw my late father, who struggled to buy the place in 1956, wrestling a bed frame through the front door and then, twenty years later, my newly widowed mother being consoled by friends and family in the small living room.

Two years after my mother's death, in 1997, my wife and I moved into the house. Being there gave me a deeper connection to my parents than I had felt in my younger years. I better understood all that they had endured.

On winter days, the drafty house comforted me like a warm blanket. From its back windows I could see Pierce Elementary School, where I had spent four pleasant years of my childhood. The building's continued presence—right there before me, all day long—reassured me that our friendly neighborhood wasn't changing, despite what reality had been whispering in my ear.

Once a prosperous working-class neighborhood of Hamilton, Lindenwald became my family's harbor of safety. We knew every family on our block and many on the other blocks. It was the quintessential American neighborhood, a small town within a city, and Pierce School was its focal point. The 1920s school, which my mother attended for a couple of years, offered space for community meetings and athletics programs for local kids.

Months after we moved into my boyhood home, my mind started mixing childhood memories—of the school, of the neighbors—with the present. By then, Pierce had become a little weathered but still proud. Before retiring to bed every night, I'd look out at it like a sailor does the North Star. In frigid weather, the warm glow of its lighted classrooms always comforted me. I felt confident knowing that the school and its neighborhood had survived the Great Depression, the cold war, and the personal tragedies of my parents and neighbors. With the school serving as a backdrop, I'd write at a little desk in my office (my sister's old bedroom), pausing every fifteen minutes or so to glance out the window onto my backyard and Pierce, two blocks away. There was always a memory to see out there—like the time my friend Tom, a paperboy, smacked me with a rolled-up *Cincinnati Post* and broke my little finger on our way home from school.

Now, decades on, the *Post* is gone, Tom is retired and living in New Mexico, and Pierce is closed. A senior living complex could replace it—appropriately, I suppose, as my baby boomer generation ages.

I pondered these things as I roasted in the frame garage—a vengeful oven filled with the day's heat and humidity. I worked mostly alone, sifting through treasures that had been buried in the loft for decades. I rejected offers to help. After all, only I could know that a dusty wooden kite box must be saved for my high school friend, Larry, and that a broken Zorro sword—aren't they all broken?—is a piece of pop culture history.

I understood that the price of moving is your life—you throw it away, piece after piece, while you relive times long forgotten. You can't help but think of your family. The years go by quickly, like chapters in a forgotten novel. They are not all pleasant. A place belongs forever to whoever claims it hardest, remembers it most obsessively . . .

As I stood listlessly in the sweltering garage, looking out at the driveway, in my mind's eye I could see a red-haired boy slugging a Wiffle ball and running baselines chalked onto a newly blacktopped street. Over the cheering of young teammates I could hear the familiar tick, tick, tick—the white plastic ball bouncing across the hard surface. The sound echoed through my mind as the ball rolled past the fielders and into Mr. Martin's driveway and infinity.

This occurred on our little patch of planet: a small postwar subdivision in an old neighborhood where my mother, my two aunts, my maternal grandparents, my great-grandparents, and others once lived, dating back to the late 1800s.

In 1996, Lindenwald and its people became a chapter in my book *Ghosts*. The neighborhood was, after all, a ghost of Ohio's past and a critical part of Hamilton's present. Fourteen years later, after debating the matter for months, I finally decided to leave because things weren't the same—not even close. My street had begun to feel like somebody else's. Who are all these people? Too many newer residents, often renters, shared neither my passion for the neighborhood nor a modicum of common sense.

Despite this, moving was still difficult. The neighborhood's collection of aging trees had always comforted me—my bit of permanence in an impermanent universe. On a walk around a half-dozen blocks, I could see all kinds of trees, architecture (including 1920s bungalows with cherry banisters and mudrooms), and, of course, the ubiquitous Cape Cods. When I walked down the street, I could at once see many homes, their histories, and their people—past and present. In Lindenwald, I always knew what was and what is. I liked that. Sometimes I'd glimpse the long ago, peripheral images that ran through my mind. I saw my friend Michael Cahalane walking with me along the railroad tracks as we solved the world's problems in a less complicated time. This was before he left for Vietnam, a war from which the heroic Marine did not return. I could also see my aunt and uncle, who lived two blocks away, working in their yard, flowers blooming everywhere. In my mind my aunt greeted me with a hug while my uncle watered his dahlias.

As I cleared out the garage on that August afternoon, wiping my face and daydreaming of past victories on the blacktopped ball field, an unfamiliar woman walked up the driveway. Her mouth was moving, but I could not hear her until I snapped back into reality. She was saying something about the house being attractive; she was assuring me that it would sell even in a weak sales market. But I didn't hear her at first. Suddenly I realized she was someone else's real estate agent. "Don't worry about cutting the grass," she was saying with a smile. "My client won't mind. He'll be coming by here this evening—if you don't mind."

I tried to smile. I thought, Strangers in our house?

As her late-model Japanese sedan pulled away from the curb, I needed a break—in more ways than one. Inside the house, I sat on a metal folding chair in an empty beige living room. Slowly I scanned the four walls.

"Mom," I said aloud, "I'm going to miss the old house." My voice echoed as it struck the bare hardwood floor. The emptiness of the room—of the moment—bothered me. I'd never seen the house so bare.

Resuming my personal archaeological dig in the garage, I sorted through the musty artifacts of my past. One after the other, they came and went—thin cardboard vacation signs my father had brought home, including the ubiquitous "See Rock City"; old family pictures, their colors faded now; schoolwork with my first grader's handwriting; my old red sled; an Australian Wobble board (used in the early 1960s hit record "Tie Me Kangaroo Down, Sport"); a dusty cowboy gun called a Buntline Special; a Davy Crockett book; and so many other things that I hadn't seen in years.

I descended the stepladder, turned, and focused on dark pencil marks scribbled on the white door jam, in my elderly uncle's hand: "Roof on, '98; siding, 1988, AC '01."

Moments later I heard the cackle of a middle-aged neighbor. She asked if I needed help. She didn't wait for my answer. Hoisting a crammed metal garbage can as if it were made of balsa wood, she lumbered toward the curb. With a grunt she slammed it to the sidewalk like a wrestler heaving his opponent to the mat. "Get it on!" she bellowed, grinning like a wild woman. Built like a basketball, she went braless, wore a bandana and tank top, sipped a warm can of beer, cursed and laughed constantly, and called me "baby."

"I'll prepare the house for sale," I told her solemnly, "but that might take some time. I might need some cleanup help later."

She looked me over, then said softy, "So tell me the truth: What do you really think about leaving?"

I just sighed.

"I know, baby," she said, gently patting my shoulder. "I know."

. . .

Two months later, my wife and I were settled into another house in another part of the city. The new neighborhood didn't feel right to me yet, but she liked it. I felt restless.

On an unseasonably warm day, I called my mechanic on a whim.

"Roger, do you have time to tow my Jeep?"

"You stranded?"

"Well, not on the highway."

It was getting late in the year to start another journey, I knew, but something nudged me. Perhaps it was the pleasant air, or maybe the changing leaves. Whatever the reason, I wanted him to make my Jeep Wrangler roadworthy again. The last time I drove it, a good eight months earlier, the brakes had gone out about a block from my house. Soon after, the battery died. Since then, the Jeep had been waiting patiently—begging me to prepare it for another trip into the Ohio countryside.

Three days and $800 later, I picked up the Jeep. A mechanic asked, "Well, was it worth it?" I assumed his question was rhetorical. I'm sure he would have been surprised to hear me say no, for he knew the Jeep was special. Although equipped with a sometimes-cranky driver and a crankier carburetor, the old Jeep had been a most agreeable road companion for me. In 2001, I bought the used Sahara model to replace my old American Motors Eagle, a four-wheel drive touring car that I'd used on trips while working on *Ghosts*. In 2006, I took the Jeep on my travels for *Lost Ohio*. And now I planned to take it again, although this time only on shorter trips. A car—and smoother ride—would be better for the longer rides.

After writing the two other books with the same theme—the loss of Ohio's small-town roots and its cultural identity—I started this one with a different attitude. No longer did I mourn the loss of something good. I knew that it would not be coming back.

No, this time it would be different. State financial crisis notwithstanding, it seemed everything was changing. I'd read a newspaper story titled "Tiny Towns May Be an Endangered Species." In it I learned that Ohio and other states were considering closing some small towns and townships to save money. To do the job, Ohio's governor suggested creating something like a federal Base Closure and Realignment Commission. There were plenty of towns to consider. According to the U.S. Census Bureau, Ohio had 3,700 local governments, including one village with only twenty-seven residents. Finally, the legacy of the nineteenth century was about ready to smash head-on into the twenty-first century.

The problem was, these communities were so much more than lines on a government report.

When I went traveling this time, I remembered what historic preservationist Mary O'Driscoll of Montgomery had told me while looking at an old church's pew. I told her that I could see a faint line running down the middle of it, indicating where a dividing board once had been attached. She said, "In our trade, a faded image is called a ghost. To a preservationist, a ghost means evidence of something that used to be there."

And that's what this book is all about—something that used to be there. A ghost.

It is also a book about personal change. As I prepared for my trips, I was concurrently still unpacking cardboard boxes in our newly acquired house in Hamilton. It wasn't easy leaving Lindenwald, but I knew that times change and that memories don't. In time, I understood that all kinds of people—in small towns, big cities, rural townships, urban neighborhoods, and everything else in between—were also doing what I had done in Lindenwald and in my family home. Faded images—that old something that used to be there—were crowding their lives.

Soon I was again traveling through Ohio in search of more forgotten places.

For some reason, finding them made me feel better about my changing old neighborhood, the move, and the loss of a part of my own past. Out wandering the back roads again, I felt at ease with past and present. I saw more unknown towns, layered in history, still waiting to be rediscovered. I thought of unknown people who once called these towns home, and I remembered the older people I once knew growing up in Lindenwald.

Times change. Memories don't.

For now, though, I will celebrate what remains of Lost Ohio—ghost towns, fascinating characters (past and present), historic battlefields, moonshine hideaways, and anything else that catches my attention. And uncovering them will make this book a tribute to Ohio and the sturdy pioneers who tamed it.

After all, "A place belongs forever to whoever . . . loves it so radically that he remembers it in his image."

Facing page: A 1930s Ohio auto brochure helped motorists find Buckeye points of interest. (Author's collection)

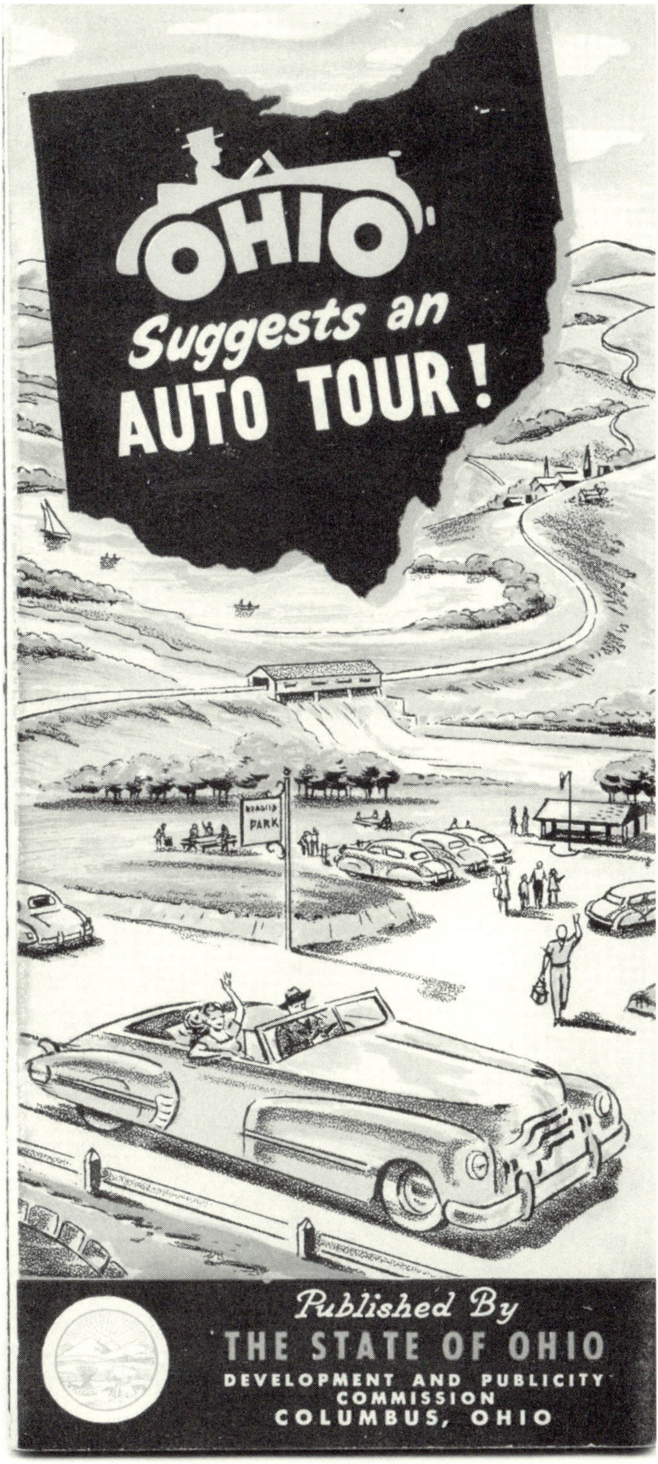

OHIO Suggests an AUTO TOUR!

Published By
THE STATE OF OHIO
DEVELOPMENT AND PUBLICITY
COMMISSION
COLUMBUS, OHIO

I

Big Dreams, Small Places

1

Finding Utopia

> The most fatal element of confusion, oppression, and violence ever introduced among mankind is the passing off of metals or any other natural product of the earth, or the earth itself[,] as pay for labor! . . . This is the origin of all forms of slavery, in all civilized countries, and of all poverty and crime.
> —*Josiah Warren, 1827*

Heading east along the Ohio River one gloomy afternoon, I stared into the March mist and tried to see a small town built on dreams and lemonade—Utopia. But the drowsy community was cloaked in gray. Everything around it was cold and bleak. Looking at the land along the banks, I recalled Joseph Conrad's words: "Going up that river was like traveling back to the earliest beginnings of the world, when vegetation rioted on earth and the big trees were kings."

In the 1800s, Utopia was a refuge for Ohio's original renegades—vegetarians, radical abolitionists, suffrage and animal-rights advocates, malcontents, and workers whose livelihoods were threatened by the Industrial Revolution. As I walked around the place, looking for its lost dreams, I empathized with the Utopian fear of technological change. I wondered why so few other "perfect" places exist today, when we feel squeezed by big business, declining values, increasing crime, global trade, burgeoning technology, and the outsourcing of jobs. I suppose every idea has its time.

Neither crime nor industry intruded when the town that's now called Utopia was founded in 1844. In those days, riverboat smokestacks belched black soot on neighboring small towns like Chilo, Moscow, and

New Richmond, all hunched along the river's bank. Today, the churning of paddle wheels has given way to the humming of rubber on the highway, though only a few visitors bother to stop in Utopia.

What is this town?
We think it's utopia.
Don't you know?
Yep. We do.

Unlike its neighbors, Utopia seems enveloped in a protective cocoon. No matter how many new subdivisions appear across suburban Clermont County, it remains unaffected. The town seems destined to remain just about as it was 150 years ago, for history's sake. But it is now merely a ghost town on U.S. Route 52—a dozen houses, barns, trailers, and the Village Market. But below the surface, secrets of communes and spirits wait to be rediscovered.

In the first half of the nineteenth century, when working and living conditions were harsh, communal societies like Utopia were established across America. Some were religious in nature, others economic. During the Panic of 1819 and the depression of the early 1820s, laborers' wages decreased and the number of available jobs declined. Some people looked to wealthy men with strange plans for a new life in commune towns. To the average family, communal life must have seemed radically different. Most groups divided their profits among all members while suppressing individual initiative. Prospective members retreated from the nation's social and political turmoil, and the agrarian past seemed a good way out. Communal societies offered economic security.

Intellectual reformers such as Scotsman Robert Owen, George Ripley, and Frenchman Charles Fourier developed their own ideas for communal societies. Segregated from the changing world, such towns protected residents from the injustices of the workplace—unfair competition, mechanization, and unscrupulous factory owners. In 1824, Owen helped establish what would become one of America's earliest and most famous communal societies, New Harmony in Indiana. In January 1826, its residents adopted a constitution that called for production without human turmoil. Owen wanted to change society "from the ignorant, selfish system, to an enlightened social system, which shall gradually unite all interests into one, and remove all cause for contest among individuals." In short, he wanted to change human behavior. No more coveting a neighbor's belongings. No more selfish acts. Everyone would work for the betterment of the socialist community to create a "New Moral World" that would allow New Harmony's people to escape society's harsh working conditions and corruption. To accomplish this, Owen believed he had to eliminate social classes. By 1827, however, his experiment was dead—the victim of its own members' laziness, self-interests, lofty ideals, and nebulous theories.

Of the dozens of different kinds of communes, the ones inspired by Fourier were most closely connected to nature. His followers wanted to restore the natural harmony of all living things by establishing phalanxes, or local groups that created their own communes. Some six years after Fourier died in 1837, nineteen Fourierist phalanxes were operating in the United States. They represented half of the nation's thirty-six reformist communities, most of them located in the Ohio and Mississippi river valleys and the Great Lakes region.

In Cincinnati, Fourier's ideas found eager supporters, including Dayton reformers Josiah Warren and Dr. J. Radcliffe. Their followers formed the Cincinnati Phalanx and planned a community on the Ohio River about thirty miles east of the city. (Later, the group called itself the Clermont Phalanx.) Radcliffe claimed that the new association "was not a mere scheme, like that of Owen's Indiana community or a Shaker society, but that it was a science—a stupendous science, far reaching, and ascending to the Most High, unfolding the laws of Divine order which reign throughout the Universe, and, at the same time descending and embracing the most lowly, the most humble things of creation." He used a blend of scientific, religious, and metaphysical language when talking about "the laws of attraction and repulsion, which hold in their respective orbits the vast number of Globes which compose the material Universe." He added, "'The music of the spheres' ... make one by correspondence with those of passional attraction and repulsion, which form and preserve the harmony of angelic societies of the blessed in heaven, and which, when understood and obeyed by men on earth, will produce the harmony of heaven in human society."

Encouraged by such wordy concepts, the Fourierite Association of Clermont County purchased 1,140 acres for a commune and farm along the Ohio in Franklin Township. The group was originally composed of twelve eastern families who wanted to move to the rural area along the river.

Warren, who once published a book called *The Peaceful Revolutionist,* supported the project but remained skeptical. He preferred what he called the equity commerce method, which would allow members to own some property. Because the new Clermont Phalanx would lack private ownership, Warren predicted that it would fail within three years. He determined this by observing other American communal towns, most of them unsuccessful. He knew what it would take to make one work—personal financial incentive. He espoused "the sovereignty of every individual over his or her Person, Time, Property, and Responsibilities; and here I add Reputation."

Always a dreamer, Fourier believed the world would soon enter a 35,000-year period of peace, and people would organize into phalanxes, each with three square miles of farmland complete with living quarters, a library, stables, and dining halls.

Two years before another communal society would be formed in Oneida, New York, Fourier's advance group chartered a steamboat in Cincinnati and headed upriver to Clermont County. On May 9, 1844, these followers—socialists, as their detractors called them—arrived full of hope and expectation. Residents occupied a newly built brick building with thirty rooms and wooden dining halls. They felt confidence in their leaders, their ideals, and their future. Member A. J. Macdonald recalled the initial event that would foreshadow the commune's demise:

> There were about 130 of us. The weather was beautiful, but cool, and the scenery on the river was splendid in its spring dress. The various parties brought their provisions with them, and toward noon the whole of it was collected and spread upon the table by the waiters, for all to have an equal chance. But alas for equality! On the meal being ready, a rush was made into the cabin, and in a few minutes more the provisions had all disappeared, and many persons who were not in the first rush, had to go hungry. I lost my dinner that day; but improved the opportunity to observe and criticise the ferocity of the Fourieristic appetite.

On July 4, a second group of members arrived from Cincinnati. They sang, read Bible verses, danced, and marched into one of the newly constructed buildings on the property. Again, Macdonald felt uneasy:

> It was at once apparent that the persons living there were in circumstances inferior to what they had been used to; and were enduring it well, while the enthusiastic spirit held out. But it seldom lasts long. . . . This Association had been on the ground only a few months; but I was told that disagreements had already commenced. The persons brought

together were strangers to each other, of many different trades and habits, and discord was the result, as might have been anticipated.

In its first year, the Clermont Phalanx claimed to have paid $3,000 of its $20,000 debt and built a sawmill, a gristmill, and craft shops. Members planted orchards and wheat fields. Yet, by the fall of 1846, the group had all but given up on the project as well as paying its mounting debt. In the end, the experiment died because of the toll of persistent flooding, jealousy, and "the want of means and the want of men," Macdonald wrote later. When progress refused to stop and the Fourierite Association's finances declined, group members fought over the things the rest of us quarrel over—money and power. Most members returned to the city, but a few did remain on the farm.

That's when reformer Josiah Warren stepped in. In June 1847, he traveled up the Ohio to the commune and met Daniel Prescott, who led one of the community's remaining six families. Prescott greeted him, saying, "Well, we have failed just as you foretold; it worked exactly as you said it would, and if you had been a prophet you could not have told more accurately what would happen. Now I am ready for your method."

So began Warren's dream of restarting the Clermont Phalanx under a new name—Utopia. He took the name from Sir Thomas More's sixteenth-century fictional account of an imaginary island operated under a perfect social and political system. Later, the book's name became synonymous with anything idealized or visionary. Certainly, this new commune would qualify.

Although Warren has been called America's first anarchist, he was not a typical communal man because he insisted that his members own property (something he would believe in until his death in 1874). Born in Boston of Puritan ancestors in 1798, he was gifted in music and mechanics. In 1823, he patented a lamp that burned more efficiently and effectively using lard instead of tallow. That same year he moved to the booming western city of Cincinnati, where he operated a lamp factory. There he refined his views on social matters and the economy and began speaking to the public about his ideas. About this time he helped found a commune in Tuscarawas County, in northeastern Ohio, before moving temporarily to Owen's New Harmony, Indiana, community.

But Warren wanted more than group ownership. He had developed stronger ideas about running communes and understood that New Harmony prospered only after Owen's collectivist dream had died.

Using $7,000 he had earned from perfecting a high-speed printing press, Warren returned to Ohio in 1847, bought supplies for the closed Clermont Phalanx, and purchased more land near the original settlement. He divided the property into quarter-acre plots, laid out streets, and started a brickyard and stone quarry. There were no organizations, rules, and lectures in town. Warren wanted to operate a village based on practical reformist ideas. "We build on Individuality," he wrote. "Any differences between us confirm our position. Differences, therefore, like the admissible discords in music, are a valuable part of our harmony. . . . With regard to mere difference of opinion in taste, convenience, economy, equality, or even right or wrong, good and bad, sanity and insanity—all must be left to the supreme decision of each individual. Peace, harmony, ease, security, happiness, will be found only in Individuality."

Warren joined with a former resident, who owned some of the land, to establish Utopia as a communal society based loosely on capitalistic principles. They believed their community would live up to the ideals of More's mythical island of perfection. The new venture soon attracted a small number of people, many of whom were excited to have found such a protective environment. "We have a home! We have a place to be!" another original member wrote after returning to the community.

After only a few months, however, Warren's grand experiment began to fail. His partner set the price of lots too high, and Utopia couldn't grow. Many of its residents, upset with the high price of land, moved to rural Minnesota in the fall of 1847. Disheartened but not defeated, Warren left for the East, where he established other communal towns.

Soon after, Warren's group sold the Utopia property to spiritualist leader John O. Wattles, who moved in with 100 followers who represented the vanguard of America's occult movement. These folks mixed some traditional Christian beliefs with the new spiritualism—a belief in communication with the dead.

By then, spiritualism had taken root firmly throughout Ohio and the nation. Wattles and his wife, former Quaker Esther Whinery, had come to Cincinnati from Logan County, where they had purchased land for a commune. After only six months, however, individual selfishness helped destroy that group. "No one can tell the inconvenience and sorrow it cost all of us," Esther wrote in her diary. "I saw how little we were prepared to live a community life and have things in common."

At the place known as Utopia, the group assembled by John Wattles was dedicated to "dietetic reform" (vegetarianism), women's rights, and temperance, practices and views that were exceptional and controversial at the time. The Wattleses renamed their new community Excelsior and described it as a place that combined the principles of religion and business in a socialistic-spiritualistic state.

In her writings, Esther did not reveal what they believed, other than generalities, nor did she say why they built a church underground. She wrote that a dozen families lived in riverside shanties that stood near a large frame building with many windows. No one suspected that the building would become the site of one of the county's worst tragedies. As she explained in her diary:

> Tho the banks of the river were twenty feet above the low-water mark, in December 1847 we woke up to find our shanties surrounded by water and the water rising fast. There was a large frame building back near the hill—but a deep ravine full of water and no way to get to it, so it was decided to all go into the new house, all incomplete as it was, and some of the neighbors were invited to share their lot with us, till we numbered thirty in all. Not near all our goods could be gotten to the new house on Tues., but such things as floated from attic windows were taken Wednesday. Moses Cornell and my husband worked from skiffs all Wed. and got most of our belongings into the new building. Mrs. Cornell and I watched them from our third-story window and wondered what our home folks would say if they knew we were surrounded by water seven feet deep and half a mile from visible land.
>
> Mr. Cornell came across the hall and said, "John, the house is settling." Mrs. Cornell said, "We could hardly get this door open"—they went on thru the hall giving the alarm. It was near eight o'clock in the evening. John had taken off his boots and I my shoes in readiness for bed. By the time we put them on again the Cornell room, next to the river, and ten feet of hall, were falling. It was no use to try to get out, for the water was seven feet deep all around us. John took me in his arms and said, "Esther, in a few moments we shall be in heaven."
>
> But—when all had fallen but our room, he said, "we must get out. God has more work for us to do." He tied bedding together and wanted to let me down on the ruins that were now above the water. I said, "No, I will not go; you must go and then you can find a way for me." Someone had put up a piece of a ladder and he found a

board that came up to our door, where the hall should have been. Mrs. Ransom with her year-old baby had walked into our room saying as she went, "What will become of this baby! What will become of this boy!" As I started down the board, she said, "Can't you take this baby?" When I got my feet on the ladder, I said "yes," and I took it from her and Husband took it from me. We expected she would follow, but our room looked so bright—and so pleasant—she did not realize the danger. . . . [She] went to our wardrobe and threw down all she could find to the people who were crying that they were freezing.

I went out on the ruins far as possible & sat down taking the baby while John took the blankets we had used in getting out, and put around us. Then he went back, hoping Mrs. Ransom would come. She did not, so I gathered up bedding [that] she had thrown down & gave [it] to those not killed by the fall of the house. He went a second time to try to get Mrs. Ransom to come, but it was too late. Our room fell and she was killed. John stumped his [toe] & pitched out toward me and was saved. . . .

Mr. Cornell & wife, son & daughter were killed. Well! 17 out of the 32 were killed in the falling of the house. We did not even get wet or in any way hurt, but were the only ones who came off so easily. The survivors made a great cry for help, so that the people at Rural, a mile away, heard us, as well as the fall of the house. And Utopia, one mile above us, heard, and both places sent boats, and called first for all the women and children. . . . I had the baby who wanted his mother and I could do no other than hold him all night and try to comfort him. Not only was his mother killed, but two half brothers and a half sister.

Despite death and financial loss, the spiritualists refused to leave Excelsior. As the floodwaters receded, the survivors buried their comrades' bodies on a hillside. "It would take a volume to tell all & then the story of the sorrowing hearts [would] be left untold," Esther wrote later. After reorganizing their quarters a few months later, the residents again experienced the river's wrath—"a whirlwind that carried the water from the river, 40 feet high. A large birch tree just on the bank where my husband had held a Sunday school class the summer before, was taken, root and branch; one mile above us the buildings were all destroyed." Then in May the group's frame house burned. A beaten John and Esther Wattles finally decided to surrender to the river. John left to scout new commune locations to the west.

Esther's account of the December 1847 disaster differs from those of other nineteenth-century historians, who claimed the spiritualists ignored warnings that the structure stood too close to the river. Those accounts assert that there was a celebratory dance on the night of December 13. On the previous night, which had brought heavy rain, the river had already started sneaking toward the camp. Yet apparently no one noticed—or cared. On the night of the thirteenth, as the fiddler played and residents danced, the walls collapsed under a torrent of water, crushing thirty-four people, many of them young. Then the river washed away the building as though it had never existed. "This disaster," one historian wrote in 1880, "occurring at night and during a terrible storm, struck terror into the hearts of the people; the history of the community from its inception to its calamitous close is the most tragic event that has ever occurred in the county."

For a while, a few of Wattles's followers tried to make Utopia a manufacturing center, but this idea failed, too, and the results have been permanent.

Now, Utopia is more countryside than town and more dream than reality.

Driving around Utopia's two narrow streets, I saw the brick house in which Wattles supposedly lived and conducted his mystic rituals. I was told that a young couple live there now. Nearby I found the gated (and locked) entrance to a 44-by-22-foot underground stone chamber that has intrigued locals for generations. I wanted to see the mysterious place for myself, to learn why it was built and what it was for. A guy at the store told me to be careful. He said the chamber was originally a church and was later used for meetings and storing food.

On a later visit, I returned to the chamber with my nimble friend Jeremy Stephenson, a ghost town photographer from Loveland, Ohio. Jeremy crawled under the fence to take a closer look and determined that he'd need a ladder to descend into the chamber below. As we gave up and started walking back to our car, a woman pulled up alongside us and abruptly asked, "You trying to get into that thing?"

"Just looking around," I said.

"For history's sake," Jeremy added.

She cocked her head. "So you guys want to go down there?"

"Sure," he replied without hesitation.

Finding Utopia

Introducing herself as Pam Meece, the owner of the property, she jumped out of her car clutching a clipboard, which she thrust into Jeremy's hands. "Sign it," she ordered, pointing to a release form absolving her of any responsibility if we should be injured.

After we'd signed, she pulled a ladder from the back of her vehicle, unlocked the gate, and slid the ladder down the shaft leading to the chamber.

Jeremy looked at me and raised an eyebrow. "Let's go."

We descended into the dank chamber, which had openings on both ends and four vented fireplaces. As we stood there looking up at rows of old stones in the ceiling, we wondered how the place had survived a century and a half.

"If not for these fireplaces," Jeremy said, "the place could pass for an ice house. I wonder why four of them were needed in such a small space. That just doesn't make sense." He paused, then added, "If the

One of four fireplaces in the underground church in Utopia. (Photo by Randy McNutt)

spiritualists went to the trouble of building an underground church, then they must have wanted to practice their religion in secret."

I glanced around at the cool stone walls, shot a picture of Jeremy and a picture of the fireplace, and left quickly, not wanting to breathe the air down there. He stayed and prowled around for at least ten more minutes, shooting photos and imagining what once happened inside the chamber.

Back above ground, I learned from Meece that the chamber was indeed built by the spiritualists and that the locals believed some sort of unknown psychic force remains below. "We believe the chamber was used by the Underground Railroad as well," she said. "I've been opening it up to tour groups. One day I hope to restore it, if I can get some grant money."

The longer we talked, the more she relaxed. She told me how "one night, while a small tour group was down there, an electrical storm hit suddenly. Members of the group saw an apparition. One guy got hit in the chest by some invisible force; another felt something hit him, too. The group—four people in all—freaked out, and came rushing up the ladder. The last guy to come up was pretty shaken."

Meece walked over to the shaft and peered down, apparently looking for Jeremy. We could hear the clicking of his camera's shutter. She said, "I've seen orbs on photos taken down there. Now, I realize that some people think the spots are just dust particles or something like them, but some of these orbs were"—she placed her hands two feet apart—"this big. That's not a piece of dust." Orbs are considered to be energy, or spirits of some kind.

She looked down again and saw Jeremy's head emerging from the entrance. "Awesome!" he told her. She smiled.

I asked, "Do you have any uninvited guests, other than 'the force'?"

"Oh, sure," she said. "I've had to put three padlocks on this gate. Vandals broke off the first two. But this one's tough. It can't be snipped off."

Meece stared at the squeaking ladder as Jeremy finally emerged from below. She said, "I had a medium go down there once. She told me, 'This place feels like a gateway. It doesn't feel like a church.' I said, 'It isn't your usual church; it was a spiritualist church.' At least that's what historians tell me."

She told us that the remnants of the old spiritualist building still remain in the lowlands along the river. "You can see the outline of the

Finding Utopia

foundation from the air," Meece said. "It's a fitting location. People see and hear strange things in this town."

Jeremy and I poked around down in the lowlands, looking for the building's foundation. We couldn't find it, but county historian Richard Crawford once assured me that it still exists. In fact, he leads tours there on Halloween. He said many people have reported seeing ghosts and hearing wailing in the area. The theory is that the flood victims continue to relive their horrible deaths, when they were trapped in the building during the dance.

That makes Utopia more than just a ghost town. It is a haunted ghost town.

Crawford said some people believe the spirits are those of early spiritualists still walking the lonely path from the river. "That is the legend," he said. "There are rumors of things happening in Utopia, especially on rainy nights. Wattles's home is visited by six people: a woman in a blue dress wearing a blue hat, a man in a black suit with a hat, a teenager, and three children. They go in through the front door and walk up the stairs to the second floor and disappear." She said that a young girl and several adults who lived in the house in recent years reported seeing spirits. Perhaps the river won't allow them to forget.

At Jeremy's house later that afternoon, we viewed his digital photographs on a computer and discovered white dots—some large, some small—on the images taken inside the underground chamber. Skeptical, we thought the spots were reflections, but then we realized that such a dark place would not produce reflections.

"They're probably orbs," Jeremy said, matter-of-factly. "I don't know what to make of them, but some are as big as basketballs."

"I don't understand," I said. "Nothing was down in that nearly dark place but us. There was hardly any light."

"Yes," he said, his voice trailing off.

We did not speak of the matter again.

And so, season after season, life has continued in Utopia. Gilbert Craig tends his tobacco farm—the "last one in Clermont County before you cross over to Brown County"; a cow roams the front yard of a mobile home; fishermen reel in big bass from the mouth of Bullskin Creek; and cars continue to roll past the Village Market.

When I visited some time later, the biggest news in town was a break-in at the store. Everyone was upset. "Why, I didn't even know we had county deputies until this," Craig said.

Nowadays along the river, Utopia and its original concept remain ever elusive. The Grand Experiment—the commune—never did revive itself. Instead, the community became an isolated haven of peace and tranquility known only to the people who lived in the area. Through it all, the town has remained, always waiting for the river to rise.

2

The Pull of Magnetic Springs

> I was surprised on my return to see the improvements made while I was gone—to see men and women that I thought could not live long had thrown away their crutches and were walking about our streets as if nothing was the matter with them.
> —*A resident returning to Magnetic Springs, 1883*

When a friend first suggested that I "look into Magnetic Springs," I wasn't sure what he meant. "Do you mean car springs?" I asked, and he laughed. He was talking about a town in Union County with a restorative spa that flourished in the days before physicians offered chemical and therapeutic alternatives.

Our brief discussion about the water cure fad of the mid-nineteenth to early twentieth centuries fascinated me.

"Oh," I said, "the town was like Saratoga Springs in New York."

"This one was different," my friend said. "It spouted magnetic water."

Based on this claim alone, I had to see the place. (Forgive me for saying I was drawn to it.) Within days I was driving through the streets of Magnetic Springs, population 320, about thirty miles northwest of Columbus. I was not impressed with the town. It looked like any other aging community struggling to cling to its spot in the countryside. On back streets I searched for any evidence of the town's glorious past but saw nothing. I saw Victorian houses, a sports field, and a historical marker. Predictable.

Today, few people come to drink and bathe in the curative waters from the springs, which means that Magnetic Springs has become another candidate for the endangered town list.

Council member Robert Baughman can't deny reality: The town is slowly fading. Sometimes he looks around it and wonders, What if Magnetic Springs had learned to adjust in a fast-changing health resort market? Then he realizes that it could not have adjusted. Progress moved too fast.

On that warm autumn day, I knocked on his door at random. He answered with a smile. "We're still incorporated," he said on his back porch. "But I don't know for how much longer. We don't have enough money. At one time we operated with a fifteen-mill tax levy. Now we think five mills would be a lot." In 2005, when he was mayor, the town again asked voters to approve an operating levy that would have provided the town with $32,800 a year. "It failed by five votes," Baughman said with disgust. "I tried to get people interested in passing it, but only four out of ten of them bothered to vote. It's a shame, too. This could be a nice town if it had new sewers."

We stood silently for a moment, looking at the old houses. He said, "Can you believe that the Ohio State and Purdue football teams used to come here to practice and take mineral baths? Nobody knows us now. I compare us to Tombstone, Arizona. I visited there on a vacation years ago. Once, it had 40,000 people, and when I saw it had 2,000 or so. But then that's the way towns go. They lose their means of support, and suddenly they're a lot smaller or else they're not even around any longer."

In 2005, the town council voted to ask the state attorney general for advice on dissolving Magnetic Springs. The town couldn't even afford to hire its own lawyer. But it never was dissolved, Baughman said, and it continues to struggle. Since then, the town's finances haven't improved significantly, he said, and few people seek elected office. Other problems included the lack of a building code, an old sewer system that's clogged with mud, and too many dilapidated houses that would each cost $7,000 to tear down. The village generates only about $11,000 a year for its general fund.

"We can't adequately repair streets and perform all the duties that people expect of a town," Baughman said. "It wasn't always like that, though. The place was booming in the '30s, '40s, and '50s." He pointed to a house on the main street. "Over there, that was a bank—right there. We had big hotels, too. My own house here was a boardinghouse for the tourists at one time. The local population was much larger then, of course. There was also a golf course and a vineyard. These days, you'd never know they were ever here."

. . .

Before leaving for Magnetic Springs, I read a clipping sent by a friend from an undated and unnamed newspaper—free of logic, science, and political correctness—from the late nineteenth century. My friend believed the story to be from an Ohio newspaper, but I wasn't so sure. For a moment I even wondered whether the writer was serious.

> MORE WONDERFUL CURES BY MAGNETIC SPRINGS—As often as once a quarter some mineral spring is discovered with all-healing properties in its waters. Paralytics, rheumatics, and cripples of every kind are seen traveling over the country from one extreme to another to reach the newly discovered springs. They remain at one place till hotels are constructed, and then they depart for some newly discovered spa. . . . As the story goes, paralysis is cured in four days by the use of these wonderful waters. One invalid who had bathed freely at the springs for a week became so thoroughly impregnated with the magnetism that he dare not enter a hardware store. He went into the village blacksmith's shop and thoughtlessly seated himself upon an anvil. When he left he found the anvil a permanent fixture. The blacksmith is the loser.

The town's story began with John E. Newhouse, a descendant of pioneers and the owner of a nursery called Green Bend Garden. In 1879, while digging a 68-foot well to obtain water for a pond, he discovered the springs. To his surprise, the water had magnetic properties. At first, Newhouse didn't consider its value, other than using it to fill the pond. He agreed to allow an arthritic Presbyterian preacher named Rose from Richwood to take home some barrels of water for drinking and bathing. Soon feeling better, the preacher returned and asked Newhouse to open the site to the public.

"Rose chastised Newhouse for keeping the secret of the water from all of suffering humanity," local historian Bob Parrott wrote in *Magnetic Springs Centennial Cookbook* in 1983. Until then, Newhouse had worried that hundreds of people might damage his vegetables. "Newhouse formed a corporation, which built a bathhouse to test the curative powers of the water," Parrott said. Apparently he liked the results, for in October he formed a spa company and erected a simple bathhouse with three zinc-lined tubs. They attracted visitors who wanted to bathe at Newhouse's nursery, near his 500,000 sweet potato plants, yams, tomatoes, and beets. A year later, his bathhouse attendants were giving 100 baths a week, and Newhouse was thinking more of magnetic water than the size of his tomatoes.

Even before he built the bathhouse, Newhouse had already decided to build a town around Green Bend. He had laid out streets and invited people to come there to live. He named his post office Kokosing. (In 1883 the town officially became Magnetic Springs, to better reflect the essence of the place.) But Newhouse understood that more money could be made in baths than in yams, so he decided to create a spa empire. In 1882, he bought a highly sulphuric spring that the locals called Blue Spring, a quarter mile east of Magnetic Springs, and built a new resort he named Maple Dell. That year a local reporter wrote, "The spring is four feet deep and so clear that you can see a pin at the bottom. The place has been graded and two hundred maple trees were planted. A marble bowl will soon be placed around the spring. This spring is considered best for liver complaints."

Local water also helped rejuvenate the body, said Jesse Conrad, a Marysville accountant and the grandson of hotel owner J. F. Conrad. "Soak a knife in the water for twenty-four hours and it will pick up a nail. It's magnetic. The water within a three-mile radius of Magnetic Springs has a unique analysis—and the same properties."

To entice more people to come to Magnetic Springs, Newhouse established Eagle Park on the west side of town. Its purpose was to provide entertainment and enjoyment for residents and visitors. He built wooden bridges and hiking trails and dug more wells so that people could drink fresh spring water.

In the 1880s, Magnetic Springs's reputation grew beyond Ohio's borders. First Lady Frances Folsom Cleveland ordered a cask of local water for the White House. An Indiana doctor who suffered from painful paralysis in one eye came to town. The doctor had tried the waters of Hot Springs, Arkansas, but found no relief until, as a reporter explained, "he came here (to Magnetic Springs) two weeks ago, and after bathing a few days imagine his delight on recovering the perfect use of his eye."

Before long, people from all over the nation were coming to stay in the huge Columbus and Park hotels, the Ballard Inn, rooming houses, and even in private homes. Local doctors owned some of the hotels. In the 1880s, finding money in Magnetic Springs was no problem, for it flowed from the hands of tourists who came to be cured or entertained or both.

Some people who came seeking a cure or relief never left. In 1880, Sue Robinson came from some unidentified town to seek help for her painful paralysis (she called it "nervous rheumatism") of the spine that she had suffered for ten years. She said, "[I] commenced bathing and drinking the water. I improved from the beginning and am now almost as well as ever in my life." She bought a property, dug a well, and built Aunt Sue Robinson's Boarding House. It became popular because of her kindheartedness and good cooking. In 1886, she changed the name to the Beehive House because "it is always full and stirring about."

Kate Milikan of Washington Court House said she felt like burning wire was wrapped around her brain. Physicians couldn't help. "During the first bath it seemed that some unseen hand had loosened the torturing bands from my racked brain," she said, "and immediately following came a sensation of such ineffable and blessed relief from pain, as I had not hoped for this side of the grave."

In 1883, the year the town incorporated as Magnetic Springs to better reflect its essence, an estimated 10,000 visitors came between Memorial Day and Labor Day.

When Newhouse noticed that Magnetic Springs also was attracting healthy people, he had another idea: make his spa businesses so opulent, so intriguing, that anyone would want to visit simply for entertainment. The idea worked. Thousands of people crowded the streets on weekends. "Newhouse and Staats are sparing no pains or more to make Maple Dell the most attractive resort in the West," one reporter wrote. "Their conservatory is equal to a visit to Florida. You will see the stately palm trees, oranges and lemons hanging on trees in their golden ripeness, with buds and blossoms on the same tree, filling the air with delicious fragrance."

While people were getting well, Newhouse tried to make them happy and comfortable with revivals, camp meetings, bicycle trips, cookouts, hikes, ice cream socials, fireworks, parades, brass band concerts, and parties at which the guests toasted with magnetic drinks.

As Newhouse's ventures grew in the late 1880s, Magnetic Springs had two newspapers, *The Magnet* and the *Magnetic Reporter*. Judging by their stories, the towns offered more than any visitor expected: "Newhouse & Co. have their steamboat placed on the creek"; "Ed Newhouse has stocked Eagle Park with live alligators, which he brought from Florida"; "Another attractive feature is the cascade falling over rocks into the lake from a height of 20 feet"; "The banana and fig trees, century plant and cactus are there with many tropical productions, in all their native luxuriance."

By then, the town was busy serving even more people from all over the state and nation who came to seek a cure for their conditions, including neuritis and rheumatism. It was estimated that tourists took 14,000 baths over a three-year period. Entrepreneurs built hotels, stores, theaters, and various other tourist accommodations. Electric trolley lines, including the Delaware and Magnetic Springs Railway, arrived from Delaware, bringing more people to town. When the automobile pushed the trolley lines out of business in 1919, people came by car.

Guests were not disappointed by the accommodations. The Sager Hotel, built in 1911 by physicians E. T. and Ora Sager, was often called the most attractive building in the county. Made of tapestry brick, it had "hot and cold magnetic water in every room; steam heat; electric light; and service unexcelled. Each floor opens onto . . . spacious porches which are cool and comfortable in the summertime. These afford a wonderful view of the surrounding countryside." In a yard next to the hotel's bathhouses stood a large tablet that listed the water's chemical ingredients, including iron.

Other hotels thrived, too. The Park Hotel, "the showplace of Magnetic Springs," offered 400 rooms and a well-equipped bathhouse with "skilled nurses and masseurs in attendance at all times. If sick, we will do you good after medicine has failed." The hotel claimed it could improve

Postcard of the Park Hotel, one of Magnetic Springs' larger hotels in the 1950s. (Author's collection)

The Pull of Magnetic Springs 29

conditions such as sciatica, neuralgia, nervousness, rheumatism, and ailments of the kidneys, bladder, liver, stomach, and bowels.

"Even so," Conrad said, "the town's big four hotels couldn't hold all the visitors. So the boardinghouses sprang up. It was a booming community." In 1904, Jesse T. Conrad's grandfather, a medical doctor, started the Conrad Hotel and Sanitarium (also known as the Conrad Hotel and Bath House or the Conrad Bath House) that his father, a chiropractor, ran later. It became one of the more popular health spas in town. Because so many of his wealthy guests came from out of the state, J. T. Conrad built an airport north of Magnetic Springs.

According to Conrad, "Grandfather bought his hotel to supplement his income, as an adjunct to his practice. In 1905, fire destroyed grandfather's hotel, but he rebuilt it and continued to operate it until he got too old to go on. I was born in his [second] hotel, and I lived there until I turned nine, and then I moved only a block away and lived there until I was eighteen. I did about every job in the hotel over the years—working at the front desk, doing the dishes, waiting on tables. I saw everything that happened. Every Friday night, grandfather used to give health lectures in the lobby. Later, he compiled them in a book called *The Road to Health*. He also staged boxing matches in the lobby for entertain-

The Conrad Hotel and Sanitarium was one of Magnetic Springs' most popular destinations. (Author's collection)

Methodist-Episcopal Sunday School members at Magnetic Springs pose for this postcard from the early 1900s. (Author's collection)

ment. Many of the hotels offered boxing as entertainment back then because there wasn't a lot to do in town. All the hotels are gone now. The last one closed in the early 1970s."

Dr. Conrad urged his patients not to drink anything with meals. He believed the food digested better that way. His regimen of treatment, aside from fresh country air and wholesome foods, consisted of drinking the local water and taking three weeks of bathing treatments. Each treatment took an hour and required patients to take a hot shower, soak in a tub of hot water, enter a steam cabinet, receive a saltwater massage, and, finally, to take another shower to clean off the salt. "You had to take the baths," Conrad said. "They were integral to the treatment. The water got the poisons out of the system. I saw people come to the hotel by ambulance, unable to walk. We had to carry them to their rooms. Three weeks later, they would walk out of their own power."

Word of the "miracle water" spread nationally. A big sign hung near one of the springs near Ballard's Hotel read: "Magnetic Springs . . . HIGH TEST . . . You can tell by the taste."

Some people simply came to town to get free water, which was available at public pavilions. Others came for the regular Magnetic Springs treatment, which involved spending at least twenty-one consecutive days in the bathhouse, where one-hour treatments included sitting in a steam room, then bathing in a tub of hot mineral-laden water, and then being rubbed down either with salt or alcohol. A retired bath attendant once recalled that in the summer attendants worked seven days a week, with only Sunday afternoon off. "I think in the 1940s I was giving more than 2,000 baths a year," Anthony Hall told a reporter.

Some of the bathhouses and hotels wanted their patients to sweat—"Open the pores and remove the poison," was the catchphrase. Bathhouse operators instructed visitors to step into the "magnetic waters." Some baths lasted two hours, depending on the patient's condition, and cost one dollar per bath in the early 1900s.

"The town is one of those unique places," Conrad said. "It wasn't unusual to have 3,000 people in town on a weekend. The hotels couldn't hold them all, so the boardinghouses took care of many people. The mafia used to come, too, not so much for their health but because things got too hot for them elsewhere. The housekeeping ladies used to find machine guns stashed in the hotel closets."

In the 1930s and later, football teams came to town. Ohio State University signed a contract with the Park Hotel, which provided workout space and rubdowns, and the Brooklyn Dodgers and Chicago Bears trained, played practice games, and received treatment.

Back then, it must have seemed to the townspeople that their main business—taking care of the sick—was destined to go on forever.

Something interesting happened in Magnetic Springs all those years ago. Exactly what happened, scientifically speaking, I'm not sure. The Internet is filled with stories, old and new, about magnetism and magnetized water. (You can even buy a "magnetic wand" that will magnetize your water.)

In the 1800s, hucksters sold all kinds of magnetic things to improve people's health. They advertised a magnetized "electrical belt" that could help men cure everything from baldness to impotence. I remember a time, in the early 1990s, when a friend insisted that I buy a magnetized wristband to help my sore arm. I didn't believe him. After visiting Magnetic Springs, I started thinking that maybe he was right.

Magnetically treated water has more hydroxyl ions, which form alkaline molecules. Spring water is usually hard water, meaning it contains supersaturated hardness ions, which bring out carbonates, which often means a lot of sodium. Early in the twentieth century, a state chemist analyzed the water at Magnetic Springs and found properties such as silica, iron and aluminum oxides, calcium carbonate, magnesium carbonate, calcium carbonate, calcium sulfate, magnesium sulfate, sodium sulfate, and sodium chloride.

In modern times, many scientists dismiss claims that magnetism helps your health. As one writer put it, "Magnetized water is a pseudoscientific fraud."

But please don't mention this to Jesse Conrad. As a boy he saw what the water could do for the infirm. "I'd say it still works," he said.

Interest in Magnetic Springs declined slowly, as medical science advanced with physical therapy, antibiotics, and vaccines. If an arbitrary date must be set, the decline might have started—imperceptibly—on October 18, 1932, in the worst days of the Great Depression, when visionary founder and gardens architect John E. Newhouse died at age eighty-nine. Still, people continued to flow into town to seek cures and have fun. But the glory years were numbered. Time and progress were catching up.

By the mid-1970s, Earl "Frenchy" LaMarr maintained that he was the last working bath attendant in town, and had been for the last ten years. He was giving three to four baths a day. He recalled that once visitors had to make reservations to get a hotel room and a bath. Summer was his busiest season, but LaMarr and other attendants worked year round. It wasn't uncommon to see people walking around town dressed only in a bathrobe after taking their treatments.

By the late 1950s, the town had all but lost its appeal. To boost the fading local economy, the town founded the nonprofit Magnetic Springs Foundation, a center for rehabilitating polio and accident victims. But the Foundation went out of business in the 1960s, after so many Americans had received the polio vaccination.

The Park Hotel, the town's jewel, closed and reopened three times between the 1950s and the early 1970s. Once, it tried to make it as a nursing home but closed finally in 1973. That left only the Incor Hotel, and its time was running short. It burned in 1980, followed by the Ballard in 1981 and then the Conrad Hotel. So in 1983, the centennial year of Magnetic Springs, only the empty Park Hotel and Conrad Bath House remained standing. Debris from the burned hotels still littered the ground.

That year, the town's Save Our Springs Committee published a centennial cookbook to raise money for improvements. A mix of town history and residents' recipes, the book became a testament to the town's past and present. Committee members wrote:

> From this spring flowed more than just magnetic water; hope for a suffering mankind to alleviate their ills and cure their afflictions also bubbled forth. Hence began a dream, a hope, a town . . . Magnetic Springs. It is in dedication of this dream that we compile this cookbook, 100 years since the town was incorporated—filled with recipes passed down from mother to daughter—memories of years gone by, and reminders of a town built on a dream. It is our hope that this dream will never be extinguished.

Robert Baughman gave me a copy of the book, and we said good-bye. (It is the most fascinating historical cookbook I have ever seen.) As I walked the streets that afternoon, looking at the history all around me, I met a woman named Tina Stovall. I asked her if she remembered how the town used to look, and she smiled. "In 1968," she said, "my first husband and I bought Ballard's Hotel. People came in there all crippled up. We'd give them baths and massages, and when many of them left, they could walk. Ballard's was one of the last of the old hotels."

I also spoke with a man named David Scheider, who told me that his grandfather founded Ballard's, and his father worked as a masseur in another hotel. "All his brothers and sisters did the same kind of work," he said. "After we sold the hotel years ago, we bottled water and shipped it out. We thought people would be glad to get it. But the process got too costly, and we sold the rights."

Stovall said, "Old people used to come here for years. Mennonites came over from Steubenville. Then, it all dwindled away—all the business we had just left, and a lot of people lost their jobs. Think of all the hundreds of people that were employed in the hotels, restaurants, and stores."

She paused and looked around. "One day people just woke up and saw their booming town going bust."

3

In Search of the Believers

> Death plows its yearly furrows across their already aged ranks and new converts . . . are very few and far between. . . . There is something so strange, weird and pathetic about Union Village as it stands in all its splendor today. . . . There is a spirit of dreariness that broods over these children of one idea.
> —*A Cincinnati newspaper, early 1900s*

I circled Shaker Heights on my road map and imagined sleek furniture and functional buildings. But when I saw a big sign welcoming me to the city, I knew I'd entered another place and time. One after another, I passed broad green lawns with large, older houses—some Tudors, some foursquares, and all roomy family homes from the early twentieth century. It reminded me of Pasadena, or some other affluent California city—not of anything resembling the Shakers, known for simplicity and frugality. Eventually, I understood: All that remained of North Union, the Shaker village that started here in 1822, was its name.

Winding through several more grand neighborhoods, I finally spotted a house where the past and present connected—16740 South Park Boulevard, the Shaker Historical Society's museum, which opened in 1947 to celebrate the community's early years. I followed a sign directing me to a few parking spaces at the rear of the property, which resembled an English garden house. A wall plaque informed me: "This home is located on land once owned by the North Union Shakers. The front lot was part of the Shaker apple orchard. The Shaker vegetable garden was at the rear. This home was built in 1910 of stone from the Shaker mill family quarry."

Obviously, this house was built after the Shakers—members of the United Society of Believers in Christ's Second Appearing—had left. After all, developers had demolished most of the original Shaker buildings between 1905 and 1920 to make way for what we now know to be Shaker Heights. Yet, the museum had a timeless feel to it, and it provided glimpses of multiple cultures and histories. With all the Shaker artifacts hanging from the walls, the house seemed to take on an older appearance as well as the characteristics of some vague and unspecified period.

Docent Mickey Horner welcomed me and asked why I'd come. When I told her I wanted to see what remained of the Shakers, she said, "We're sorry we don't have more pieces." With that, we walked through the house, looking at antiques in glass cases. It became clear to me then that this place celebrated the Shakers and their ideals of health and purity as well as the memories of wealthy Clevelanders who came here to live in the early twentieth century. "We don't have any Shaker sisters here, or brothers," Horner said, smiling. "They all left when the colony dissolved in 1889."

By then, the Shakers had been living in America for more than a century. In 1774, persecution forced founder Ann Lee (the faithful called her Mother Ann) and her small group to leave England. Two years later, the Believers, as they called themselves, established communities in New York and, a few years later, New England, Ohio, Kentucky, and Indiana. Lee considered herself a messenger inspired by God; her followers saw her as a female Second Coming. The wife of a blacksmith, she taught celibacy and believed that God was both Father and Mother. She sought simplicity in everything.

The sect's name came from its members' animation while in worship. In the throes of religious fervor, members fell down and swooned, danced, and shook. People called them the Shaking Quakers, and later the Shakers. The Believers didn't object. These optimistic and spiritual people lived simply and built solid, practical furniture, which is what they are best known for today. Their self-contained villages were divided into groups, or "families," and they managed to blend agriculture and light industry with a religious and communal lifestyle.

By 1815, the Shakers had about 1,000 members nationally. Their first western outpost, Union Village near Lebanon in southern Ohio, was founded in 1805, after three Shaker missionaries from New York had converted prominent local farmer Malcomb Worley and Presbyterian preacher Richard McNemar. As Union Village grew, its members founded Shaker communities in other areas and states: Pleasant Hill, near Harrodsburg, Kentucky; South Union, near Bowling Green, Kentucky; Watervliet, near Dayton, Ohio; West Union, near Vincennes, Indiana; and North Union, near Cleveland.

The Shakers tried to live quietly in rural Ohio, growing crops, creating beautiful and functional household products, and worshiping God. Their strict beliefs trapped them between the enlightened and unenlightened, between their consciences and their human lusts. The group grew through assimilation of volunteers, including whole families with children. With no government social programs available then, many people sought refuge with the Shakers. Some stayed permanently.

North Union (also known by its spiritual name, the Valley of God's Pleasure) started in 1822 when local farmer Ralph Russell and his family converted to Shakerism and offered their farm for a village site in Cuyahoga County. The Shakers built dams along Doan Brook to supply power to gristmills and sawmills, and the colony grew, peaking in the early 1850s.

"Three hundred people called it home," Horner said. "It was a thriving place that didn't exclude anyone. They welcomed blacks from the South. The women had as much say as the men. The group was friendly and progressive. But its younger people could see how much money the people in Cleveland were earning. Many left as more manufacturing became mechanized, and fewer things were being made by hand. All this helped in the demise of the Shaker community. Despite this, the Shakers built a gristmill and they ground all the grain for the farmers in the area. Local farmers got ideas from them. The Shakers were not secretive."

Author Edward Deming Andrews wrote in 1953, "Progress of the community of North Union [had] two factors basic to the success of religious communism . . . the bequest of good land and strong leadership . . . Ashbel Kitchell, the first presiding elder, was a gifted administrator, commanding in stature, just, intelligent, iron-willed." After his departure, the community continued to operate with able leaders.

When the Civil War broke out in 1861, disrupting important southern trade markets and Ohioans' lives, the village declined swiftly. By 1865, its population stood at only twenty-seven. Yet the Shakers persevered.

"The Shakers tried to raise silk worms, but the community was too far north for that work," Horner said as she led me to a related exhibit.

"Their main thing was sheep—for wool—and orchards—lots of orchards—and herb gardens. They sold seeds at markets in the city as well as in packages. The Shakers were doing this before Burkee." Their community also operated a broom factory, a woolen mill, and a carpenter shop. Later, in the 1870s, they bought vineyards in Lake County and grew grapes, making wine to sell to "the world"—anyone who was not a Shaker. A Shaker brother wrote that the wines "are a delicious way to administer a gentle stimulant—that's all—a nice medicine." The wine bottle labels read: "Shaker Communists, Shaker Wine, made only for medicinal purposes by the Shakers." (In this pre–Karl Marx day, "communist" referred to communal life.) But because the wine was intended for medicinal use, it wasn't particularly tasty and didn't catch on. It was soon discontinued.

By hiring field hands, North Union's dwindling population managed to hold on another decade. But by 1889, the end had come. The group dissolved its community and then sold its holdings—mills, houses, workshops, and man-made ponds—to developers for $316,000.

As I strolled through the museum and saw its varied contents, I became, for an hour or so, an unwitting time traveler. Exhibits hurled me from 1822 to 1922 in a matter of minutes as I looked at old photographs, artifacts, and portraits of important people in Shaker Heights—especially "the Vans," brothers Oris Paxton and Mantis James Van Sweringen, Cleveland developers who turned the former Shaker commune into a rich man's community. Their Shaker Heights became both the antithesis and the embodiment of Shaker ideals. While the Shakers didn't embrace a wealthy lifestyle, they did strive for healthy, rural living and good organization. The Van Sweringens, prominent builders and moneymen, wanted Shaker Heights to have both.

"The brothers were the movers and shakers of Cleveland," Horner said, intending no pun. "They knew this land would be good for a development, but the people down in Cleveland didn't want to come up here in the early 1900s because the roads were too bad. The brothers wanted to sell lots here, so they had an architect draw up plans for a whole garden-style community. It was a planned one; all the streets were laid out before the people came here to live. Eventually, the Van Sweringen Company sold the lots and made Shakers Heights a desirable community. In time, about all that remained of the Shakers was their name."

The brothers operated their development with strict rules. They wrote a restrictive clause—called the Shaker Standards—that limited who could build what and how. Shaker Heights became the Cleveland area's most exclusive community.

In the late 1920s, the brothers owned holdings worth $3 billion—on paper. To better serve Shaker Heights, they bought railroad companies on credit and extended commuter service. (Their real monument is Cleveland's Terminal Tower.) In doing so, however, they overextended themselves financially. When the stock market crashed in 1929, so did the Van Sweringens' grand plans to fully develop Shaker Heights. Under high stress, M.J. died in 1935, O.P. in 1936. (Reportedly, O.P. had just $3,000 left at his death.) But their planned community continued, becoming a city in 1931. "They didn't want all millionaires or all laborers living in Shaker Heights," Horner said. "They wanted a mixture."

On a wall of the museum hangs the company's original plans for "Shaker Country Estates, 1928"—in contrast to the washstand, butter churn, kitchen table, applesauce crock, chairs with woven seats, and seed boxes that occupy the same space. "If you look closely," Horner said, pointing to a seed box, "you can read the names of the Shaker sisters and brothers."

In Warren County, near Lebanon in southwest Ohio, I headed north on State Route 741 and stopped at the sprawling Otterbein Lebanon Retirement Center, built on the site of North Union's parent town, Union Village. I wanted to look at the architecture. Unfortunately, I arrived a few days too late. A big crane was smashing the smooth brick walls of Bethany Hall, pulverizing a big piece of the town's Shaker history. At the time of its completion in 1844, Bethany—the Shaker Center House, or office—was supposedly the largest brick building in Ohio. The Shakers fired the bricks on site.

I felt a sense of loss and sadness as chunks of the building collapsed. I asked an elderly Otterbein resident what he thought, and he shrugged. "No big deal. Management wants to replace it with some kind of 'complex.'" Specifically, it was the planned $3 million Life Enrichment Center, a fitness and community center that "management" believed was essential to keep elderly residents healthy—and to remain attractive to prospective residents. Bethany simply became too expensive to maintain, especially since it occupied a prime piece of real estate.

The trade-off—prominent 166-year-old Shaker icon swapped for hard-cash practicality—created an intellectual and sentimental dilemma among some residents and local historians. After all, the Otterbein and Union Village stories had been closely intertwined for a century. After the demolition, only two Shaker buildings still stood out of the 100 at Union Village in 1912. During the twentieth century, many of the structures were razed or burned, relegated to sites for firefighter training.

Reaction to Bethany's fall came from preservationists in New York, Georgia, Massachusetts, and even England. Clearly, the demolition disappointed Lois Madden, president of the Western Shaker Study Group, who recalled the spring day when she traveled to Lebanon to eat at the Golden Lamb Inn and, on a whim, decided to drive five miles west to see Bethany Hall for the last time. "I thought I was emotionally prepared for what I'd see . . . [but] that assumption proved false," she said. "Nothing could have prepared me for my reaction to the devastation wrought in so little time—all that was left was a pile of rubble. What a very sad ending to that once magnificent structure that served the Shakers so well. The loss of the building is a tragedy unto itself. What struck me on a deeper, more profound level was the loss of the imprinted memories contained within its walls."

North and south of the Bethany site, Otterbein Retirement Home support buildings lined Route 741. One of them, Marble Hall, was the oldest and, at one time, most notable building at Union Village. Oddly enough, it doesn't look anything like a Shaker building. Former Otterbein archivist Mary Lou Warner, who agreed to show me around, told me that renovations in the 1890s added two towers to the structure and embellished interior hallways with marble and expensive woods. "The Shakers did it," she said. "They refurbished the building when their membership was dwindling. I suppose they wanted to show the world that they were 'of the times.'"

In doing so, they eliminated some prime Shaker architecture. To get a full view of the large Marble Hall, I walked across the street and stood next to an old tree. I read a little sign attached to its trunk: "Mulberry tree planted by original Shakers." Sadly, I noted that the tree had outlived most of the historic buildings. Looking over the horizon, I found it difficult to imagine a 4,500-acre Shaker farming community flowing as far as the eye could see.

The peaceful landscape of the nineteenth century hid the drama that unfolded when Union Village became the first Shaker community established west of the Alleghenies. To the pioneers, the Shakers must have seemed odd, practicing sexual and racial equality, pacifism, and celibacy. Their then-radical theology—not to mention communal living—created animosity and misunderstandings among many local people, who circulated a false rumor about the Shakers keeping women and children without their consent. On August 27, 1810, a crowd of 1,500–2,000 people converged on Union Village. Some were curiosity seekers, some were there to protect the Shakers, but many were there to force the Shakers out. The conflict became one of the first great tests of religious freedom in Ohio.

As the editor of *A History of Warren County* described the event seventy-some years later: "Many men living in the vicinity of Union Village believed that the leaders of the new sect were designing impostors, living in secret sins of the darkest dye, and [neighbors] were ready to wage a war of extermination against them, or drive them from the county." In that daylong standoff, Shaker opponents—armed with pistols and whips—bullied and threatened and argued with the Believers to either give up their faith or get out of town. But the Shakers stood their ground. As the tense day wore on, opponents were allowed to meet with relatives who they claimed were being forcibly kept in the village. At the day's end, the crowd dispersed, but lawsuits, public bickering in the local newspapers, and mistrust continued for years. Then mob organizers and the Shakers began talks that were mediated by local community leaders, including Francis Dunlavy, a county Common Pleas judge. He was not a Shaker, but some of his relatives were prominent in the faith.

Lebanon's Shaker opponents likely found the new faith baffling. From early on, the communal residents kept to themselves, writing hymns, working on the farm, and discussing their theology. They printed books of Shaker theology on presses at the village, and they also opened their worship services to the members of the public, who were sometimes surprised and sometimes mocking. During one service, the Shaker minister shouted, "There goes the devil!" Six elders claimed to see the devil running out the front door. "The congregation rushed madly out," the *Cincinnati Commercial-Tribune* reported, "and at last the elders claimed that the devil had been 'treed' in a straw stack. This was immediately set on fire and entirely consumed while the Shakers formed a dancing circle about the blazing straw, shrieking and howling all the while."

In Search of the Believers 41

Visitors disillusioned by the sect's unusual religious doctrine and practices were further put off by its communal rules. When a man joined the group, he had to give all his possessions—including land—to the commune. When a couple "of the world" joined the group, they were no longer considered married. Their children were required to live with the other Shaker children; when minors reached maturity, they could decide whether or not to join the group. Such rules angered relatives, who felt slighted on issues such as personal property and child custody.

People also must have been frightened by the Shakers' visions, especially if they came during open church services. In these visions, history's greatest people returned to Union Village for a few minutes or several hours. "Sometimes George Washington came, Napoleon perhaps, and Mother Ann," said Martha Boice, a leader of the Western Shaker Study Group. "Some Union Village residents did not participate in the dreams, which brought dishonor upon them from the elders. The elders tried to get rid of some other members, saying they were unworthy. They were trying to eliminate the people who were not getting these dream 'pictures.'"

Even to some members the dreams seemed macabre. By the late 1830s, during a time the Shakers called the Era of Manifestations, members were hearing heavenly trumpets, speaking in the voices of deceased Shakers, falling into trances, receiving drawings from spirits, seeing the ghostly presence of historic figures, and being knocked off their feet by spirit visitors. "The beholder is compelled to acknowledge the finger of divine agency in this work," one member wrote. Many more spirits came: a French woman who skated with the spirit of a woman from Iceland; long-dead Native Americans; a black slave named Dinah the African, who spoke through a Shaker sister (members asked her what she wanted, and she said, "Love"). Another time Pocahontas "touched an inspired [Shaker sister and visionary] on the head, who forthwith began to speak in the Indian tongue; and could then, & for sometime afterwards, speak only in the Indian tongue." During one meeting, the Shakers received sixty messages from spirits. Other sessions brought spirit poems, drawings, and confessions. When founding members McNemar and Malcomb Worley expressed some skepticism, they were banished from the village. McNemar, sixty-eight years old, appealed the decision at Shaker headquarters in New York and won, but he died soon after returning to Union Village.

The Era of Manifestations continued into the 1840s, and then, as if the spirits had tired of making personal appearances, it all ended. The

Shakers concentrated on growing medicinal herbs, making furniture, and selling their goods to the world. For the remainder of the nineteenth century, the Shakers of Union Village stood fast, eventually winning over their skeptical neighbors with their determination, integrity, and industry. At its peak, the village was home to 600 residents and had dozens of homes, farm buildings, and shops, where Shaker craftsmen produced everything from steel to brooms to wool caps and stockings.

Union Village became known for its agricultural advancements. Shakers introduced Merino sheep to the region, became championship cattle breeders, developed a new breed of hog called the Poland-China, sold hundreds of varieties of medicinal herbs and plants as well as the famous Shaker Sarsaparilla, and sold small packages of garden seeds. At the start of the Civil War, Union Village still had 364 members, despite its rule of celibacy. But the war damaged the Shakers' southern markets, and potential converts became more intrigued by cities and industry than religious communes.

By the early 1900s, the village's industry had declined, and so had the number of Shakers. In a *Dayton Daily News* story on January 28, 1911, reporter Findley P. Torrence observed: "There is something very pathetic in the Shakers' predicament. As they saw the light they followed it, but the light failed." The Shakers had followed their beliefs by founding the community, but, in time, their following either left or died. Only a few elderly Shaker members remained.

In 1912, Union Village died quietly when the village property was purchased by the United Brethren Church. Eventually, the complex became affiliated with the United Methodist Church (hence, Otterbein's Methodist connection). In an interesting turn, the church turned the village into a home for the elderly—which, in a way, carried on the Shaker tradition of group families.

On a chilly and cloudy October day, I returned to Otterbein to take a bus tour of Union Village with members of the Western Shaker Study Group and a group of Chicago Shaker enthusiasts.

We stopped in a cemetery to see a marker for Union Village residents who had been veterans of the Revolutionary War. One woman noted, "Imagine! In 1805 the land here was covered with oaks that were 300 years old." Then we turned west on Route 63 and entered the Lebanon Correctional Institution, a state medium-security prison built on old

Shaker farmland. Another prison, the Warren County Correctional, abutted to the west. Inmates tended the farm across the highway from where the Shakers used to grow crops.

Our little group got out of the bus and walked a short way to an old brick agricultural building on the prison property that was shedding its white coat of paint and whose roof was collapsing. Inside, farmer-inmates stored tractors, tires, and related parts. "This building," Martha Boice told us, her eyes scanning the interior, "is Shaker. We know that much. But we don't know what it was used for. It's a mystery." Again, most of us stared at the cold, dirty walls.

"Perhaps it was a slaughterhouse," one gentleman said as he looked up at the bricked-up windows and a door. "Up there," he said, pointing to a spot high on the wall, "I can see nail blocks for hanging peg rails. If only we knew more . . ."

Boice added, "You can see a lot of shadows in masonry—things that were."

My next Shaker pilgrimage took me south to White Water Village on Oxford Road in Hamilton County's Crosby Township. White Water was one of twenty-four North American communal villages founded by the Shakers between 1787 and 1824 and is the only surviving village that's left of their four Ohio communities. Although parented by Union Village in Warren County, White Water operated autonomously from 1822 to 1916 as an agricultural community. Twenty-two structures still stand, including two homes, three shops, a brick Shaker meetinghouse, the trustees' office, barns, corncribs, smokehouses, and other smaller buildings. Other structures include the brick wash house (built in 1853); the brick office (1855); a barn and brick laundry; a frame dwelling (1843); the boys' frame residence (1830); and the frame broom shop (1876).

Today, White Water is a forgotten piece of Americana. At Miami Whitewater Forest park near Harrison, volunteers opened a display of local Shaker artifacts with the help of the county park district, which between 1989 and 1991 acquired about 1,300 acres in the area, including the village and its 600 acres, most of them in Crosby Township and a few in Morgan Township in neighboring Butler County. However, the county park district has not yet opened the buildings to the public. "But we're going to change that," Richard Spence vowed. "It will open. We've been working hard on the project for years." As president of the nonprofit Friends of White Water Shaker Village, Spence has worked closely with vice president Jim Innis to apply for restoration grants totaling $500,000. Meanwhile, volunteers continue to donate money and repair the buildings.

Displayed in the visitors' center are photographs—a dozen or so children dressed in suits and wearing ribbons in front of the small white school, a farmer standing in front of two barns with milk cans, and three Shaker men in suits standing in front of the Center Family's trustees' office. There is also a timeline: "1822—a community starts near Okeana in Butler County; 1827—a brick meeting house is erected; 1829—Shakers build a sawmill and gristmill; 1839—seventeen acres of broomcorn raised and made into brooms; 1850—the census counts 73 women, 64 men."

A respected Shaker historian, Spence has been fascinated by White Water since the 1980s and has been actively trying to save it since the 1990s. "The village is a treasure we should save," he said. "But that will take time and money. The park district could put a trail down to the village pretty easily. The trustees' office building could be opened to the public with some work. The other buildings would need more attention, so they could be taken care of later. This would be an authentic Shaker village for people to see up close. I'm sure there would be a lot of interest because it has a fascinating story."

The Shaker's life was one of hard work, religious faith, and dedication to agriculture. Joseph Berne, an Episcopalian minister who as a boy lived at White Water, remembered it fondly when he visited in 1887: "I attended divine worship, and as they stood in their ranks and sung, how I thought of the time when I had my place among those pure people. Sad thoughts came over me. . . . Of course, I missed the large company of former years, I missed the exercise of the stepping, the round dance, the shuffling, and all those beautiful forms of worship I once knew so well and which I think help on the life of a Believer."

According to Spence, "A lot of people joined the group in the 1830s, but then the cholera epidemic hit and thinned the population out," he said. "Then the Millerites, a traveling group of religious people, stopped here and joined the Shaker group. That helped. But, in time, celibacy could not be overcome and the group slowly died out. The last Shaker left here in 1916."

But the process started much earlier, as indicated by an article in the

Harrison News on April 19, 1877: "Still they depart, one by one and two by two they go. Within the last two or three weeks, several Shakers have bid their friends good-bye, to try a life among the worldlings."

Growing more curious, I drove about five miles north to see the village. I was surprised to see that it stood across from modern homes.

Oak versus particleboard.

4

Autumn at SunWatch

> Let us probe the silent places,
> Let us see what luck betide us.
> —*Robert Service*

Ten minutes south of downtown Dayton, beyond sprawling warehouses and smoky paper mills, I took a two-lane road freckled with autumn leaves. As I approached the Great Miami River, the horizon dropped and the air felt damp and heavy. The quiet patch of lowland was an anomaly near Interstate 75.

Soon I saw the parking lot for SunWatch Indian Village/Archaeological Park. A series of timeline markers compressed 15,000 years of our earliest history: The Paleo-Indians, descendants of people who migrated from Asia 40,000 years ago, came to Ohio about 16,000 years ago; the Archaic people, 5,000 years ago; the Adena, 2,500 years ago; the Hopewell, 2,000 years ago; the Fort Ancient, 1,000 years ago. Later came the Shawnee and other "modern" tribes that were here to greet the first settlers. To put this timeline into perspective, consider that the great pyramids were built about 2800 BC, Stonehenge was constructed in 2000–1800 BC, Viking explorer Leif Erikson sighted North America in 986 AD, and Columbus started his first Atlantic voyage in 1492 AD.

The Adena tribes lived in what is now Ohio from about 1000 BC to 700 AD; the Hopewell from about 200 BC to 600 AD; and the Fort Ancient from about 1000 AD to 1700 AD. The latter's culture was not as advanced as the Hopewells, who fashioned copper artifacts and traded regularly with other peoples.

SunWatch, a reconstructed Fort Ancient town and interpretative center, opened on five acres near the Great Miami in 1988. The name refers to the villagers' fascination with the sun. During its brief existence, 1180–1250 AD, SunWatch was a planned community, with public and private places surrounded by a stockade. The village's size, about 250 people, was large by New World standards.

It took only one glance to convince me that this was as good a place as any to start my search for lost Indian towns. It was a journey that would lead me to excavation sites, mounds, and museums across Ohio, but it would not answer my most obvious question: What happened to the early tribes?

When people think of the state's lost towns, they usually don't consider those that existed long before the settlers arrived in the Northwest Territory in the 1780s. I know we shouldn't try to compare the SunWatch people to modern families, but early Indian towns were communities in every sense — places where people loved, fought, reared children, married, rejoiced, quarreled, worried about their religion, and buried their dead. Their impact on the land was much less harsh than ours because it occurred over a longer period and without heavy industry and chemicals. Prehistoric and some early tribes lacked metal-tipped farm implements, axes, shovels, primitive guns, and draft animals. Yet, by hard work, they tore down trees, built towns, and hunted to sustain themselves and even flourish.

I had set up a tour with the best guide in town — James Heilman, a SunWatch founder and the curator of archaeology at the parent Dayton Museum of Natural History. In the oval-shaped village, five reconstructed lodges poked above low-hanging fog. Heilman explained that archaeological excavations have revealed evidence of eighteen more lodges. "People can't believe what exists out here by the river," he said as he scanned the cloudy, gray horizon. "We've been excavating since a man called us in 1969 and suggested that a prehistoric town was here. He had found some items. We were skeptical at first, but he was right. It was one of Dayton's best-kept secrets. Eventually, we decided to show what life was like here 800 years ago. We continue to uncover pieces of bone used for fishing hooks and pipes carved from slate. The way the place looks now is probably how it looked about AD 1200."

Using evidence collected by archaeologists, museum volunteers duplicated one-room lodges complete with wooden frames, grass coverings, and mud-packed walls (for wind resistance). The largest lodge served as the men's gathering place. Inside the low-ceilinged room, a fire burned in a ring in the middle of the earthen floor. No ventilation. Wooden shelves on the walls held crude pottery and tools. Despite his tall frame, Heilman darted effortlessly into the open lodge and dropped a log on the fire. The room felt as cool as a cave. "I lived here for one week last winter with eight people," he said. "The lodge was comfortable, but the smoke bothered us. It was so dark inside that we lost a twelve-inch skillet for three days. We used 150 pounds of firewood every twenty-four hours, just to keep the temperature inside at fifty-five degrees. The best thing about the stay was the lack of a telephone."

If settlers had not stripped the countryside of trees, Heilman said, the Indians would have done so in time because they needed large amounts of firewood. The image of the Indian as the great ecologist is not completely accurate, he said, because their villages created garbage and their people exhausted the soil. White settlers behaved similarly, once measuring prosperity by how many farms a man had worn out.

At SunWatch, the villagers dug pits that held up to forty bushels of corn. Because they were lined with blue stem grass and animal skins, the pits resisted mold and water. Other SunWatch pits contained wastes. By rummaging through these pits, archaeologists have learned how the people lived. They coped with harsh winters, termites, crop failure, kids, dental cavities, predatory animals, and in-laws—the same problems that people face today. They were not eco-fairies running innocently through the woods. They were attracted to the Great Miami for the same reasons that white settlers would be later: river transportation, fishing, rich soil, good drainage, and trails. Heilman said SunWatch villagers also chose the site because it was then on a pocket prairie. They didn't have to clear any trees, he said, and a wooded area nearby provided plenty of firewood and building materials.

Related by a common female ancestor, SunWatch people lived in families, or clans. Archaeologists have determined that the SunWatchers were of the Wolf Clan. "The village was broken into quadrants by families," Heilman told me. "After marriage, the wife's mother moved next door—or in with—the couple. Despite the arrangements, we don't know if women gave the orders." In Fort Ancient villages then, the average family consisted of parents and three or four children. Each family produced its own food, tools, and clothes. Men hunted, fished and did the heavy work; women farmed, collected firewood, and maintained the household.

Autumn at SunWatch 49

In 1200 AD, Fort Ancient villages were scattered throughout southern Ohio, including along the Little Miami River, in the Scioto River Valley, along the Great Miami, and on various creeks and other rivers. Archaeologists, the detectives of history, don't know if all the villages were occupied at once. If so, the region had a relatively large population for the time. The remains of a large Fort Ancient town in Hamilton County, called the Madisonville site, was discovered in 1879 by Charles Metz, who found 1,200 graves and many artifacts.

SunWatch people fashioned animal skins and feathers into clothing and also wove coarse cloth, strung necklaces, made spears and arrows from stone and flint, and carved armbands from shell, bone, and stone. They were also the first Ohio River Valley people to make the bow and arrow. Villagers ate whatever they could kill, including Indian dog, skunk, toad, wildcat, crane, and owl, besides the usual deer and bear, and they planted corn and beans. At one point in the tour, Heilman picked up a couple of ears of dried corn and rubbed his fingers across them. He said, "Decayed human teeth show a dependence on corn, which caused malnutrition and dental problems." Women cooked in a large community pot, and the people ate what they wanted. They piled earth on top of their wastes. Over time, the villages sat a few feet higher.

By our standards, the early Indians were short—the men were five feet four inches and the women five feet tall and slightly stooped. They lived only about twenty-seven years. By the Adena period, both men and women averaged two inches taller. Their lifespan didn't change much, though. They were dark and Asian in appearance. By the 1200s, the Fort Ancients had changed physically, representing different racial and cultural backgrounds.

As I ended my visit, I noticed the interpretative center's logo: a sun—in yellow, red, and black—with clock hands on eleven and lodges with thatched roofs. To these early farmers, the seasons—not time's hourly passing—were all-important. Their religion tied the elements to everything. The tribes believed that the heavenly bodies were living entities, and that supernatural forces controlled the weather through their surrogates, the wind and rain. They also believed in a supreme being and showed thanks at seasonal planting intervals by conducting ceremonies that included music with drums and flutes. By using a special pole, Sun-

Watch villagers developed a complex system of charting time based on observing the sun. When the pole's shadow hit the main lodge, the Solstice House, the time had arrived to plant crops. Using solar astronomy, they determined when the frost would leave so they could plant corn. (This happened while many twelfth-century European astronomers were still doing horoscopes.)

Heilman showed me through the rest of the village, stopping every few minutes to point out something he found fascinating.

> Evidence suggests that villagers left during the winter for smaller quarters, but we don't know where they went. There is a lot we still don't know about them, and we wish we had the answers. We know a lot of esoteric stuff, but we also know that they fished in the river and worked land that is among the richest in Montgomery County. They were good farmers. Their land seldom flooded. We know that because if it had, we would see silt in the old food storage pits. We think one reason they abandoned the village after only fifteen to twenty years was that they had a major impact on their environment. We can't prove it, but we're strongly suspicious. Each year they had to go farther afield to look for wood, and their field fertility was going down.
>
> And they had other problems. All wasn't gleeful in the neighborhood. Either the wolves were exceptionally aggressive, which they were not, or the villagers had trouble with bipedal animals. We have seen triangular pieces stuck in their chests, so I don't think warfare was uncommon to the area. You don't build a stockade for nothing.

His enthusiasm for archaeology and the early people made me want to learn more.

For reasons unknown, Fort Ancient towns decreased in number after 1250. In 1450, only two large villages remained in the Miami Valley. By the late 1600s, the Fort Ancients were gone. A few decades later, when the Shawnee returned to the Ohio Country, their ancestral home, they probably absorbed the few, if any, remaining Fort Ancients. Heilman said a popular theory is that the Fort Ancients became the Shawnee. The trouble with that thinking, he said, is that the Shawnee tribes were not matriarchal. Another theory is that the Fort Ancients' demise coincided with the rise of the warrior League of the Iroquois, an upper–New York confederacy that later dominated American Indians and the fur-trading business. So perhaps the Iroquois destroyed the Fort Ancient society. Other people believe that the Hopewells and Fort Ancients declined gradually as they mingled with other tribes, or that plague or drought ended their reign.

When the pioneers arrived in the late 1700s, they didn't even know the Fort Ancients had farmed successfully in the area a few centuries earlier. In fact, only in the last 100 years have we started to understand what they accomplished.

Now all that remains of an entire culture is a few dried bones, pieces of pottery and flint, and a sketchy idea of who the Fort Ancients were. It is only when I think of the interpretative center's sidewalk markers that history takes on new meaning to me—15,000 years. Fifteen thousand years in the future, what we call Dayton might have been leveled and rebuilt fifty times over. Or it might be scorched earth.

Future archaeologists might have as much trouble understanding our society as we have the Fort Ancients. We just have to hope that an archaeologist in 17,000 AD doesn't pull plastic jugs from a twenty-first-century landfill and conclude that Dayton was only a disposable community, one unworthy of reconstruction or interpretation.

5

Knights of Shawnee

> Nobody in Cincinnati knows anything about Shawnee, and yet Shawnee is a type, an evidence showing forth of what every intelligent business man in Cincinnati ought to be thinking about. When you see in this country a dark streak of earth on a side hill, they say it is a "blossom of coal." So Shawnee is a "blossom" of what this section is to be, and which will rival and perhaps exceed, in wealth the best portion of the [coal] region of Pennsylvania.
> —*A Cincinnati newspaper, late 1800s*

While refueling my car one afternoon in southeastern Ohio, I read a sticker someone had slapped onto the pump: "Save our industry! Stop Cap and Trade!" Referring to a federal plan to reduce carbon emissions by limiting the use of coal, the sticker implored the faithful to protest to their elected officials. I could understand why some people, particularly those in the southern Ohio, were against it. Even my hometown, Hamilton, keeps a huge mound of coal standing next to the city's power plant on the Great Miami River. For many Ohio cities, coal remains a major energy source.

Coincidentally, later that day I arrived in a semi–ghost town named Shawnee in Perry County. The old town once boomed because of coal mines; and now, despite having lost many of its people, mines, and businesses, Shawnee refuses to march into history's dark night.

When I first drove down Route 93, I saw the town perched on the hillside like a collection of toy buildings. The first thing I noticed was Shawnee's unusual appearance. When I mentioned this to Cindy Hartman, who owns the Community Gift Exchange Shop with her husband, she chuckled. "It does look different," she said, noting it was built on a hillside. But I was referring to its empty streets. To me, Shawnee looked more like a movie set, all weathered and apparently deserted, yet still intact.

I asked Hartman if the town was growing, and she said emphatically, "Oh, no. In the last year, the post office and the library have both closed. We have only five businesses left, including a furniture store, which is doing pretty well, and a couple of carry-outs."

Shawnee wasn't always a good candidate for a movie set. Once it was an active small town supported by local businesses and the booming coal industry. Then the coal business went bust, and people started leaving town. In 2000, Census takers counted just 600 inhabitants.

The whole area has been affected by the decline in coal production. In the early 1900s, coal companies employed 50,000 workers and operated more than 1,000 mines in Ohio. Many workers lived in company towns, especially in southeast Ohio. Many of Perry County's coal-mining towns—called the Little Cities of Black Diamonds—were operated by the Sunday Creek Coal Company. These days, Ohio's coal production is about half what it was in the 1970s, only about 3,000 miners work in 130 mines. The decline in production made ghost towns out of Bogus, Rain Rock, Moonville, Rendville, Hamburger, Hobo, Mudsock, and San Toy.

Nowadays, Shawnee is more about the past—coal, rural America, and union workers—than the present. There also is a secret labor history to the place, one that's ignored by most history textbooks. If you talk to the locals long enough, they will tell you proudly that their town was instrumental in the birth of America's earliest organized union, the Knights of Labor, founded in 1869. I didn't doubt their sincerity, for the story of Shawnee's union connection has been passed down through the generations, like great-great-grandfather's pocket watch. Regardless of who's correct about the leadership—historians or locals—there is no disputing that the Knights were an important force in Shawnee and Perry County in the late nineteenth century.

As I walked around town, I couldn't imagine what life was like back then, when the words "union," "radical," and "socialism" were spoken in the same breath. I had with me a copy of a page from the *Cleveland Plain Dealer* of September 3, 1984, which had an Associated Press story, datelined Shawnee, Ohio, that carried the headline "Home of Labor Movement Quiet on Workers' Day." In part, the small piece read: "Secrecy surrounding the organization's [Knight's of Labor's] early activity obscured its true birthplace. Many historians acknowledge that

Philadelphia and Shawnee were the only places where early Knights of Labor headquarters were located." Above the Shawnee story appeared a more revealing headline: "Protests, Celebrations Mark Labor Day."

A street scene from Shawnee. Note the run-down buildings. (Photo by Randy McNutt)

On the road leading into town, a sign boasts, "Shawnee, capital of the Knights of Labor union movement" from 1870 to 1880. If Shawnee wasn't the union's first headquarters, then it must have been one of the more important towns for the group, which encountered more than bare-knuckled opposition from company owners and figurative brick walls in many quarters of society. Imagine the reaction of wealthy company owners when they learned that their coal miners had organized for their own welfare. The gall—an eight-hour day! Safer conditions!

"Children worked in the mines during the 1880s," said Shawnee historian John Winnenberg, author of a children's book called *The Little Cities of Black Diamonds: The Story of Our Community*. "Mining was dangerous. People were hurt and [they] died due to cave-ins, explosions, and a lack of air when a tunnel would be closed off. The biggest mine disaster in Ohio was in the little town of Millfield in Athens County. Eighty-two miners were killed in an explosion there."

In those days, mine companies controlled nearly every facet of their employees' lives, owning company housing, stores—just about everything that workers used or needed often came from the owners. Nevertheless, union members—in Shawnee and across the nation—did make some progress in the last three decades of the nineteenth century. Published in 1905, *A History of the Coal Miners of the United States* described the Knights of Labor of Shawnee as "one of the best in the state," as offering the "best educational institution for workingmen ever devised." To help educate their members, the Knights in 1881 erected a three-story building at Main Street and School House Hill. The Knights of Labor Opera House featured a stage, a library, and the offices of United Assembly No. 169. (When the Knights weren't using the building's stage, they rented it to Field's Minstrels.) The Knights rented out one meeting room and used the other for their lodge hall. "At every weekly meeting," the book said, "original essays were read and discussion held on industrial subjects to educate and train members for the varied duties of American citizenship."

At their meetings, the Knights—a mix between a fraternal group and a union—also conducted elaborate rituals modeled after the Freemasons. Early in the Knights' history, members' names had to remain secret, for employers often fired employees who joined the union or tried to organize workers.

Most other historians maintain that Uriah S. Stephens and his fellow tailors founded the Knights of Labor in Philadelphia in 1869. Many people in Perry County claim their coal miners joined and helped turn the union into a political and educational organization. "Its purpose was noble and holy," *A History of the Coal Miners* asserted. "It taught that industrial moral worth, not wealth, was the true standard of individual and national greatness."

As the group expanded in size, appeal, and strategy, Terrence Powderly became the union's national leader in 1879. He ended its policy of secrecy and aggressively sought new members, including women and African Americans (but not Asians). In Ohio, the union was particularly strong: in 1880 it had only 800 members, but by 1887 more than 17,000. Meanwhile, the group's national membership continued to grow, thanks in part to several strikes that brought attention to the Knights.

Those days were difficult ones for workers, who had few, if any, rights. Business barons ruled by intimidation and exhaustion. Workers toiled ten to twelve hours a day six days a week, often alongside child workers. Management paid little attention to safety issues. Naturally, the Knights took root quickly if not quietly, attracting workers who labored in the nation's lumber and rail yards, packinghouses, garment factories, tanneries, and coal mines. They appreciated the Knights' motto: "An Injury to One Is the Concern of All."

The union and other reformers called for an eight-hour work day, a graduated income tax, equal pay for equal work, elimination of child labor, improved working conditions, government ownership of telegraph and railroad lines, and better wages. In an effort to improve the morals and lifestyles of its members, the union also supported the temperance movement. By 1886, the Knights had 700,000 members—called "producers," who made products. Members included factory workers and even some business owners, but not "non-producers"—bankers, lawyers, teachers, and people in other service occupations.

As the Knights of Labor tried to assimilate and ally with the smaller unions, it continued to discourage strikes, saying they were disruptive and dangerous. The Knights sought to improve members' working conditions through boycotts and negotiations. Some of the group's leaders disagreed with Powderly, however, and encouraged workers to strike in the larger cities.

The Knights' demise began on May 4, 1886, at Chicago's Haymarket Square, where farmers gathered to sell produce. A day earlier, police had arrived at the McCormick Harvesting Machine Company plant to protect the company's strikebreakers. Striking McCormick workers sought an eight-hour workday. During a brawl, one man was killed and several were injured. The violence attracted Chicago's anarchists, who called for 20,000 people to join them the following day in a rally at Haymarket Square. A crowd estimated at 2,000 people showed up. Defying orders, police entered the crowd to break it up. Someone threw a pipe bomb, killing seven officers and wounding sixty people. In retaliation, officers fired into the crowd, killing four demonstrators. Ultimately, eight anarchists were charged with conspiracy to commit murder; seven were convicted, four of whom were hanged, and one committed suicide.

Inflamed by newspapers, Chicago officials panicked over the anarchist menace. National public opinion quickly turned against the Knights, who were blamed for the so-called Haymarket Riot. (Yet no evidence ever linked any of the defendants directly to the explosion.) As a result of the riot, public opinion turned against organized labor. Of course, the eight-hour workday seemed doomed. As the Knights' influence started to decline, a more moderate union, the American Federation of Labor, founded in Columbus, began to grow. But it welcomed only skilled tradesmen; no women and African Americans. In 1890, a specialty union, the United Mine Workers, also began operating in Columbus, siphoning more members from the Knights.

Because Powderly failed to rally and unite his group at this critical time, he resigned his post in 1893. His leaving didn't help much, however. Membership continued to decline as new unions began to form. In 1900, the Knights had only 100,000 members left. But in Shawnee, the group remained strong and influential. From 1881 to 1900, it spent $15,000 to remodel the Opera House. In 1902, the group finally sold the building to the local chapter of the Knights of Pythias, a fraternal organization.

As I drove on the back streets of Shawnee, listening to the radio news and stories about a reeling economy, I realized that some things had changed for the better in labor relations and politics in the last century, but many had not. Workers were still the first to be laid off, while company officers earned millions in "golden parachutes"—buyouts or retirement income—when they left.

For many workers, the Knights of Labor's original dream—employers developing a moral worth—remained a largely unfulfilled dream.

. . .

When Shawnee was a premier American coal town, Perry County became the destination of thousands of miners from across the nation. Its towns were rough-and-tumble places. The after-hours antics drew the attention of newspapers across the state. As far away as Cincinnati, Cleveland, and Toledo, newspapers looked to fill small holes in their pages with Shawnee's odd stories. In the early 1900s, the *Cincinnati Commercial* ran this one-paragraph piece:

> SHAWNEE, O., August 15—An altercation between Thomas Lomax and James Kennedy, last evening, ended with Kennedy striking and killing Lomax. John Perkins and Frank Wade [also] had a pitched battle, and razors and chairs were freely used. Perkins was badly cut up. Wade and Kennedy were arrested.

In the 1800s and early 1900s, violence among Hocking Valley laborers became legendary. When fistfights involved many people, Perry County residents gave them fanciful names such as the Tunnel Hill War, which broke out in 1854 when some railroad laborers failed to receive their pay, and the Hippodrome War, which occurred at a traveling circus in Somerset in 1853. "The melee [Hippodrome] did not last fifteen minutes, but seemed an hour," a county historian wrote thirty years later. "A great many persons were bruised, cut and otherwise injured in the fight, only one fatally." The fight resumed the next day and continued for days.

Other unusual occurrences in the valley received attention statewide, many of them involving coal. In 1956, a headline in the *Cleveland Plain Dealer* read: "Perry County Widow Digs Crazy Cellar: Woman Has Coal Mine in Basement." A Mrs. William Leaver didn't have to call the coal company truck to provide heat for her house. She hadn't needed a delivery since 1917. That's because she had her own coal mine in her basement. In 1916, she and her husband moved into his grandfather's house in Shawnee, population 1,145. The Leavers went to the basement and examined the walls. To their surprise, one was made of pure coal. Mr. Leaver built a door on the wall to cover an open mineshaft. Whenever he needed coal, he'd crawl into his little mine—fourteen feet high and 150 feet long—and start digging, just as his grandfather had done for the last thirty-nine years. When they purchased the house, the Leavers had also bought the mineral rights to the property, a lot next door, and an adjacent lot. In 1956, Mrs. Leaver told a reporter that she had an estimated 1,000-year supply of coal.

A major economic boost to the area came in 1870 when the railroads arrived. They carried coal out of the Great Vein—a coal-rich area around Monday Creek, a tributary of the Hocking River. A new town, New Straitsville, made up of mostly English and Irish immigrants, sprang up within months. Other coal towns also popped up quickly, and some existing towns expanded. Drawn by jobs in mining, railroads, construction, and other fields, workers flooded into the three counties in search of jobs.

Shortly after being platted in 1872, Shawnee started growing—fast. Miners came looking for work; mine owners hired them. Shawnee became the Hocking Valley's third largest mining town, despite the financial turmoil of the Panic of 1873. The Hocking Valley mining district would come to dominate the economy in parts of Ohio's Athens, Hocking, and Perry counties until the 1930s.

At its peak, Shawnee had four physicians, a dentist, many secret societies and fraternal groups, two large public schools and one parochial school to accommodate 550 children, eight churches, sidewalks made of boards, muddy streets into which wagon wheels sunk, three large company stores (miners were required to shop there), and a number of hotels, boardinghouses, and company houses located outside of town in Whippoorwill Hollow, Shield's Hollow, and other places. Several hundred miners worked in six mines near Shawnee, including Upson's and the Double X, and in four blast furnaces, including the Fanny and the New York.

As the twentieth century dawned, Shawnee's *People's Advocate* saw its town as "rude in appearance . . . [but] in many respects like a progressive little city" of about 4,000 people, making it Perry County's largest town, made up of representatives of "nearly every land under the sun," mainly English, Irish, Welsh, Scotch, and German. Meanwhile, in 1900, Nelsonville's population hit 5,000 and Glouster and New Straitsville topped 2,000. Smaller towns such as Jacksonville, Murray City, and Corning reached 1,000, as did a number of area company towns. Rendville attracted many African Americans, while towns like Shawnee and New Straitsville discouraged them from moving there. John Fleming, the newspaper's editor, once wrote that for many years a worker named John Lilly was the town's "sole representative of the Negro race. . . . During the gubernatorial campaign of 1893, Johnny told Governor

McKinley that he held the Negro vote of Saltlick Township in his vest pocket. As a Negro citizen of the town, Johnny has not had a successor."

Today, Shawnee and the Valley's other neglected communities are linked by a common supporting organization, the Little Cities of Black Diamonds, which represents "small towns and the townships that surround them, with a significant portion of the land in the region being part of the Wayne National Forest."

The group borrowed the name from Ivan Tribe's *Little Cities of Black Diamonds,* "the book that got the history fever started." Through the Black Diamonds group, the communities have tried to keep alive local history, culture, and traditions. In a statement on their website, group leaders acknowledge that their member towns have "shared a common story of economic decline, community decay, environmental degradation, and population loss during the decades since the 1920s, that has resulted in the Little Cities region becoming one of the least politically potent regions of the state." The region's huge population losses have finally given way to steady growth, although "in many ways there is an

The tiny coal museum in Shawnee draws few visitors these days. (Photo by Randy McNutt)

Knights of Shawnee 61

on-going battle between restoration and decay. Which force will prevail still remains uncertain." The leaders hope that if local people continue to learn about their region's story, they might become more active in helping restore their own towns.

That battle continues today in Shawnee, although at first glance the visitor might not know it. To outsiders, the town looks like it is on life-support.

In the 1880s, things were different. Shawnee boomed. Through ups and downs in the coal market, the town persevered. In time, however, the depressed coal market affected even Shawnee. "In retrospect," Tribe wrote, "we now know that long-term stability eluded the mining camps and by the 1980s, some have vanished or become virtual ghost towns. The depression of the mid-1890s proved a trying period for the

On the street in Shawnee, where many buildings have deteriorated. (Photo by Randy McNutt)

62 *Finding Utopia*

local populace; they survived one set of hard times only to be hit by another a generation later."

By modern standards, the coal towns of the Hocking Valley—including Shawnee—were tough places where men worked hard and played harder. Naturally, the town councils tried to restrain their rougher element by enacting laws against public drunkenness, fighting, carrying weapons, profane language, and other infractions. In Shawnee, the mayor heard 1,292 cases—576 of them for public intoxication—from 1874 to 1900. Tribe researched them and determined that the most unusual was the case of Jack Evans in December 1880: "Jack Evans having been . . . charged with drunkenness . . . being so covered in filth was discharged from custody without a trial."

In 1875, a traveling reporter from Cincinnati marveled at seeing sixteen-month-old Shawnee. "Here is a town . . . which looks as if it had been built last night, and the boards look like they had not got dry since they left the lumber region! Here is a marvel. We left Newark with the idea that Shawnee had 1,200 people . . . and [when we] arrived at Shawnee and we found the census had been taken last week, and it [population] was 1,830! From what I saw I have no doubt that when this letter is printed . . . [the population will be] over 2,000." The reporter noted that in 1870 the coal-rich land around Shawnee was selling for $65 per acre. In February 1872, he said, 150 of those acres went for $150 per acre. The next month, amid speculation that a community would rise from the hillside, 600 acres sold for $500 per acre. "Shawnee is at present the terminus of the railroad and the outlet of the coal mines. . . . Shawnee will probably reach 5,000 inhabitants before its peculiar advantages cease," he added.

The reporter, identified only as E.D.M., left the train on that warm September day and walked around the young town. He marveled at the activity. In those halcyon years, Shawnee's streets ran "over the sides of hills in every direction, for there is not an acre of level ground," he said. "The principal street ran along the foot of the hill, and may possibly be carried a mile." As he walked along another street, he observed people in motion—working, playing, talking, and no doubt fighting.

"Just opposite of me," he went on, "is a store, just built and opening. The lot is only 25 by 70 feet. After the town was started, this lot was sold for $450; then for $900! This seems to be about four times what it is worth, but I have not the least doubt the owner will make a great profit on this lot, and get profit on his store. Fifty thousand dollars per month are [being] paid out here for wages, and that gauges the value of lots. Now mark: sixteen months ago the only buildings in Shawnee were a house and a barn! This is an indication—a mere sign—of what this country is to be."

Even before the Great Depression began in late 1929, Shawnee and the Little Cities of Black Diamonds were experiencing tough times. The depressed economy made things even harder in Perry County than in many other Ohio communities. Nearly all the local brick plants and coal mines closed. Railroad lines canceled passenger service to Shawnee and a few other county towns. Shawnee's banks closed, never to reopen.

When the twentieth century neared its halfway point, Shawnee—and the coal mines—slipped. The *People's Advocate,* founded in 1929, ceased publication in 1943. People started leaving town after World War II, and the next decade wasn't much better. The 1960s weren't good for Shawnee, either. More families slipped below the poverty line. New highways were built, sending cars and trucks away from downtown. More Main Street businesses closed—even the town baseball diamond. High schools were relocated outside of town and existing schools got older. The residents who remained started driving to other towns to do their shopping.

This postcard of Shawnee is from the early 1950s, when the town was still filled with businesses. (Author's collection)

As I drove around town, looking for life, I passed street after street and saw no one. So I parked my car and started walking. I took photographs of what appeared to be an old theater, an empty insurance office, and other forgotten storefronts. What an eerie sight—all the empty buildings.

Now, like a big museum, Shawnee offers its weathered buildings for all to see. One of the town's oldest is the frame town hall and firehouse at 103 West Walnut Street. When it opened in 1874, its tall steeple gave Shawnee a stately appearance. Now ready for renovation, it is listed on the National Register of Historic Places. The building cost $685 to construct. It served as the town hall and jail until the end of 1889, when a new town hall replaced it, costing $1,532. Early on, the first floor was used as a fire station and the upstairs as the town hall and a makeshift classroom.

A few doors away, I thought I saw a man and his wife, about sixty years old, sitting on their porch. I walked up to them to make certain they were not a mirage. The man looked at me as though he hadn't seen a human being in weeks. "Hello!" he shouted.

His house appeared to be recently painted white, and his flower garden added color to the front porch.

"What happened to Shawnee?" I asked.

He shook his head sadly. "Many people have left," he said. "This process has taken many years. The population keeps dwindling. Sometimes I feel like we're alone. We don't know what the future will bring. All we know is, there will be one. Shawnee has survived this long; it will survive longer."

He leaned toward his wife, smiled, and put his arm around her shoulder.

"Somehow," she added.

Lost Legends

II

6

Army of the Damned

> A good general is never taken by surprise.
> —*Little Turtle*

Thirty minutes before dawn, on November 4, 1791, General Arthur St. Clair heard gunfire crackling along the Wabash River. Then a hideous howling sliced the morning air. The malevolent sound raised the hair on inexperienced soldiers' necks. Aching with gout, St. Clair limped from his tent, clutching a plain dark coat and a tri-cornered beaver hat. "Indians!" shouted an aide. As musket balls ripped through the snowflakes, waves of painted warriors smashed the army's camp on three sides. The general and his officers tried to rally their troops, but the volunteers bolted in panic. Above the turmoil they could hear the natives' howling growing stronger, as though it originated from the depths of hell. One soldier later described the angry chorus as "an infinitude of horse bells suddenly opening to you."

Soldiers began fleeing into the woods, dropping their muskets and shedding their shoes and jackets to attain greater foot speed. The lucky ones managed to outrun the warriors, who preferred to plunder the campsite. There, wounded soldiers and civilians were mutilated, scalped, and killed—in that order.

On that grim day, along a tributary of the Wabash in what is now Mercer County, Ohio, Little Turtle's tribal confederation won the Native Americans' greatest victory ever over an American army. More soldiers died there than on any other battlefield in the country, a statistic that would stand until the Civil War. (By comparison, General

George Custer [another Ohioan] lost only 271 soldiers at the Battle of the Little Big Horn.) St. Clair lost more than 600 soldiers. His debacle is the only major battle in American history with no official name. It was usually called St. Clair's Defeat, but it was also known as St. Clair's Shame, Battle of Bloody Run, and Battle of the Wabash. A local stream, Buck Ditch, was called Bloody Run because the blood of dying and wounded soldiers turned its water red.

It took St. Clair's troops thirty days to march into infamy, and only about a week to run back to Fort Washington on the Ohio River.

Exactly 219 years after the battle, I left Cincinnati and drove north on U.S. Route 127, passing urban neighborhoods founded in the early 1800s. It was generally the way St. Clair's army headed north in that chilly fall of 1791, although it passed through a much different terrain—isolated, hilly, heavily wooded, and filled with bobcats, bears, cougars, poisonous snakes, and other dangerous animals.

At Hamilton, I stopped at the site of Fort Hamilton, a supply post built by St. Clair's troops on the Great Miami River. A plaque marked the fort's location. I stood and looked at the western hills I knew so well and wondered how they looked in 1791.

Unlike the cold late autumn of 1791, the weather for my trip was relatively warm and pleasant. Farther north on Route 127, red and gold leaves blew from scattered clumps of trees. I marveled at how St. Clair's ragged army managed to march this far—fifty, sixty miles by now, maybe—in only a few days and under such strenuous conditions.

As the sun slowly warmed the interior of my car, I felt tired after ninety minutes of driving. My allergies bothered me, so I turned on the air conditioner for a short time while listening to the radio as a diversion. A male talk-show caller complained about illegal immigrants. As a large cloud of crows flew over my car, I randomly turned west onto a small side road, between patches of brown stubble that covered the flat horizon.

Farmland—sleeping cornfields—rolled toward the horizon in northern Butler and Preble counties. I couldn't imagine all the hardships that the troops—the army of the damned—must have endured on their march toward oblivion. By the time I reached Darke and Mercer counties, all I could see was autumn's handiwork. Silver silos guarded a blue horizon; occasional rural towns looked like outposts on the two-lane highway. Gazing around, I finally realized what the settlers and the Indians wanted with this land: food, natural beauty, independence.

The Ohio Country was the prize.

While assessing the battle's terrible aftermath, St. Clair must have wondered how this could have happened. His recent past had been one of only power and success. Only seven years earlier, at age fifty, he was safe and secure as the president of the Continental Congress. Then, in 1788, he was offered the post of governor of the newly created Northwest Territory. St. Clair accepted, in what he would later call the "most imprudent act in my life." He felt obligated because he had fought with George Washington in the Revolutionary War.

Three years later, President Washington summoned the governor to Philadelphia to discuss a planned offensive against the Indian coalition that had been growing stronger north of the Ohio River. In March 1791, Washington warned him, "General St. Clair, in three words: Beware of surprise."

When he arrived at Fort Washington from Philadelphia, St. Clair began having doubts. Henry Knox, the secretary of war, had enlisted 2,000 levies—soldiers who served under federal orders for six months— and local militia. But the levies consisted of mostly untrained, undisciplined, and drunken soldiers. St. Clair ordered them to dry out at Ludlow's Station, near the fort. He soon discovered that his troops had been issued poorly made equipment by Quartermaster General Samuel Hodgdon, a friend of Knox. The inept Hodgdon also had ordered four-pound shot for St. Clair's three-pound cannons and arranged for the army's musket ammunition to be handmade in an onsite laboratory, which St. Clair considered dangerous and inexact. The newly arrived gun carriages were unfit for service, and soldiers hadn't received new shoes. When they finally did arrive, courtesy of Knox's friend and New York financier William Duer, they wore out in only a week.

Yet, inexplicably, St. Clair informed Knox that "the troops seem in perfectly good condition." Winthrop Sargent knew better. The troops "were generally wanting the essential stamina of soldiers," he wrote later.

> Picked up and recruited from the off-scourgings of large towns and cities; enervated by idleness, debaucheries, and every species of vice, it was impossible they could have been made competent to the arduous

duties of Indian warfare. An extraordinary aversion to service was also conspicuous among them, and demonstrated by the most repeated desertions, in many instances to the very foe we were to combat. The late period at which they had been brought into the field left no leisure or opportunity to discipline them. They were, moreover, badly clothed, badly paid, and badly fed.

With physical pain from his old nemesis gout, St. Clair was already exhausted by the time the march began. At times his men had to carry him on a stretcher. At Washington's insistence, the army continued north, walking through soggy woods and muddy plains. In this wild and dangerous country a confederation of Miami, Wea, Shawnee, Piankeshaw, and other tribes watched and waited.

Meanwhile, St. Clair bickered with his second in command, Major General Richard Butler, a Pennsylvanian who doubted St. Clair's ability for "managing Indians." At forty-eight years old, Butler had impressive experience as an Indian agent and, later, the nation's superintendent of Indian affairs. But St. Clair shrugged it off, telling people that Butler was "soured and disgusted." Both men had fought with distinction in the Revolutionary War—Butler at Yorktown, Saratoga, Monmouth, and other battles and Sinclair as aide-de-camp to General Washington—but this time they were marching into the Ohio Country. Indians did not fight like the British, as General Josiah Harmar had learned painfully a year earlier, when he marched on a similar path to disaster. St. Clair's mission—"the humbling and chastising of the savage tribes"—came from Knox, who also had provided Harmar with insufficient manpower. Harmar's defeat had reflected poorly on St. Clair as territorial governor, and this time federal officials back East expected him—now that he was both governor and general—to chase the Indians out of the settlers' backyards.

But Natives Americans considered the Ohio Country their backyard. They maintained—and they had a logical case—that the Ohio River was a legal and natural dividing line between settlers and Indians. Yet the settlers continued to flow down the Ohio, build fortified towns on the north bank, and interfere with Indian ways.

Butler doubted St. Clair's ability to lead an army against the united tribes. During the journey, the two generals disagreed on how to build roads through the woods. They also disagreed on strategy. Their relationship continued to worsen, so they avoided each other.

When troops looked for tools to cut down trees, they discovered that the quartermaster had sent them too few. At the Great Miami River, about twenty-five miles north of Fort Washington, they paused to build a supply post, which St. Clair named Fort Hamilton. As his army left there on October 4, Indian scouts tracked its movements. By then the weather had turned colder and the troops were weary from the long march.

Yet St. Clair had his orders: destroy Kekionga ("blackberry"), a large Miami town, and then build an American fort there (near the present site of Fort Wayne, Indiana, near where the St. Joseph and St. Mary rivers form the Maumee). St. Clair called Kekionga "the headquarters of iniquity"—a major British fur-trading post and a town with streets, sidewalks, a ballroom, a council hall, framed paintings, a five-seat outhouse, and a brothel.

As the army kept marching north, through fields and thick woods, Butler asked St. Clair for permission to take 1,000 of his best fighters and quickly attack the town before freezing weather arrived. On refusal, St. Clair said later, Butler "liked to have laughed in my face." Continuing north on October 22, more deserters slipped away. Twenty militiamen had walked off the previous night. More soldiers left the next morning. Officers demanded that St. Clair teach disobedient troops a lesson. He ordered two captured artillery deserters hanged, but executions did not dissuade more men from fleeing.

At 9:00 A.M. on October 24, on a calm and cloudy day, the shrinking army left camp, unknowingly surrounded by Indian scouts who would follow the soldiers on their march north (a route that roughly paralleled present-day U.S. Route 127). Meanwhile, even more militia members continued to desert. Some soldiers who remained grumbled that they should steal the army's food and weapons and then leave.

Five days later, while marching deeper into enemy territory, St. Clair foolishly closed his army's eyes by ordering twenty valuable scouts to leave on an unrelated mission. By then, the army was twenty miles off course. As he approached an eastern branch of the Wabash, St. Clair thought he was coming to the St. Mary's, near Kekionga.

On October 31, as the group pushed north and the number of desertions increased, St. Clair issued a fatal order: The regulars of the crack 1st Regiment, his only reliable and trained unit, were to leave for the rear of the column to protect provisions and chase deserters. A melancholy Sergeant Major Withrop Sargent wrote, "Our prospects are gloomy. But the general is compelled to move on, as the only chance of continuing our little army." By this time, St. Clair had only 60 percent of the troops that had started with him at Fort Washington. Knowing this, and knowing the dangers, why, then, did he believe the Indians posed no immediate threat? Did he not realize that Little Turtle's confederation was preparing to attack? The Native force, meanwhile, shadowed the army.

I knew every rock and crevice on and around Route 127. I had driven back and forth on Route 127 many times. I counted the small-town signs that I could remember—Ansonia, Versailles, Fort Loramie, Minster, and St. Henry. They dotted a flat horizon of corn and wheat fields.

I saw no sign of Indians, cougars, and bears, except their sports-team logos on the sides of rural schools.

St. Clair's army kept trudging through flat wetlands, soaking their shoes and spirits. On November 3, they arrived at a wooded dry spot along the Wabash. St. Clair ordered his weary soldiers to make camp and leave it unfortified, thus ignoring President Washington's advice about surprises. Kentucky sharpshooter Robert Branshaw observed:

> The main camp was pitched in a level wood by a small stream which was one of the branches of the Wabash River; on higher ground about a quarter of a mile across this steam, the militia and a company of rangers had been on duty through the latter part of the night and were prepared for an attack by Indians whom we knew to be in front of us. We supposed them to be a mere scouting party sent out to gather information about our movements. We did not think that they planned anything more serious than to pick off some of our number and to get a few scalps if they could do so without serious risk. Certain it is, we were not prepared for what took place.

St. Clair's lack of planning continued to worry Butler, who suspected trouble. In his tent late that night, Butler told his aides, "Let us eat, drink, and be merry, for tomorrow we may die."

Early on November 4, the troops awoke tense, hungry, and tired. Their stiff fingers barely moved in the morning cold. A light snow started to fall. More men contemplated leaving. St. Clair hadn't slept well; he was wracked with pain. He had no way of knowing that his army would make history on this morning and that his name would forever be equated with defeat.

Sleepy Branshaw peered into "the gray of the morning, before objects had become distinct at any considerable distance." He recalled,

> I was standing near one of the fires conversing with a comrade. Suddenly I saw twenty or thirty painted savages dodging around among the trees in front of us, as if they planned to attack by surprise. Supposing the ones I saw to be the entire party, and think it a good chance to bring down one of them and at the same time to alarm the camp, I instantly raised my rifle to my eye, took quick aim, and dropped the nearest Indian. The smoke had not cleared away from my rifle when a terrific volley was poured upon us. It was accompanied by appalling yells from a thousand throats. At the same instant I saw Indians spring from behind their covers and rushing down upon us in overwhelming numbers. Instantly, I turned to fly and stumbled over the dead body of the comrade with whom I had been conversing. He had been shot through the temples, and he was the first dead man I saw on that fatal day.

Little Turtle's warriors blew through the militia camp like a tornado. At the sound of the whooping and charging Indians, the militia panicked and ran toward the main army in the center—straight into the artillery camp, which was quickly overrun. Cannons couldn't be fired because Indians were immediately behind the fleeing militia, who by then were surrounded and trapped. The Indians started slaughtering the frantic troops and piling their bodies as high as the artillery. At the sound of the howling, Darke said, many soldiers ran "like a mob at a fair." Warriors quickly identified the officers because they wore colorful insignia on their uniforms and rode horses. One by one, the Indians picked them off, leaving the troops without enough leaders. While the soldiers fled, the Indians hacked, bludgeoned, beat, choked, shot, and stabbed to death not only soldiers but more than 300 horses and fifty-six women camp followers—soldiers' wives, workers, prostitutes. One officer observed that women's bodies lay strewn about, "some of them cut in two, their boobies cut off, and burning with a number of our officers on our own fires." Between 100 and 250 white women were captured. Only three women escaped.

To Major Ebenezer Denny, the scene was déjà vu. He had the dubious honor of participating in Harmar's defeat a year earlier, and now he was involved in another massacre. "The savages seemed not to fear anything we could do," he wrote in his journal. "They could skip out of reach of bayonet and return, as they pleased."

Kentucky militiamen dropped their guns and started running. As Sargent put it, "The enemy was shooting them down with pleasure from behind trees and most secure covers."

St. Clair's regulars fought bravely, but soon they became surrounded and then picked off by musket fire. Pandemonium reigned. One Indian bragged later that he tomahawked so many soldiers that he could not raise his arm later that night. Lieutenant Colonel George Gibson shouted to the levies: "Fight them! Fight them!" But when he fell dead, the men around him ran. "The levies were lost forever," Sargent said.

Branshaw recalled:

> As we fell back, the militiamen behind us discharged their pieces at the approaching savages; then they turned and fled in the wildest alarm through the little hollow back toward the main camp. Many of them never reached it, for by this time the Indians were firing rapidly from all sides and were following up the advantage with their murderous tomahawks and scalping knives. All the while, they were screeching with such appalling effect that I believe some of our men, who might otherwise have escaped, became bewildered, stupefied, and lost.
>
> As for myself, I had some very narrow escapes. Although I was a pretty good runner, I had been singled out by an ambitious young warrior, who, in a race of about two hundred yards, had almost caught up with me. With a good reach of his arm, he might have sunk his tomahawk in the back of my head. A glance over my shoulder showed him about to strike, and instinctively I threw myself down to avoid the blow. As fortune would have it, he struck his foot against one of mine and pitched headlong over me. His weapon flew from his grasp. Before he could recover himself, I was upon him, driving my hunting knife through his throat and severing his jugular vein.
>
> As I again sprang to my feet, I beheld three other savages close at hand, bounding toward me with yells of rage. I had no hope of escaping from them; but still I ran, straining every nerve to its utmost. Fortunately, they were not as fleet-footed as the one I had killed, and to my unspeakable joy, I found that I was outdistancing them. Each Indian

carried a gun in his hand, but I had thrown mine away during my first race. This probably gave me some advantage. Seeing that they could not overtake me, they suddenly stopped; one of them took deliberate aim and fired. The ball sung loudly in my ear, the outer portion of which felt as if it were touched with a live coal. A small portion of my ear had been shot away.

On parts of the battlefield where the fighting had ended, it is said that Indians rejoiced and played torture games with survivors. According to nineteenth-century histories, the Indians rammed stakes into women and, for carnival-style amusement, tied living soldiers to trees and threw knives as close to their heads as possible.

So badly did the warriors' victory shock white America that writers would continue to tell tales of St. Clair's Defeat for the next 125 years and describe Little Turtle's warriors as fiends, devils, and demons.

As the afternoon grew warmer, somewhere north of Greenville, I stopped at a small country library to search for any trace of the ill-fated Ohio army.

I asked a library assistant, "Do you have information on General Arthur St. Clair?" She looked puzzled. I added, "He was the governor of the Northwest Territory. Leader of the pioneer army . . ."

"I'm sorry," she said, shaking her head. "I'm not familiar with him." She pointed to a shelf behind me. "Over there we have several books on the Civil War . . ."

Amid the chaos on that bloody November morning, individual stories unfolded like sad little plays. William Wells, a white man who grew up Indian, scalped so many soldiers that day that his arms went numb. (A few years later, he would switch sides.) A camp woman named Red Headed Nance outran six Indians who momentarily forgot that a battle was going on when they saw her flowing red hair. They coveted her scalp. She outran the warriors—even the soldiers—and lived to be an old woman with a story to tell. St. Clair fought hard that day, despite his gout pain. Four horses fell from under him and eight musket balls ripped through his coat. (He never had time to dress in full uniform.) Miraculously, he escaped unharmed and was among the last to leave the

Army of the Damned 77

battlefield. Soldiers found the only surviving packhorse and placed the general on it. Boldly, Colonel Drake gathered some men and charged the Indians in the center, creating a wedge that allowed St. Clair and a small number of soldiers and civilians to escape to nearby Fort Jefferson.

Denny later testified before Congress, saying,

> The wounded were taken to the center [of the camp], where it was thought most safe, and where a great many, who had quit their posts unhurt, had gathered together. The general, with other officers, endeavored to rally these men, and twice they were taken out to the lines. It appeared as if the officers had been singled out; a very great proportion fell, or were wounded and obliged to retire from the lines early in the action. General Butler was among the latter, as well as several others of the most experienced officers. The men, thus left with few officers, became fearful, despaired of success, gave up the fight, and, to save themselves for the moment, abandoned entirely their duty and ground.
>
> As our lines were deserted the Aborigines contracted theirs until their shot centered from all points, and now meeting with little opposition, took more deliberate aim and did great execution. Exposed to a crossfire, men and officers were seen falling in every direction; the distress, too, of the wounded made the scene such as can scarcely be conceived—a few minutes longer, and a retreat would have been impossible—the only hope left was, that perhaps the Savages would be so taken up with the camp as not to follow. Delay was death; no preparation could be made; numbers of brave men must be left a sacrifice, there was no alternative.

The brave Butler—one of three Butler brothers who fought that day—threw himself into the battle and was wounded twice. Four soldiers wrapped him in a blanket and carried him to the surgeon. They placed him in a sitting position, against a tree. As the doctor examined him, a single Indian lunged forward, rammed a hatchet into the general, and scalped him before his attendants could prevent it. His two brothers, both officers, watched helplessly. (Reportedly, the warrior who killed Butler acted on orders from the renegade Simon Girty.) Later in the battle, the younger Captain Edward Butler fulfilled his dying brother's last request by saving Major Thomas Butler, who had been seriously wounded in both legs.

General Richard Butler died at St. Clair's Defeat. Butler County was named in his honor. (Author's collection)

The only reason the Indians didn't destroy St. Clair's entire army was because they stopped midpursuit to gather up the booty—the army's abandoned supplies, valued at $32,810, a fortune in those days. (The Indians didn't know what to do with eight captured cannons, so they tried to hide them.) In retrospect, the militia's instinct to throw down their weapons and run might have saved some of their comrades, for the lure of muskets-for-the-taking was simply too strong to resist. "The most disgraceful part of the business," St. Clair wrote after he returned home, "is that the greatest part of the men threw away their arms and accoutrements, even after the pursuit . . . had ceased. I found the road strewed with them for many miles."

Sargent described the situation as a battlefield hell that can't be imagined: "Heads, body extremities and sexual organs were severed and mutilated. Persons still living were sometimes tossed on campfires to burn in excruciating pain. At least one female captive was spread-eagled, and then stakes 'as thick as a person's arm' were driven through her body. . . . The road for miles was covered with firelocks, cartridge boxes and regimentals."

Army of the Damned   79

One soldier walked thirty miles to Fort Jefferson with a tomahawk sticking from his head, and another man, scalped and bleeding, arrived with him. By 9:30 A.M., November 5, a sick and weary St. Clair rode a skinny, slow-walking packhorse into Fort Jefferson. A journey that took two full days on the way up took the troops only ten hours in retreat.

Meanwhile, the Indians tortured wounded prisoners by gouging out their eye sockets and filling their mouths with dirt. ("As if in a grim, hideous satisfaction of the white man's demand for more land," an early 1900s historian observed.) Severed limbs were scattered everywhere. The Indians scalped practically everyone (a gruesome ritual not limited to the Indians; American scalps could always be sold to Henry "Hair Buyer" Hamilton, the British lieutenant governor of Canada).

The warriors also enjoyed disfiguring corpses on the battlefield. They stripped flesh from bones. According to an often-told story, they cut out Butler's heart, distributed its pieces to each tribe that fought, and ate them to celebrate. (Years later, however, Little Turtle denied this.) One survivor observed that all the scalped white heads looked like "pumpkins in a cornfield in December." An American captain reported that the nightmare on the Wabash "continued often for two or three days, if they can contrive to keep the prisoner alive." Back on the battlefield, the heads of dead soldiers were scattered across the field like rotting fruit while bodies were laid like broken scarecrows in the light snow. Overhead, turkey buzzards circled in triumph, ready to claim their prizes.

Sharpshooter Branshaw would never forget that day.

> It seems like a wild, horrible dream, in which whites and savages, friends and foes, were all mixed in mad confusion. They melted away in smoke, fire, and blood, amid groans, shouts, shrieks, yells, clashing steel, and exploding firearms. I fired eleven shots and had the grim satisfaction of seeing nine savages go down before my aim; four of them fell within ten feet of me. While I was loading for the twelfth time, a ball struck my right wrist and fractured the bone. I dropped to the ground and bound my wound as well as I could. Finding that I could be of no further use where I was, I started for the rear, feeling weak and faint. I had eaten nothing that morning, which was the case with nearly all of the army. On my way to the center of the camp, I met pale, frightened men running in all directions. Numerous dead bodies, some of them scalped and presenting ghastly spectacles, proved that many of the Indians had been there before me. Wounded

> soldiers called to me and begged for help and water. But I could do nothing for them, and I hurried on. When I came within sight of the spot where the women and children had been collected, I beheld a large body of Indians busy at their work of slaughter. Turning in another direction, I ran down the road.

Fortunately, he found an unattended horse and mounted. Fugitives clogged the trail ahead, but he surged forward, passing them before the order to retreat could be given. "I was spared the painful sight of seeing the whole army in flight, with the victorious savages in hot pursuit, butchering at every step," he said.

When Branshaw finally reached Fort Jefferson, twenty-two miles from the battlefield, he fainted when told he was safe. "The remnant of the army arrived about dark, and nothing was heard that night but sounds of lamentation and woe," he said. "Subsequently, my arm was amputated. My career as soldier ended with that disastrous day, in which nearly a thousand gallant men and two or three hundred women and children had been killed or wounded. Oh, woeful, woeful day!"

It took the tribal coalition only three hours to destroy St. Clair's army, which represented 65 percent of the United States land forces. Indian losses were light—estimated at 66–400 warriors (most likely fewer than 100, though more recent estimates are as low as 21).

What amazes me are the numbers of dead soldiers. According to Major Denny's preliminary estimates, 500 out of about 1,400 American soldiers escaped, and the remainder were listed as dead or missing. Sixty-nine of the army's 124 officers were killed or lost in action, including General Butler.

In his book *Blue Jacket: War Chief of the Shawnees,* Allan Eckert reported that 852 whites died; 39 of 52 officers were killed and 7 were wounded. Of the 868 regulars and militiamen, 593 were killed and 257 wounded. He wrote that 220 of the 255 camp followers died, and all the rest were wounded. Of the total 920 soldiers available to fight that day, only 24 returned uninjured; 264 of them were wounded and 632 were killed.

In December 1791, Denny arrived in Philadelphia to personally explain the details of St. Clair's Defeat. He knew the story all too well. Of course, President Washington had already heard the news. It had

Army of the Damned 81

shaken the entire capital and damaged the new federal government's credibility.

When he first heard about the massacre, the usually mild-mannered Washington was said to have cursed St. Clair and stomped back and forth across the floor in a rage. When Denny left the president's office, a still-hot Washington told Knox:

> It's all over—St. Clair defeated—routed—the officers nearly all killed! The men by the wholesale—the rout complete! A surprise into the bargain! Here in this room I took leave of him and wished him success and honor. "You have your instructions," I said, "from the secretary of war. I had a strict eye to them and will add—beware of surprise!" He went off with that solemn warning ringing in his ears. And yet to suffer that army be cut to pieces, hacked, butchered, tomahawked by a surprise. The very thing I guarded him against! Oh, God! He is worse then [sic] a murderer! The blood of the widows and orphans be upon St. Clair! How can he answer for it to his country!

St. Clair's Defeat spawned one of the earliest media frenzies. A song, "Sainclair's Defeat," circulated around the country. Opposition politicians and newspapers blamed President Washington for the fiasco. A Boston paper printed the names of the dead officers, a brief description of the battle, and two rows of black coffins across the top of the page, with skull and crossbones below, near a drawing of Butler.

At Washington's insistence, a despondent St. Clair resigned his army commission, but he remained governor of the Northwest Territory. The defeat sparked the first congressional investigation, which resulted in St. Clair's exoneration. As a result, Washington used executive privilege to withhold from Congress important papers related to the battle. He claimed the information would injure the public. Congress voted against issuing an official report on the battle, which disappointed St. Clair. He wanted to clear himself of the allegation of incompetence, although it was commonly thought that he did not train and discipline his troops. Ultimately, Congress blamed the defeat on the quartermaster and the private companies he had hired to provide supplies. Knox, in turn, blamed the defeat on a lack of good troops, insufficient discipline, and the lateness of the year.

St. Clair could not escape the verdict of history. His name would forever twist in a field near the Wabash, and a refrain from a popular song would haunt him:

Saint Clair was our commander as it may remembered be
For we left nine hundred lying in that cursed territory.

A Village of Bones

Major Butler was wounded the very second fire;
His manly bosom swell'd with rage when forc'd to retire;
And as he lay in anquish, nor scarely could he see,
Exclaim'd, "Ye hounds of hell! Oh revenged I will be."
  — *"Sainclair's Defeat," late 1790s*

The village of Fort Recovery is an old battlefield on which layers of history are superimposed, like coats of red paint. A rural town of 1,400 people, it lies on the northwest corner of the Treaty of Greenville line, a few miles north of the headwaters of the Wabash River. Its streets bear familiar frontier names—Washington, Wayne, Butler, Harrison. Boundary Street was once the line that divided Indian and white territories. Until the mid-1800s, everything north of the line was officially Indian country.

The names that will forever haunt this place are the ones that I grew up hearing—names as familiar to me as my own. There is Butler—for Butler County, where I live; Gano and Reily, both pioneers who helped build my county; and, of course, Harrison, the man who would become president.

Ever since the terrible morning of November 4, 1791, life on the land around Fort Recovery has been quietly deceiving. On the outside, everything is rural and quiet, like any other old country town. Deep down, however, something unusual stirs. The town simply can't escape its bloody past. While old souls pace the fields and relive that cold morning, two reconstructed blockhouses stand guard behind the town, as if to protect it from an old enemy who's expected to return.

But he never does. Only a few visitors come into town, looking for legends. They find a tamed landscape, a farmer's dream. In 1933, artist Frank Wilcox couldn't understand how St. Clair's troops endured their march north. Lacking man-made drainage systems, Wilcox said, the heavy forests must have made the area a "flat, wet, and dark jungle."

When I arrived, no real forests remained. Farms surrounded the town. I passed several farm homes that were hosting high school graduation parties. On that warm, gray Sunday, no litter blew across Broadway. No deafening bass lines—audio litter to me—thumped from passing cars. People said hello and smiled. Fort Recovery looked like most other older small towns, mostly late Victorian and brick, but was somehow friendlier and cozier. Only a few stores were open on that afternoon before Memorial Day, but community pride showed in the storefronts. Businesses proudly displayed the village name in large letters on their front windows, tourist brochures touted the town's slower pace, and the local Case implement dealer arranged his tractors in neat and precise rows, like tanks ready for deployment.

I found the Fort Recovery State Memorial, built in 1956 and located just west of the business district, to be surprisingly realistic. Here the past of the Northwest Territory reveals itself in an eerie conjunction of ramparts, battlefields, lost settlements, St. Clair, Indian ghost towns, dead soldiers, chiefs Little Turtle and Blue Jacket, and, of course, the white phantom himself, Anthony Wayne, whom the Indians called "the Wind."

In January 1792, General James Wilkinson, commander of Cincinnati's Fort Washington, asked for volunteers to bury American soldiers at the site of St. Clair's Defeat, the worst defeat of American troops by Native Americans. He also planned to attack an Indian settlement about fifteen miles to the south. One hundred and fifty men signed on, including Captain John S. Gano, Butler County pioneer John Reily, and Ensign William Henry Harrison. The night before they planned to leave, a storm dumped two feet of snow on the hilly ground. Provisions, baggage, and equipment had to be transported on sleds. Attesting to the extreme cold is the story of how, while bivouacking on the first night in Sycamore Grove, near Fort Hamilton, Reily's head slipped off his "pillow" (his saddle) and froze to the ground. His frozen "cue" (hairpiece) prevented him from standing, and Reily was able to rise the next morning only when helped by another soldier.

Near Fort Jefferson, about sixty-five miles to the north, Wilkinson finally decided that the weather was too bad to carry out the planned attack on the Indian settlement on a branch of the Wabash River (near present-day Mercer County). So he ordered the regulars to return to the fort and the volunteer grave diggers to continue on to the infamous battleground where St. Clair's fallen soldiers lay.

Historian James McBride told the rest of the story in 1869:

> On their last day's march, when within four miles of the field of battle . . . the scene, even though covered with snow, was almost melancholy. The bodies of the slain lay strewed along the road and in the woods on each side. Many of them had been dragged from under the snow and mutilated by wild beasts. One of the party counted seventy-eight bodies between the point where the pursuit terminated and the battlefield. No doubt there were many more who, [when] finding themselves disabled, crawled to a distance out of sight of the road and there perished.
>
> The great body of the slain [was] within an area of forty acres. The snow being deep the bodies could be discovered only by the elevation of the snow where they lay. They had been scalped and stripped of all their clothing that was of any value. Scarcely any could be identified as their bodies were blackened by frost and exposure, although there were few signs of decay, the winter having been unusually early and severe.

Gano and others identified one of the corpses as Butler's: "Having dug a large pit, a work of much labor, as they were poorly supplied with spades and other implements, they proceeded to collect and bury the frozen bodies. Probably not more than one half, however, were interred, as they worked at it only on the day of their arrival. They [the bodies] were so numerous . . . that when all piled together and covered with earth, [they] raised quite a mound."

Desperate for frontier leadership, Washington turned to Anthony Wayne, another trusted Revolutionary War general, to lead America's army against the tribes. As old and unfriendly rivals from the Revolution, Wayne and St. Clair were comets shooting in the opposite directions of history. War and gout were all they had in common. Wayne, in stark contrast to St. Clair, trained an effective fighting force called the Legion of the United States and started building more wilderness supply forts. His army left the women and the liquor behind.

General Anthony Wayne as he appeared about 1795. (Author's collection)

In December 1793, Wayne arrived at Fort Greene Ville for the winter. He ordered Major Henry Burbeck and 200 soldiers to march northwest to build a new fort on the battlefield of St. Clair's Defeat, where the village of Fort Recovery is today. It was a bold and dangerous order. (Of this march, a nineteenth-century historian wrote that "the very heart of Fiend-land was penetrated.") When the troops arrived, they couldn't pitch their tents because so many American corpses were rotting on the battlefield. Burbeck's soldiers had to pick up and bury hundreds of skulls and bones. Perhaps motivated by their grisly discovery, the men built a wooden fort—a "work impervious to savage forces"—in only five days. It included four twenty-foot-square blockhouses attached to rectangular picket walls. After considering the names Fort Restitution and Fort Defiance, Wayne settled on Fort Recovery—because the land had been recovered from the Indians. Wayne believed the name would send a psychological message to both Indians and pioneers.

With such a name, almost a challenge, the garrison must have suspected that something big had to happen there again. And on June 30, 1794, it did: 1,500 Indians—Shawnee, Miami, Delaware, Potawatomi,

Ottawa, and Ojibwa—attacked supply trains and relief columns. Fifty soldiers died. Then the Indians charged the fort and its garrison of 200 soldiers. This time, however, the Americans weren't taken by surprise. After thirty-some Indians were killed and wounded, Little Turtle withdrew and called for peace.

His confederation became disillusioned and began to divide. Blue Jacket took over the smaller group. Suffering heavy losses from American cannon fire, the Indians withdrew two days later. In an even more decisive battle fought two months later, Wayne's army defeated the Indians at the Battle of Fallen Timbers, in what is now Lucas County. The battle destroyed the Indians' ability to mount a major campaign against the settlers.

The next year at Fort Greene Ville, the largest fortification on the frontier, Wayne personally negotiated a treaty with Little Turtle and other chiefs that would open Ohio to peaceful settlement and effectively remove the Indian threat. His victory improved conditions so rapidly that statehood followed in 1803.

Fort Recovery began the transition to peace. A town grew around the fort.

Memories of the two battles lingered there for generations, like blight in the soil. As late as 1903, during the state's centennial, one Ohio historian smugly wrote: "The savage has been pushed back. His hunting grounds have been appropriated for better and higher uses." Today's "higher uses" include the farms of Mercer County, Sunday volleyball games in the front yards of farmhouses, and strong community pride.

The characters in Fort Recovery's saga—both white and Native American—have been swept into the dark corners of history. Yet these fighters persisted for years after serving in the bloody battles around Recovery. Nowadays, most people wouldn't recognize their names, let alone their differences and successes.

Little Turtle, the Miami strategist and early peacemaker, realized that he could not defeat Wayne's highly trained army and gave up his leadership of the tribal confederation, although he stayed with his warriors during the battle. He reluctantly signed the Treaty of Greenville. The next day, his wife died, and, in a show of goodwill, American soldiers carried her body to her grave, played military music, and fired a three-gun salute. Over the coming years he would ask for help in teaching his people how to farm like the whites and try to convince the white government to ban the sale of liquor to his tribe. He claimed liquor killed more of his people than the battles. Unfortunately, he "grew gouty and slow and dependent upon his new white masters," author James Alexander Thom wrote. "He was scorned by those like Tecumseh who chose not to sign treaties but to fight on." A century after his death in 1812, Little Turtle suffered the ultimate insult: he was exhumed, and his possessions were sold to a white collector.

Black Hoof, a Shawnee chief who was famous in his time, claimed he fought in fifty battles, including the Battle of Fort Recovery. He died in 1832, reportedly at the age of 105. He is practically forgotten today by all but the most knowledgeable of Indian scholars. The Shawnee, who lived in the Scioto River Valley, were perhaps the region's most hostile tribe toward whites.

Blue Jacket, another Shawnee, replaced Little Turtle as the Indian confederation leader. He lost at Fallen Timbers in 1794. Later, he moved west of Ohio and died at Sandwich, Canada, in 1810. He signed the Treaty of Greenville and never broke it.

Anthony Wayne commanded the American forces in the biggest battle ever fought on Ohio soil—Fallen Timbers. More sites, roads, buildings, and government entities carry his name than any other military figure who walked the fields of Fort Recovery. Near Detroit in 1796, the arrogant Wayne, age fifty-one, died at the Presque Isle blockhouse while still wearing the uniform of the Republic. In a controversial move, his body was dug up in 1809 and boiled in a big vat. The boiling separated flesh from bones. The bones were taken back to his home in Radnor, Pennsylvania, and buried, and the flesh was reburied in the original grave.

Tecumseh began reorganizing the tribal confederation after the tribes' defeat at Fallen Timbers. An iconic American character who was perhaps born near Xenia, he is the subject of Thom's novel *Panther in the Sky* and Allan Eckert's play *Tecumseh!* Both writers believe he scouted for the tribes during St. Clair's Defeat and perhaps chose the Indians' attack points. Years before it started, Tecumseh predicted the War of 1812. To prepare, he traveled widely for three years to recruit new tribes for his coalition. When the Americans and British finally did go to war, the Indian position had weakened significantly with the defeat of 1,000 warriors—while Tecumseh was still away—by William Henry Harrison's army at the Battle of Tippecanoe near Lafayette, Indiana. By the time Tecumseh tried to assemble an Indian army, white soldiers had secured more of the western territory. He once asked Harrison to come out and fight and not hide "behind logs, like a groundhog." Harrison obliged. In 1813, Tecumseh died during the Battle on the Thames in Ontario, Canada, taking a musket ball in the head. Thom noted that Richard Mentor Johnson "rode to the vice presidency in 1836 on the jingle 'Rumpsey dumpsey, rumpsey dumpsey, Richard Johnson killed Tecumseh,'" although no one could prove conclusively who killed the Indian leader.

Arthur St. Clair lived longer than any of the other principals, but his popularity declined. He was a frank, open, honest, and accessible man, yet the Indians preferred to deal with Wayne because they trusted—and feared—him. Haunted by his tragic military defeat, the once-confident St. Clair slipped into a political sinkhole. He resisted the idea of Ohio statehood and was replaced as territorial governor in 1802. Yet he left behind some permanence; St. Clairsville and many other communities in the Northwest Territory still carry his name. Broke and unhappy, he returned home to Westmoreland County, Pennsylvania, to run an inn owned by his son. Creditors attached the governor's $60-a-month federal pension. Before he died in 1818, he was still being asked to explain his defeat. One period writer called the government's neglect of St. Clair in his old age "a disgrace to the nation," considering what it was spending on retirement pensions for Revolutionary War soldiers. Masonic brothers paid for a simple gravestone, which read: "The remains of Major-General St. Clair are deposited beneath this humble monument, which is erected to supply the place of a nobler one due from his country."

While walking around the reconstructed stockade at 1 Fortsite Street, I tried to envision the terrain on Christmas Eve 1793, when Wayne's troops arrived to reclaim the battlefield. But I couldn't imagine it; the whole story seemed too surreal. On this bloody ground, once a bone yard, history runs straight down Broadway. Surrounded by fields of corn and wheat, the town now helps feed people of every color, including Native Americans. So "normal" is Fort Recovery that its old-fashioned business district could pass for the set of a movie about small-town life. Few traces of the conflict remain, except for the fort, the memorial, and older historical markers around town.

As I strolled past a store, I nearly bumped into a black metal sign pole that jutted from the middle of the sidewalk. It read: "Gen. Richard Butler was killed by Indians beneath a tree which stood on the site of this building . . . in . . . St. Clair's Defeat, November 4, 1791."

Looking down the street, I saw other state historical markers commemorating the defeat. One identified the area as once Indian hunting grounds. Another said, "When American pioneers attempted to settle the Northwest Territory following the Ordinance of 1787, the Indians, aided by the British, fought fiercely for their homes.... After a furious battle, St. Clair's troops broke through the enemy encirclement and retreated southward here on this field. They left approximately 900 dead and wounded, in what is, relatively, the most disastrous defeat ever to befall an American army. Victory was yet to be won."

Perhaps by necessity, however, the people of Fort Recovery, far removed from the bloodshed that created their town, have written their own separate and distinct community story. It's not that they ignore the military's sacrifice. They simply do not overemphasize it. Through the years, villagers have tried to show that their town is like any other. Local histories focus on typical people and places: post–Civil War buildings such as the Fort Recovery Depot, built in 1879; the Stirrup Factory, built in 1895 and once called the world's largest exclusive manufacturer of wooden stirrups; the Cigar Factory, where in the 1920s workers earned five cents per hour and the factory's specialty was called Mike's Twins; the Old Fire Hall, built in 1878; the Fort Recovery Banking Company, built in 1881 with an outdoor clock that is still wound every day; and the Opera House, which opened with much enthusiasm in 1888 but lost popularity when the movies came to town in 1910.

In 1889, old Fort Recovery High School's first class—all two members—graduated in ceremonies at the Opera House. The Trinity Evangelical Lutheran Church, built in 1871 at a cost of $9,000, still stands at Broadway and Wayne Street. At first I thought it was an older Catholic church because it looked architecturally powerful—gothic, in a way. Then I realized it was German and Lutheran. Its early members are still remembered for their unique holiday practice. In the 1880s, church members chopped down a sycamore sapling, stripped its branches, and fastened evergreen branches to the trunk. They trimmed it with popcorn, apples, paper flowers, and large white candles. It was a Fort Recovery Christmas tree.

Saint Wendelin Catholic Church has its own story. Eighty-four-year-old Ed Lefeld has rung the church bell every day for fifty-six years, which is unusual in a time when most churches use automated ringing systems with recorded bells. (The truth is, he never wanted to ring the bell for so long. "Once you're committed," he said, "you just keep on.") He also used to mow the grass and start the furnace, but now he's too old for those chores. But he said he'd continue to ring the bell until the church council finds someone else to do it.

In contrast, just down the street the town's darker past coexists—on markers, in the museum (the only mounted dragoon exhibit in America), and in the school district's mascot, the Indians. And the word "fort" is still used liberally all over town. People haven't tried to change the town's name to something less forceful. It is the community's essence.

The Miamis lived in western Ohio, including the land around Fort Recovery. If Little Turtle and Anthony Wayne (or, as Little Turtle called him, "the Chief Who Never Sleeps") could visit the town today, they would think they had awakened on another planet. The physical and emotional planes have changed that radically. The proud Miami are long gone. So are the Shawnee. On driving into Fort Recovery, I had seen a homemade sign that congratulated Miami University's winning football team. The university, named in honor of the tribe, nicknamed its athletic teams the Redskins long ago. In the 1990s, the name riled many students, faculty, and administrators—though satisfied most politically incorrect alumni and fans—and in 1997 the name was changed to RedHawks. Would Little Turtle believe that a university established by whites in 1809 is named for his tribe? Would he believe students planned to hold an "Indian Theme Party"? Would he mind being called a "Redskin"?

At Fort Recovery's museum gift shop, I bought a slim booklet of Shawnee words that were recorded in 1786 by Major Ebenezer Denny, who in 1816 was elected the first mayor of Pittsburgh. The Shawnee word for "I'm glad to see you" was *Awassoleponeneaway*. The word for "I'm sorry" was *Wallamelawessalepo*. "Very drunk" was *Alamawanetho*. "You lie" was *Keenanhotchemoh*. "Mouth" was *Tonee*. "Night" was *Tapahkay*. Now, these words are foreign to even most Indians, but Shawnee leaders are working together to revive their old language. The last time I checked, however, only one person was conversational in it. I also bought a piece of old sheet music titled the "Miami Scalp Song," cowritten in 1914 by a Miami University professor and administrator named A. C. Upton. Its cover featured a detailed sketch of an Indian warrior, printed in red. Being a Miami graduate, I was intrigued. Coincidentally, at the time of my trip the university was trying to stop student-led bands from playing the song at Miami's football and hockey games. In one story I read, an administrator said the song should be eliminated from the school's musical repertoire, as the Redskins name was eliminated in 1997. Several students pointed out that it was done only as an instrumental these days. They said they enjoyed hearing it—then putting their hands to their mouths to utter a whooping sound.

Since the school was founded in 1809, many other things have changed about the Indians, the whites, and the Ohio land that they all coveted. All around Fort Recovery, where an army died on the wooded ground, forests and prairies have been transformed into rich farmland that grows soybeans, corn, and a wheat crop to help feed the world. Gone, too, is the hatred, as if it never existed. Before Wayne, Little Turtle, and other Indians signed the Treaty of Greenville in 1795, awarding 25,000 square miles to the United States and setting up the Ohio Country for statehood, enterprising pioneers could earn $136 for every ten Indian scalps they turned in like pelts. Of course, the Indians sold white scalps to the British in Detroit. The whites called the scalpers "hair-lifters." The prices of scalps on both sides fluctuated, as stocks do today.

Browsing in the fort's museum that afternoon, I learned how Wayne's soldiers hunted, ate their meals, dressed, and used packhorses to build Fort Recovery's walls. The museum displayed ancient Indian artifacts as well as pieces left by the pioneers. Life-size figures of 1790s soldiers of the 1st American Regiment, dressed in blue with red and white trim, stood guard while an Indian warrior, complete with nose ring, defiantly raised his hatchet. On the walls hung portraits of St. Clair, Wayne, Little Turtle, and Blue Jacket. Glass cases held fragments of a sword hilt; a piece of the original fort's wooden flagpole, unearthed in 1836 when a well was dug; forged spikes and wrought-iron hooks; and a curry comb, a skillet handle, hook rings, a teapot spout, a gin bottle, a snuff bottle, and other examples of everyday frontier life. Another display explained how the Congress in 1792 provided for America's first regular military—four infantry regiments, a squadron of dragoons (cavalry), and four companies of artillery, for a total of 4,563 men under optimum conditions.

Outside, a reenactor from the 1st American asked me if I'd like to shoot his musket. I looked at the heavy, formidable stock and tried to imagine lifting it to my shoulder. "Oh, come on," he said. "It won't kill you." I said no, but he insisted. To avoid embarrassment, I picked it up and tried to aim it. It was so heavy that I had trouble keeping it at arm level. As I held it, the gun slowly tilted toward the ground. I boosted it back up, and when I squeezed the trigger, the butt kicked my shoulder so hard that I nearly fell down. Smoke swirled around my face and my ears rang. I felt as though I had been kicked in the shoulder by a mule. "That'll wake you up fast," he said. When I came home later that day, I took off my shirt and noticed a wide bruise on my shoulder where I cradled the gun. My ears didn't stop ringing until the next morning.

When joining the original 1st American in the 1780s and 1790s, soldiers received a hat, coat, four shirts, stock and clasp, one pair of buckles, a blanket, socks and four shoes, bread, meat, vinegar, soap, candles, and, most important, whiskey. The regiment did its share of drinking. Whiskey became not so much a drink as recreation. Most soldiers exchanged their pay for liquor. It was also given as a reward to good soldiers, who often got drunk and fought with one another while serving in wilderness forts.

At the Battle of Fallen Timbers in 1794, members carried the French-made Charlesville flintlock musket, which fired .65-caliber lead balls. The musket weighed about ten pounds. Using a smoothbore barrel with an undersized musket ball for easy loading, the flintlock was dependable at only about eighty yards. But Wayne was an innovator. When his men stood tightly together and fired at once, their volley was devastating. He also ordered that bayonets be welded to gun barrels so that the soldiers couldn't lose "their steel."

In 1790, the 1st American was sent to the Northwest Territory, where it was ordered to build eleven forts, control immigration, negotiate treaties with the Indians, and protect surveyors and settlers. The regiment periodically traveled up and down the Ohio River to keep the peace in the new territory. Not even its disastrous campaigns against the Indians in 1790 and its participation in St. Clair's Defeat a year later could destroy the unit.

After St. Clair was defeated, the 1st American was absorbed into Wayne's new Legion of the United States. Wayne trained the men vigorously and organized a force based on classic Roman models. Each legion was divided into four sublegions, each with distinctive uniforms. The oldest regiment in the army today is the 3rd Infantry, which traces its lineage to the 1st American.

. . .

Helen LeFevre welcomed me warmly. She helped tend the fort's shop, which sold everything from maps of Indian towns and the Northwest Territory to books on Ohio frontier life. As a member of the Fort Recovery Historical Society, she escorts students on tours and tends the displays. A day earlier, she and other society members had finished erecting hundreds of white wooden crosses on the wide lawn at the Fort Recovery memorial, where many of Wayne's and St. Clair's soldiers are buried together. LeFevre said:

> We painted names on some of the crosses, but only the officers' names. We simply couldn't write every soldier's name. After all, there are 1,000 crosses out there. The sight of them standing together in one place really brings home just how many people died in battle here, especially the first one. It means more to people when they can see crosses standing side by side, than to read about them in a book. You have to see it to get the full effect. St. Clair came here with about 1,400 men, and a few hours later left with one third of them. I find that hard to believe. One soldier who fought on that awful morning returned here to live. I'm not sure I could do that. The memories— bad ones, I'm sure—must have been all over the place for him. How traumatic. But then, some veterans refuse to talk about their war experiences while others talk about them all the time. Talking is a part of their therapy. Maybe living here was his therapy.

Standing behind a glass case filled with toy Indians, frontier maps, key chains, area histories, coloring books, and various fort-related souvenirs, LeFevre explained that the village of Fort Recovery is unusual because two important battles occurred in one place. "Imagine—a town covering a battlefield," she said. "This place was literally built right on top of it. Years later, when the bones of dead soldiers started washing up after rainy seasons, this became a gruesome place. In 1851, two boys were playing when they found some bones. More appeared later. Then more. People started keeping them and putting them in big wooden boxes. There were plenty of bones scattered around here from St. Clair's Defeat. It was an amazing battle because of the number of officers killed—about sixty-seven. Their names are inscribed all around our stone monument. For most armies, such a crushing defeat would have ended any interest in returning to this place on the banks of the

Wabash. But the Americans weren't finished. They came back here and built a fort named Recovery. And they never lost heart. Think of the courage it took to conquer this wilderness, not to mention the Indians. I don't think people today would have such strong will and courage."

After leaving the store, I walked along the streets again and shot photographs of buildings and markers. The downtown looked almost deserted. I wondered, Could this town be haunted? And if not, why not? At a gas station, I asked a man for directions to St. Clair's battlefield. He thought for a moment and said, "Mister, you're practically standing in it—over there, behind the library. Actually, it's about everywhere in this town."

On an entire village block on Butler Street (Route 119), I found half of St. Clair's frontier army buried beneath a 101-foot granite obelisk in Monument Park. The Fort Recovery Memorial Association was originally formed to conduct commemorative events and to petition the federal government to build a monument, which ultimately cost $23,700 and weighed 800 tons. Thanks to lobbying by Association members, the federal government erected the impressive Washington Monument replica in 1910, after strong winds had toppled the original wooden monument. One of its brass plaques, the "Roll of the Dead," lists many of the commissioned and noncommissioned officers killed in the battle, including General Butler.

I wandered along the street and looked down at the first row of white crosses put up by the historical society. Lieutenant Samuel Boyd, Lieutenant Winslow Warren, Ensign Maxwell Bhines, Ensign William Balch—the row of officers' crosses seemed to go on forever.

The town square is filled with grass and marble. In the typical hyperbole of the era, large bronze plaques on the monument told the story of Fort Recovery's two battles.

> This monument marks the sacred spot where lie buried the fallen heroes who so bravely met and gallantly fought the savage foe; who as advance guards entered the wilderness of the West to blaze the way for Freedom and Civilization; who sacrificed home and life to the great duty of securing for a future inheritance vast dominions and great institutions. It stands as a loving tribute of a people in grateful appreciation of the undaunted courage and patriotic devotion of the illustrious dead; and may this lofty shaft forever proclaim the glorious achievements and undying fame of the heroes of 1791 and 1794.

Stone marker at Fort Recovery, where the early American army suffered its worst defeat at the hands of Native American tribes. (Photo by Randy McNutt)

Next to the monument is a weathered black metal sign erected by the Mercer County Medical Society during Ohio's sesquicentennial in 1953: "Dr. Victor Grasson, a hero of the Indian Wars, was killed while caring for the wounded during General Arthur St. Clair's defeat here." Nearby a marble slab set into a stone reads: "Honor the Dead. Five dollars fine for defacing or climbing on this monument."

Forty years after St. Clair's Defeat, a passerby discovered a cannon buried in the mud near the mouth of the creek. He sold it to a volunteer artillery company near Cincinnati for $60. In 1838, Robert G. Blake found the remains of Major McMahon, one of St. Clair's officers, and his companions. Their bones were reburied in the Pioneer Cemetery in Fort Recovery. A few years later, a farmer struck a metal object while plowing near a decayed tree. Authorities uncovered a locked wooden box containing 900 gold and silver coins then valued at $14,000. Later, they learned that it was the army's paymaster box, hidden under the tree on orders of General St. Clair.

When two boys found a human skull on a street in 1851, townspeople were sickened. Later, on finding sixty skeletons "in a good state of preservation," the town held a burying ceremony. The *Indiana State Journal* covered the event.

The ceremony of reburying the remains of the soldiers slain at the site of Fort Recovery during St. Clair's Defeat took place on September 24 [1851]. When we arrived there the preceding afternoon, the hotels and many of the private houses were crowded to overflowing. People continued to arrive throughout the night and until noon the next day. The number who attended was variously estimated at from five to seven thousand, and it was impossible to make a closer estimate. Two thousand persons formed a procession. The sons and the grandsons of those who were to be carried to their last resting place were present.

The occasion was one of solemn import. If these bones had heretofore been neglected, it was only through ignorance of the spot where they lay. Now that mere chance had exposed the grave, the citizens were enthusiastically playing that respect which is due from every true and patriotic American. These men died to maintain liberty and the peace and quiet of the fireside. There were some old gray-haired veterans present with recollections of the defeat vividly stamped upon their memories.

The bones were placed in thirteen coffins, representing the thirteen original states. They were buried in one large grave in the village cemetery. Peace to their ashes. Beneath the sod in one common grave lie the bones of officers, soldiers, and citizens. May their memory live in the heart of every American.

But that didn't stop more bones from pushing to the surface. Over the next forty years, the bones of dead soldiers continued to pop up around town. Shocked by the repeated discoveries, county officials decided to preserve the remains by interring them in thirteen (in honor of the thirteen states of 1791) large black walnut coffins that would hold the bones of the soldiers, camp women, men who worked for the military, and reportedly a few children who were killed in the battle. The townspeople held a special ceremony, which they called Bone Burying Day. Five thousand visitors from Ohio and Indiana attended the ceremony in the town of only 200 people. "While the coffins were being filled," wrote Celina historian S. S. Scranton, "the people were permitted to examine the bones, many of which bore marks of the bullet and tomahawk."

By 1880, all that remained of the original Fort Recovery was its wood flagstaff, which was removed and later taken to the relic room of the Capitol Building in Columbus. In 1891, even more bodies were discovered, and reburied in another patriotic ceremony in the middle of town.

. . .

On a warm day in recent times, 1st American Regiment reenactors cleaned flintlocks while camp women cooked in iron pots behind the tents. Smoke rolled from the camp like thick dust. The regiment's cannon unit prepared for a demonstration. They moved quickly, with purpose, each doing his job to perfection. In only twenty seconds, one soldier crammed gunpowder into the barrel while another prepared to light the other end and yet another tapped out a staccato on a drum.

"Rapid fire!" an officer commanded.

"Prepare to fire!" a crewmember shouted to his men.

The cannon belched black smoke and fire over the lawn. A concussive blast of air popped my eardrums. Spectators covered their ears as the deafening sound ripped the air.

"Good timing, soldier," the officer said.

"Thank you, sir!" the soldier replied. "I had a good, experienced crew."

For a time I stood around watching the soldiers as they drilled and broke down the camp. I saw a high school boy and girl walking over to chat with one of the regulars.

"Can I see your rifle?" the boy asked.

"Sure. It's a muzzle loader, a musket, like the ones used here when Ohio was on the frontier, the Old West."

The boy looked puzzled. "You mean the Wild West?"

"Not that West. We're talking about what was then the western United States."

"Were wars fought around here?" the girl asked.

"Bloody wars."

"Were Indians around here?"

"Oh, sure," the man said. "The 1st Regiment fought them—right here."

"Awesome," the boy said.

"Don't you kids ever study history?"

They did not reply. They had already grasped each other's hands and begun walking away, lost in their own world. I watched them as they strolled nonchalantly over land on which an army once ran headlong into oblivion.

8

The Road to Fort Laurens

> Our sick naked, our well naked, our unfortunate men in captivity naked!
> —*General George Washington, December 1777*

As small towns disappear across the nation, so do pioneer cemeteries, historic homes and schools, and old forts and battlefields of varying importance. One day I went looking for any military survivors in northeast Ohio. It didn't take long to find the ghost of one near Bolivar in rural Tuscarawas County—as well as forgotten revolutionaries.

Impressed by freshly mowed, lush green fields, I visited Bolivar (it rhymes with Oliver). There on the main street are a number of businesses, including a couple of antiques shops. I stopped in one to look around.

"You a collector?" the owner asked. I explained that I was looking not so much for antiques but for the ghosts of Ohio's past. He replied, "Oh, then you should visit our fort. There's plenty of 'ghosts' out there. Just follow the signs."

An arrow directed me to a blacktopped path to a museum near Interstate 77 and the Tuscarawas River. I considered the depth of history around me—the river, fort, canal, and interstate, all within sight of one another but occupying different times. The nineteenth-century towpath, on which mules once pulled stubby canal boats, is the twenty-first-century's walking and biking trail—three miles of it on level land along the Tuscarawas River. In my mind I tried to superimpose old and new towpaths but could not. The original seemed an alien place inhabited by mule-driving children who the locals contemptuously called "hoggees," which originated from an English word, Hogler, meaning poor field workers. Poorly fed and forced to work in foul weather, many of the hoggees died before turning sixteen.

As I walked, my mind tried to hit fast-forward a century and a half. When work crews wanted to build the interstate, they "relocated" a part of the river and poured the highway's concrete on top of the then-dry riverbed. Native Americans called the river the Mooskingum (meaning elk's eye), but white settlers named it Tuscarawas, a corruption of the Tuscarora tribe's name.

A sign alerted me to Fort Laurens, the only American Revolutionary War outpost in the land that is now Ohio. Built nearly thirty years before Ohio became a state, the log fort is long gone. But it is the site of a small museum operated by the Ohio Historical Society.

Walking through the quiet and attractive park, I thought of rough-hewn logs and quadrangles, of freedom and keeping it. I could see the interstate directly in front of me, but I could barely hear the humming of tires. As I entered the museum, manager Tammi Mackey greeted me with a smile. I was the only visitor in the building. She asked if I wanted to watch a documentary film. "When it's finished," she said, "you can walk around on your own. Everything's self-explanatory."

I sat in the attractive theater and scanned walls decorated with reproductions of old regimental flags. The brief movie explained that General Lachlan McIntosh, who built Fort Laurens in 1778, intended to "chastise and terrify the savages" of the region for not siding with the Americans. He named the fort for his friend and patron Henry Laurens, president of the Continental Congress.

Laurens might seem an unlikely namesake for a Revolutionary fort, for he loved England and its people and stood to lose a fortune if the colonies won their independence. But he also abhorred its tax system and its increasingly authoritarian ways. Slowly he began leaning toward supporting his native Carolina (now South Carolina), where he was born in 1724 to a well-to-do saddler. At age twenty, Laurens was sent to England to learn a trade and there studied under a successful merchant. Three years later he returned to Charleston—shortly after his father's death—and expanded his family business. He sold saddles to New York, imported rum from the West Indies, and exported items such as lumber, silver, gold, and deerskins. He became one of the wealthiest men in the American colonies.

When the Revolution started, Laurens emerged as a prominent state leader and was elected to the Continental Congress in 1777. He and other members of Congress fled Philadelphia when the British army occupied the city that year. In 1780, he sailed to the Netherlands to negotiate a treaty with that country but was captured by a British warship on his way. Charged with treason, he was taken to the Tower of London and imprisoned. Eventually, British authorities exchanged him for Lord Cornwallis, the lieutenant general of British forces in the United States. Once free, Laurens helped negotiate the treaty between his country and Great Britain.

In November 1778, General George Washington ordered American soldiers to march into the Tuscarawas Valley and build a fort. On the recommendation of Laurens, Washington appointed General McIntosh to lead the expedition.

I wondered what hardships McIntosh and his men endured when they came to the area that is now Bolivar—the weather, the hard labor, the loneliness.

When the movie ended, I walked around the circular display area and saw mannequins dressed as Indian warriors and British and American soldiers of the Revolution. One display noted that the British soldier often carried sixty pounds of equipment and was "expected to do so without complaint." One sign read: "Here lie the remains of American soldiers who died at Fort Laurens between January and August, 1779." Their names were listed at the bottom of the sign.

McIntosh, a Georgia native, is one of those tragic historic figures who tried but could not earn respect. His obsession with rules and personal honor often got in the way. In 1777, he dueled the popular Button Gwinnett, a Georgia representative who had signed the Declaration of Independence. Shooting at each other from a distance of only twelve feet, both men were wounded. Gwinnett died from his wounds, and McIntosh was blamed, even though Gwinnett had harassed him and challenged him to the duel. Gwinnett had never gotten over losing a military appointment to McIntosh.

He was not well liked by his men, who considered him too strict. He blamed the early American army's politics—detractors and angry subordinates—for his shortcomings. Later, he tried to defend his military record, but people always remembered him for killing a patriot.

In the winter of 1779, 172 men and women defended the quadrangular fort with four bastions. A raiding party of British troops and their

Indian allies attacked and killed more than twenty American soldiers, but they did not take the fort. Reinforcements eventually saved the defenders. The soldiers who died were buried near the fort's hospital.

Between display cases filled with arrow points, deer bones, silver trade ornaments, fishhooks, knives, scissors, bayonets, clay pipes, and buttons was a large sign asking, "How hungry would you have to be to eat your shoes?" This told the story of what happened on March 23, 1779.

When a relief column finally arrived with supplies for the starving soldiers, Fort Laurens's soldiers fired celebratory shots with their muskets, which frightened the loaded-down packhorses and sent them scurrying away into the dense woods. Many of the new supplies were lost. So again, that winter the soldiers were forced to "boil cowhides and moccasins to make soup." Troops lost their patience. They openly called the place Fort Nonsense, and officers could only agree. The men tried to rebel that cold winter of 1778–79 but were stopped by officers. After one Indian attack, the soldiers were afraid to go hunting. Two men sneaked out, shot a deer, and dragged it back inside the gates. The starving group ate it within minutes. Some didn't even bother to cook the meat.

The fort's design was typical of the period, made of logs and shaped like a square with protruding parapets on the corners. It featured a wooden blockhouse, twenty feet square, and huts that could house up to 200 men. I couldn't imagine a small company of colonial men poking through the woods—filled with hostile tribes—just to build a fort.

After arriving here, McIntosh wrote to his superior, Colonel William Fleming, on December 7, 1778: "I have advanced thus far and built a good large stockade for here, with barracks to contain two hundred men, or more when they can be had, to make excursions to any of the Hostile Towns who still dare offend and insult us, which I hope will secure the peace for our frontiers in this quarter at least."

Making my way through the museum, I came to a commemorative marker for the Tomb of the Unknown Soldier of the American Revolution. This nameless soldier's remains had been uncovered during construction of the museum in the early 1970s. He had died from a musket shot to his abdomen. On June 26, 1976, Ohio National Guard units and veterans groups buried the soldier with full military honors.

The fort slowly decayed after soldiers abandoned it in 1779, and then in the early 1800s builders of the Ohio & Erie Canal destroyed two eastern bastions that faced the river. Eventually, farmers started plowing the site of Fort Laurens. "The river was redirected to build the highway,"

Mackey told me. "I can't imagine moving a whole river. But it did have a flat bed."

Now, twenty soldiers rest in a crypt inside the museum; the Unknown Soldier lies in his own nearby tomb. It is a peaceful place. So peaceful, in fact, that no one would believe that British soldiers and Indians once besieged a log fort on this spot.

Since the 1990s, the idea of rebuilding Fort Laurens has been on the minds of the site's supporters, including Scott Fisher, a member of the Friends of Fort Laurens Foundation. "We're talking about Ohio's only connection to the Revolutionary War," he said. "We're talking about soldiers who spilled their blood for our freedom. When people say the fort is too far away from where they live, I talk about our heritage and the men who died." Fisher told me that Captain Abraham Lincoln, grandfather of the president, and Major Richard Taylor, father of President Zachary Taylor, both served at Fort Laurens. Fisher knows that rebuilding the fort would be expensive—about $1.4 million—but he continues to recruit new members for his nonprofit Fort Laurens Foundation, which seeks donations to resurrect this nearly forgotten piece of American history.

During Ohio's Bicentennial in 2003, for the first time in 225 years, Fort Laurens became the site of the Frontier Family Reunion. Descendants of the notorious frontier renegade Simon Girty assembled at Fort Laurens State Memorial together with the descendants of frontiersmen Daniel Boone, Simon Kenton, Lewis Wetzel, William Crawford, and Alexander McKeek and representatives of various Native American tribes. At some point in the past, Fisher said, these pioneers' lives all intertwined. Wetzel and Crawford served at Fort Laurens, which was built in Delaware Indian territory. Fisher said Kenton saved Boone's life during an attack on Boonesboro, Kentucky, and Girty saved Kenton from burning at the stake when Indians wanted to kill him. (Even though Girty did save Kenton during the Revolution, Fort Laurens became the first official American military site attacked by Girty after he sided with the British.) "Some of these frontiersmen helped defend Fort Laurens while others tried to destroy the fortification," said Fisher. "We were excited to have them all return to this site, not to celebrate victory or defeat, but to celebrate history and the role their family ancestors played in the state and nation."

After the war, the place faded into history. "Today, the area is really just a military cemetery and museum—a state memorial," Fisher said. "Just outside the museum is the Tomb of the Unknown Patriot of the American Revolution, which pays homage to at least one defender of the fort. We want to bring the place back to life, so to speak."

Fisher believes a wooden fort would attract more than 40,000 visitors annually, as the reconstructed Fort Boonesborough does near Richmond, Kentucky. In addition, he said the project might also encourage other communities across Ohio to provide financial help to regional historic sites. "Ohioans haven't fared well in teaching history," he said. "We need to remember the past. The fort would enable present and future Ohioans to understand, appreciate and support the historical significance of the outpost and the lives that were lost to secure America's independence."

While researching the fort, Fisher was surprised to find that the General Assembly approved rebuilding the fort in 1915. Governor Frank B. Willis even signed a bill into law, and legislators appropriated $5,000 to purchase land. But for some reason, the work never started. "I know the wheels of government turn slowly," Fisher said, "but I think this is way too slow. Time after time, the state has promised to rebuild Fort Laurens and each time it has failed to act. If the foundation can raise about 50 percent of the estimated cost, we feel confident that the state will come through with the rest of the money." Usually, the state requires an eighty-twenty split between public and private funds, according to Fisher, and the Foundation hopes to raise $632,500 in private donations and then also reach out to corporate sponsors. "By sponsoring particular pieces of the fort, we hope to offer potential foundations, businesses and individual contributors an identifiable portion of the fort," he said.

"We'll need about 1,800 logs just to build the stockade," he said. Foundation members also have collected more than 5,000 signatures from people who want the state to rebuild Fort Laurens. Ultimately, if Fisher can't persuade the state to comply with the legislature's 1915 act, the foundation could always sue. "I don't want to get into confrontation with the state," he said. "But we always have that option."

Fisher said he and his group refuse to quit planning the fort because of what it represents. "The price of freedom has never been free," he said.

Back Roads

9

Freedom's Towns

> This is not just black history. This is American history that has been forgotten.
> —Roane Smothers, a descendant of Longtown settlers

I found Payne's Crossing by luck while driving on State Route 595, south of New Straitsville, near the border of Perry and Hocking counties. This African American ghost town thrived from the mid-1800s until the 1920s. On a bright Indian summer day, just over a hill in the Wayne Forest, I first noticed Payne's Cemetery—a small, immaculately trimmed place with a historical monument. Intrigued, I stopped to walk the grounds. I paused to read the granite marker in front:

> Payne Cemetery, Established 1852.
> Before you is a remnant of the historic black community of Payne's Crossing. Freed from slavery in Virginia in the early 1800s, they settled here then joined the fight
> for freedom during the Civil War.

The only remnant of the community is the cemetery, which is home to many veterans of the U.S. Colored Troops who fought in the Civil War. In 1993, Lancaster's genealogical society started researching the graves, which consisted mostly of free blacks who began settling in the town in the 1830s. Some of them fought in the Civil War. In 1994, inmates from Hocking County Correctional Facility repaired and straightened the stones and restored the cemetery to its pristine condition.

On June 19, 2010, the town's descendants and other interested people gathered to dedicate a state historical marker at the cemetery. This occurred on the African American day of celebration Juneteenth, a reminder of June 19, 1865, when Union soldiers informed the last group of slaves that they were free.

Feeling so much history beneath my feet, I decided to continue searching for more black ghost towns—the Gist and the Randolph settlements, where history was waiting to be remembered.

On State Route 32, the Appalachian Highway, traffic jams and subdivisions faded to farmland as I headed east into Brown County. A few mobile home sales lots squatted on brown fields along the four-lane road. I was mesmerized by passing fence posts, white lines, and a blue horizon.

I was seeking out what remained of towns settled by former slaves from the John Randolph (of Roanoke) and Samuel Gist plantations in Virginia. In the early 1800s, when anybody could start a town on a dream and a dollar, some runaways stayed on in Ohio to build their own towns; others, including the Gist and Randolph people, came straight from their plantations—freed at the request of their deceased owners.

From 1810 to 1850, former slaves founded at least twenty-two small communities between the Ohio River and Lake Erie. They had to overcome the threat of southern bounty hunters, inhospitable neighbors, and a frustrating legal system. Occupied by African Americans from different parts of the South, these hardscrabble towns shared another common trait: both the land and its inhabitants were very poor.

Despite the presence of the Underground Railroad, Ohio was not a paradise for escaping slaves in the 1800s. Because the state bordered Kentucky and Virginia, many Ohioans feared an exodus of blacks into the Buckeye State. Questions arose: Where would they all live? Where would they work? In southern Ohio, where the reception for blacks wasn't nearly as warm as it was in the north, many white residents or their relatives had migrated from slave-holding states. Not surprisingly, Ohio seemed to say to Kentucky, "We won't be a haven for your uneducated and socially unsophisticated runaways." An unnamed citizen newspaper writer explained the position in 1819: "Much as we commiserate the situation of those who, when emancipated, are obliged to leave their country or again be enslaved, we trust our constitution and laws are not so defective as to suffer us to be overrun by such a wretched population. Ohio will suffer seriously from the iniquitous policy pursued by the States of Virginia and Kentucky in driving all their free Negroes upon us."

In 1804, the Ohio legislature required newly arrived black residents to show proof of their freedom as a condition for settlement and employment. Blacks who came here legally also were forced to register their names with county officials. In 1807, the state expanded the statute by requiring blacks to post a $500 bond to enter the state and submit signatures of people responsible for their welfare in case they should become destitute. In addition, the small black population had to comply with the federal Fugitive Slave Law. Ohio's so-called "black laws" prohibited blacks from suffrage, public education (the legislature didn't approve a segregated school system for blacks until the 1840s), and welfare and even from testifying against whites. But the laws weren't rigorously enforced.

Bequeathing freedom to one's slaves wasn't unusual, but providing money for their care and the purchase of farmland was beyond unusual—and even controversial. According to historian W. Sherman Jackson, "Many slave owners felt that freed slaves were a source of agitation. This was typical of Virginia—getting freed slaves out of the state."

By the time I finally arrived in Brown County, I was weary of monotonous highway travel. Then the small town of Fincastle greeted me—farms, a veterinarian's office, and little else. I pulled up at Peggy Mills Warner's new ranch house set on the edge of large cornfields. She had invited me out to see what remained of the Gist Settlement. Each day, she learned a little more about the grit and spirit that carried her ancestors from a Virginia plantation to farmland in Ohio decades before the Civil War. Warner's personal journey brought her back to the land she roamed as a child. In 1996, she emancipated herself from suburban Cincinnati and moved to Fincastle's Gist Settlement to preserve—and gather—history and genealogy. Ever since, she has been piecing together word-pictures of her remarkable ancestors and their friends as well as a portrait of the state and nation in an era of differing views on slavery and treatment of African Americans.

The original black settlers on this land were all slaves until Samuel Gist, their wealthy owner, died at age ninety-two in England in 1815. Gist's will established a trust fund to care for his former slaves and their children, buy property for them in Ohio, and appoint abolitionist Quakers to "attend to the comfort and happiness of my slaves and their offspring." The Quakers used Gist's trust money to buy land for the settlements and construct schools and other buildings. The land was to be inherited by future generations who could trace their lineage to the freed slaves. Gist wanted them to live on the land without paying taxes. After the Quaker trustees purchased about 3,000 acres at several sites in Ohio, a free state, the newly freed slaves began arriving from Virginia. Eventually, they ended up in Ohio's Brown, Erie, Highland, and Adams counties. It wasn't long, however, before the Erie County group grew disillusioned with the harsh climate and malaria and returned to Virginia. (Eventually, some of them returned to Ohio to settle in Highland County.)

On first arriving in Brown County in 1819, the black settlers found a wild land filled with dangerous animals and struggling pioneers. "The land was so bad, so rugged," Warner said, "that it was practically given away. Farming was tough." Nearly a century later, Georgetown's *News-Democrat* wrote that "they were dumped by [Gist's] agents into the swamps, a few rickety school houses and a cheap church structure or two, and left to hoe their own rows as best they could."

The years before the Civil War must have been uneasy times for freed slaves living near the Mason-Dixon Line. Southern bounty hunters and slave owners drifted into Ohio in search of runaways. There is no record of the impact these hunters had on the settlement at Fincastle. We do know that it and all the Gist Settlements served as stations on the Underground Railroad, removed from the cities as they were. Southern slaves heard about the settlements, of course, and sought them out on their way north. This increased tension between the settlements and area towns, however, where many people disliked the idea of living near blacks.

Several hundred former slaves lived and died with little notice on two settlements in Brown County and one in Highland County. Their towns operated beyond the mostly white, rural counties, in parallel worlds.

These days, the land around Warner's modern gray house with white columns is still quiet, green, and orderly. Corn and soybeans undulate in the wind. Tractors roam the fields like giant beetles. On a clear, bright summer day, Warner drove me down a gravel lane, through the fields and toward narrow asphalt road. Ahead of us was the Brush Creek Baptist Church, built in about 1860 and rebuilt in 1976.

"Sometimes only five people show up for services, but the church keeps on going," Warner said as she turned the wheel to enter the parking lot. "Hey, there's Earl Johnson's place; he's a descendant. Over there's Mrs. Carr's home; she's a descendant who moved here from Cincinnati a while back. Actually, there are a number of descendants left. My problem is getting them interested in our genealogy. It's important to me that my people get some recognition. It is my life's work."

When I visited Brown County's Bodman Road Settlement, all 1,120 acres of it had vanished, possibly the victim of a nineteenth-century typhoid epidemic; the other settlement, 1,153 acres near Fincastle, consisted of a few old buildings and newer homes like Warner's. Nothing on the land suggested that it was once a sanctuary for freed slaves. Warner wants to change its anonymity. She has turned her living room into a genealogical war room, with stacks of books and papers scattered around a baby grand piano. She is determined to find the names of people who once lived on the land. She has obtained old census records, courthouse deeds, and obscure little histories that mention the settlement people. "I feel their spirits are encouraging us to uncover information; they're waiting in heaven for us to act," she said. "I know some of their relationships were sad and some may have cobwebs, but I believe in the end the good will outweigh the bad. I want people to know more about these people. Unless we know where we've come from, we can't chart the path on which we'll travel."

She grew up in Georgetown, the Brown County seat, about fifteen miles south of tiny Fincastle and about twelve miles north of Ripley. It was the river town that Kentucky's slavery advocates called an "abolitionist hellhole," where the Reverend John Rankin helped hundreds of runaway slaves escape to on the Underground Railroad in the years before the Civil War. In this way, the land is historic and sacred to her. Any old house in the area could be a former hiding place, loaded with secrets that might never be told.

Warner's mother married a Georgetown man who refused to live on the settlement any longer. But Warner's maternal grandfather, James Peter Toler, remained there proudly and built houses and welcomed his granddaughter for visits. "He was a well digger; lanky, a real Lincoln of a man," she said. "My sister, who has watched the generations, said she has not found anyone who resembles him until my son." A neighbor, veterinarian Andy Purdy, who grew up in the area, remembers Toler as an old man who never stopped working. "He did everything by hand, even in the fields," he said. "People on the settlement couldn't afford tractors or horses. They were their own horses. Looking back on it, what strikes me was their work ethic. Sweat and labor. But today the settlement is known to only the people who were reared there, or connected to the land in some other way. The place is great, but it's all faded history."

Like her father, Warner had little interest in living in the settlement. While caught up in a busy suburban life in Milford, she taught music at a Clermont County elementary school and tended to her family. She had no time to study genealogy; rent meant more to her than roots. Then one day in the 1990s, in one of life's serendipitous turns, a family member mentioned that some settlement tracts had come up for sale and that they'd be a wise purchase. In fact, one of them was next door to Warner's late grandfather's place. For reasons she can't fully explain, Warner bought the property. Slowly, its murky past enveloped her. In 1996, she built a house there and moved in. "My son, who was in college at the time, cried the day I came out here to live," she said. "He said, 'It's so far out there.' He doesn't care for the country; he has no interest in this place. But I was proud and determined. I've instructed him to never sell my house and its twenty-two and a half acres. This is where I want to keep alive the memory of the settlement and erect a memorial rock with the names of the people who lived here. They will not be forgotten."

The Gist Settlement's culture and historic significance is not lost on the staff of the National Underground Railroad Freedom Center in Cincinnati. "It's a fascinating story, one with national interest," said Ed Rigaud, CEO and president. The settlements were nothing more than reservations. "We're talking about people who were free without being granted citizenship," said Oloye Adeyemon, a family traditions and oral history specialist at the Center. "The ironic thing is, the state was authorized to send them back to Virginia as slaves if they should leave. So they were tied to what was then some of the worst farmland in Ohio." They might starve if they stayed, but they would become slaves again if they returned to Virginia.

The man who granted their freedom, Gist, is nearly as forgotten as his slaves. A loyalist, he returned to England during the Revolutionary War. Some say his conscience made him free his slaves at the Gould Mill Plantation, but Adeyemon speculated that Gist did it as a memorial to himself. "He wanted to leave a legacy. He was an orphan."

In the nearly 200 years since they were granted freedom, Gist's family of former slaves has grown and spread across the country. Some of them have formed the Freed Gist Slave Settlement Foundation, which held its first family reunion in 1999. About ninety people, descendants from all three settlements, attended. Warner, who helped organize the reunion at Woodland Lake Leisure Resort in Highland County, hopes to bring relatives together every summer and possibly start a small scholarship fund for young students.

Sitting in her tidy living room, Warner lovingly pulled out several three-foot-long white paper boards on which she had written long-forgotten names—Old Ben, Sally, Maria, Rosanah, Matilda, Scott, Peter, and Old Lucky. On another sheet were written Parson Jim, Sylvia, Patey, Uofia, and George. They are just names to most people, but to Warner they represent stories waiting to be uncovered. She has studied them and thought about them for so long that she practically knows them. They are like neighbors to her. "I'm trying to build a family here," she said, pulling open an old scrapbook filled with photographs. "Just imagine where we'd be if everyone did the same. That's my dream." She paged through the book and added, "At first, I never thought that these names would be important in my life. People die, and who's left to carry the torch? All I know is, this place—this story—must survive. People who lived in run-down shacks must be remembered. If I don't do it, who will?"

In Miami County, in west-central Ohio, two towns, one black and one white, stood above the abyss of history, ready to fall in at any time.

The white town, Rossville, has dwindled down to a tiny, quiet community. Platted in 1840 by William Knowles, the original town was named for a man named Ross who owned a carding mill on the Great Miami River. Founders believed their town would benefit from thriving Piqua, just across the river. Even so, Rossville grew slowly. It was the site of a local curiosity, the Willow Cottage, a home built completely of willows that grew along Rush Creek.

Nearby, the Randolph Settlement consisted of only a half-dozen small houses, an old cemetery (with a fancy but homemade gate), a homegrown African American museum, and some tales passed down by the generations. Yet, on a deeply personal level, the settlement is still alive—a part of Ohio history that's nearly forgotten by an integrated society.

In 1846, a group of freed slaves from Virginia camped on land near Rossville. Nowadays, in a confusing juxtaposition of names, Rossville is synonymous with the Randolph Settlement, the rural black community that developed on the outskirts of the Rossville Springcreek Township.

The settlement is wrapped inside the town—or, more precisely, what used to be a town.

Helen Gilmore, president of the Rossville-Springcreek Historical Society, once told a reporter that not every original Virginia slave settled near Rossville. A few group members moved to the settlement of Rumley in Shelby County. "It was already formed by two brothers who had been runaway slaves from Canada," she said. "Rossville was the last of three settlements where the Randolph slaves lived."

On the bright summer morning I arrived in the Randolph Settlement, I could hear a hammer pounding in the distance. I noticed a couple of white men repairing a car at the end of a long driveway. Two black men came out of another yard, jumped into a 1989 blue Chevrolet, and drove slowly down the hill. They passed Jackson Cemetery, which was surrounded by a thick wall of trees and guarded by a large, empty plant container and an arched entrance sign that read, "Jackson (African) Cemetery." I suppose the sign was put up in later years, because twenty years earlier a factory owner wanted to build on the property, not knowing that it was a cemetery. Then Helen Gilmore intervened, saving her ancestors' gravesites. The first thing I noticed was the entrance sign, which was made of wood, painted black with large white letters, and mounted on two black metal poles. A large rock next to it carried a small bronze plaque that read: "Jackson Cemetery. Dedicated to the memory of the free Randolph slaves. Placed June 14, 1980 by the Piqua Chapter DAR."

Despite the blowing ragweed, I breathed deeply—fresh air! Sunshine fell on the wet grass and the trees arched so far down that they embraced me. Looking around, I wondered where all the graves had gone. All I saw was one rectangular old headstone, broken and illegible. Vandals have targeted the cemetery for years, I learned. On closer inspection, I found more graves scattered around the cemetery—all small and unassuming, some marked by the star of the Grand Army of the Republic to denote Civil War veterans. Nine former slaves buried here served in the 27th Regiment of the U.S. Colored Troops during the war. Community residents Jesse Lockyear and Paul Crouder fought with the 54th Massachusetts Regiment. They were recruited by the white abolitionist Robert Gould Shaw, who came from Boston in January 1863 looking for Ohio blacks to help form a crack Union regiment. Fortunately, Lockyear and Crouder survived their unit's bloody assault on Charleston, South Carolina, on July 18, 1863. They lived until after the turn of the twentieth century. In 1989, the regiment's story was told in the film *Glory*.

I continued to search for graves and found only one of the original slaves who came from Virginia. But later I learned that I had missed the others—130 people rest there, apparently unidentified, including original slaves named Bartlett, fifty years; Phebe, fifty years; Nancy, eighty years; John, one year; and Lindy, one year. At ninety, Old Joshua was the oldest. Catherine, three months, was the youngest.

As I wandered past more scattered and unmarked graves, I wondered, Did young people yearn to leave for the city? Did the various black settlements in Ohio communicate with one another? Did any men from the Randolph Settlement play on the Rossville Stars baseball team? No one knows.

The settlement's roots go back to Randolph, who was born June 2, 1773, in Prince George County, Virginia. Eventually, the rich bachelor—no wife, no children—settled in Charlotte County. Although he claimed to oppose slavery, he owned hundreds of slaves and argued that the federal government had no constitutional right to enact the Missouri Compromise or any other law regarding the slavery issue. In 1799, he was elected to the U.S. House of Representatives, where he served for nearly twenty years. In 1825, he was appointed a U.S. senator, and for two years he became a famous politician of his time, one of eccentric tastes in clothing and ideas. While he argued for states' rights, he also opposed a national tariff, the National Bank, and the war with Great Britain in 1812. Randolph returned to the House of Representatives until 1829. The next year, Andrew Jackson appointed him the nation's minister to Russia, where he served a few months and resigned. By then, he was said to be in poor health and a frequent user of alcohol and cocaine to relieve his discomfort. A writer once said that a premature decay gradually took over Randolph's body and his vital powers. He returned to Virginia to live alone on his plantation of 6,000 acres. He left orders that he was to be buried facing west so that he could see what his old political adversary, Henry Clay, was doing in Washington.

When Randolph finally died in 1833, his wishes were complicated by paperwork. His last will ordered that most of his slaves be sold. But in earlier wills he had granted them freedom, as well as no less than ten acres for every slave older than forty. According to legend, on his deathbed Randolph said he wanted his slaves to live free. But his brother contested the will. In 1846, after a thirteen-year legal fight, a judge finally ordered the slaves—383 men, women, and children—to be freed and sent to live on 2,000 acres that a Randolph agent had purchased for them in Mercer County, Ohio. Perhaps the agent had heard of Mercer's black connection: in 1843, educator Augustus Wattles, a Connecticut native, had started the Emlen Institute, a school for blacks, in Mercer. Under pressure from neighbors, he closed it in 1857. Full of hope, the Randolph slaves traveled 500 miles from Virginia to Charleston, West Virginia. They arrived by riverboat in Cincinnati on July 1, 1846. One glimpse of the public landing must have excited them, for Cincinnati was on the border between North and South and was a city with a reputation for freedom. Surely they knew that their long journey was finally ending; their promised land was on the riverbank.

But a writer for the *Cincinnati Gazette* had another view: "And now the poor creatures are among us!—Why should this be? . . . We have already several colored settlements among us.—And pray, why does not Virginia and Kentucky retain their freed blacks? What right have they to be pouring in upon us their helpless, new made free? We have very much fear that the common objection made in the Slave States, that we, as Free States, having nothing to do with Slavery, will turn out, on examination, to be eminently untrue, in more respects than one."

Probably the slaves never heard about the newspaper story, which was published the day after their arrival. They were too busy pushing north, a journey on which they walked and rode on wagons and canal boats to their destination in Mercer County in west-central Ohio. Unfortunately, the appearance a few days later of more than 300 blacks—enough to form a significant country town back then—provoked anger among the local immigrant farmers, mostly Germans, who feared that blacks might dominate their adopted community. As canal boats filled with black faces passed through New Bremen, a small canal town along the way in Auglaize County, an organized group met them with pitchforks and a resolution in hand that read:

> Resolved, That we will not live among Negroes; as we have settled here first, we have fully determined that we will resist the settlement of blacks and mulattos in this county to the full extent of our means, the bayonet not excepted.
>
> Resolved, That the blacks of this county be, and they are hereby, respectfully requested to leave the county on or before the first day of

March 1847; and in the case of their neglect or refusal to comply with this request, we pledge ourselves to remove them, "peacefully if we can, forcibly if we must."

Resolved, That we who are here assembled, pledge ourselves not to employ or trade with any black or mulatto person in any manner whatever, or permit them to have any grinding done at our mills, after the first day of January next.

A group of armed white men chartered canal boats and escorted the former slaves out of the area. The blacks never did take possession of the land for which Randolph had spent $8,000. Nor were they ever compensated for it. Most of the property now lies beneath Grand Lake St. Marys.

The Virginia group split up. Some members traveled southeast to Miami County, where the white residents seemed friendly, and camped near Rossville. Eventually, they settled there. Near Troy, others formed Marshall Town and, near West Milton, a place called Hanktown in Union Township in Miami County. (To make matters more confusing, maps in the 1880s also listed this community as the Randolph Settlement.)

Years before the Civil War, the "Randolph Negroes" and the issue of freeing slaves caught the attention of people across the country—with most southerners criticizing Randolph and Northern abolitionists praising him. In 1855, the *New York Daily Tribune* sent a reporter to Ohio to write a story about the fate of the former slaves. The piece said, "The Negroes were ultimately suffered to settle on their lands, and I learned that they are mostly living on farms of their own, and doing pretty well; much better, in fact, than could be expected under the circumstances."

Through the 1900s, the residents' descendants, called the Buckeyes, held family reunions to honor the original 383 slaves, whom they called the Old Dominions and, sometimes, the Originals. A century and a half after they came to Ohio, descendant James P. Humphrey would be elected Sidney, Ohio's, first black mayor. He stayed in touch with his roots by visiting the original Randolph plantation and obtaining a brick from a slave cabin. "Walking on the same ground that my foreparents walked on . . . I was thinking of the changes in the times," he told a reporter. "They were slaves, and here I was going back there as the mayor of a city. It was an emotional experience."

The Randolph Settlement survived raiding bounty hunters in the years before the Civil War and tough economic times after it. At one time the town had a grocery, a church, a one-room brick school, and a number of houses. Now, legends outnumber the buildings. A local man served as the musical town crier, waking up his neighbors every morning by playing a tune on his fiddle. Wooden planks served as sidewalks across Rush Creek. One old woman resident, Elizabeth Rankins, dressed in flour sacks and claimed she once shook hands with the Great Emancipator himself, Lincoln. Aunt Ida Bell baked prune pies and sang a song that would be politically incorrect today. Original slave Shadrach Meshach Abed-nego White (also known as Buddie Shang) drank corn whiskey and rubbed it into the bald spot on his head; nobody remembers if his hair ever grew back. The last of the Originals, Jimmy "Jeems" Rial, was over 100 when he died. He was so well known locally that he merited a picture postcard in the early 1900s. He wore a hat that looked something like an English bowler. Another resident, Albert McKnight, the son of two slaves, marched in Piqua's parades and polished brass at the bank. He wore a fresh chrysanthemum in his lapel. His headstone in Forest Cemetery read: "In Memory of a Character Who, Without Responsibility of Position, Attained Lasting Prominence."

Buddie Shang's adventure proved that whites in Shelby and Miami counties were still friendly to the former slaves. He shined shoes outside a tavern and lived in Lacyburg, a black shantytown near Sidney. One day he decided to go fishing in the canal, and on the way he argued with a young man. Shang, who was about seventy-four years old by then, felt threatened. He fired a shotgun in the direction of the young man and scared him away, but a white man who lived in a cottage came running out and accused Shang of firing at his cottage. The man, Lewis Nichols, started throwing bricks at Shang, and, in self-defense, Shang shot him dead. On January 27, 1890, an all-white jury in Sidney acquitted Shang. After the jury returned its verdict, Shang's lawyer turned to him and said, "You're free again, free for a second time, Buddie."

When I started walking around the settlement, I saw a one-and-a-half-story wooden building painted blue-gray with a colonial red trim with a gable roof and a sloping back roof and a small front porch. It was once a schoolhouse. According to architectural historian Mary Ann Brown, "it represents a house type found commonly among rural black settlements that were established in Ohio before the Civil War. . . . This repeated house type was has been identified in ten rural black settlements in western Ohio."

A sign outside identified the building as the Rossville Museum and Cultural Center. Located at the end of tiny McFarland Street, it is the focal point of the settlement today, but few people stand in line to enter. The museum opened in June 1984 in the former home of York Rial, a stonemason who built the house in 1850. In 1987, it was added to the National Register of Historic Places. On the day the museum opened, called Randolph Freedom Day, 250 guests showed up, including U.S. Representative Thomas Kindness, who came all the way from Hamilton. The museum received a letter of congratulations from President Reagan and more artifacts, including a Civil War sword, a picture of Randolph, pieces of African art, an acoustic guitar without strings that was used by Piqua natives the Mills Brothers on their first tour of Europe, a Randolph slave family's Bible, and a framed copy of the original plat of the African Cemetery, which someone had found in a basement, complete with water damage from the 1913 flood. Along with these things were old photographs, period antiques, and a book that contained the original slaves' freedom numbers—proof that they had been freed.

Now, they represent more than numbers. As a worn tombstone in Jackson Cemetery reads, "Thompson Rial. Born a slave. Died Free."

Pushing deeper into the country, I searched for another Gist Settlement, near New Vienna in Highland County.

Though there were houses and a church and a school in the old days when the settlement flourished, it was never officially a town, as towns are normally judged, and cartographers didn't bother listing it on Ohio maps. In fact, most people don't know that the place existed. What those old maps don't reveal is that a town transcends dots and lines. The people of the settlement loved and cared for one another. Does that not make the place a community?

The Gist Settlement was a social and legal enigma planted firmly in the fertile countryside. On a journey some years ago, I saw it, in an odd juxtaposition, near Kenny Davis Homes, where dozens of modular and mobile homes sprawled on both sides of the road. A sign proclaimed "Building Dreams," informing drivers that the good life was available

Freedom's Towns 121

for a handshake and 10 percent down. Not far away, the timeless fields of Penn and Fairfield townships erupted in a myriad of summer colors.

Despite the settlement's proximity to local farms, few people entered it, except to worship in the little white concrete-block Carthegenia Full Gospel Church. In the 1940s, the settlement was home to about forty-five people whose lives were circumscribed by the store, the church, and the school. Young men left for jobs in the city. As older residents died, new families—those with no history at the settlement—moved in with battered mobile homes that obviously didn't come from Davis's lot. Soon a sea of junk piled up around tattered metal shacks, and the settlement became a nearly deserted inland island.

But Paul Turner came back to cultivate corn, soybeans, hay, and history. He used to rent and farm 560 acres outside the settlement, but that didn't pay enough so he started tending 100 acres of settlement land, where he was reared. He liked the place, the feel of it. In the 1980s he learned that the county might sell most of the settlement to pay $25,210 in delinquent taxes, so he obtained loans and paid off the debt in five installments. His action was practical, not charitable. He wanted to preserve his community. As a young man, he had left it once to join the navy. He served in Vietnam and attained the rank of master chief, the highest rank for an enlisted man. He was stationed in California for nearly fifteen years.

In time, however, he longed to feel the changing seasons, to walk up the dirt lane in summer and to feel the sting of winter's wind. So in 1976, he returned to live in his parents' old house and to watch the snow pile as high as the mailbox. Turner came back out of homing instinct. The place was home, a place with a past.

That past had been peaceful and productive, focusing on agriculture. Then, in 1861, the Civil War shattered the quiet and stirred the patriotism of many of the settlement's young men, who fought in the Union Army and died on forsaken southern hillsides. They became a part of history—Isaac Day, Nelson Good, Harrison Pearl, Henry Turner, W. D. Williams, all buried now in the Gist Cemetery, their tiny headstones bleached and crumbling, with Grand Army of the Republic emblems and tiny American flags next to their graves.

Turner took me there, and we stood and viewed each grave. Except for the wind whistling across the fields, the place was quiet. The cemetery was small, filled with dandelions and brilliant green grass and little purple flowers. The headstones were small, no larger than eight by fifteen inches, with hand-carved initials and a weathered appearance. Some of the names were obliterated by time. Turner looked over the graves and said the cycle continues: "The little cemetery is filling up while I work the land of my forefathers—people named Turner and Rollins." Perspiration ran down his forehead. "It's a pride thing, I guess. I love the land. If I hadn't come back here when I left the service, I would probably have some money in the bank and be riding my motorcycle someplace by now. But I did come back. I liked the people. Now, I want this place to remain for my kids' sake. You see, I grew up extremely poor. Other than not having your health, there's nothing worse than having no money. When I was a kid, the teacher would announce that I'd get free lunches that week. I used to hate that. I remember it to this day. That's why I want to do something with the land. Be productive."

So Turner paid taxes on land that could not be legally his—at least not yet. "People will say, 'Why's he doing that?' Well, that's nobody's business," he said.

Such talk is uncharacteristic of the mild-mannered Turner. Yet, as a descendant of former slaves, the land is his historically. "Oh, I guess I could hire a lawyer and tie things up in court," he said. "But if I lose, I might have to pay $40,000 instead of $25,000. Nobody else wants to take on the responsibility of paying the taxes. I'm it."

The tax history of the Gist Settlement is more tangled than a kid's shoelace. Years ago, the county prosecutor told me that the county cannot legally award property to the Settlement's residents, even if they have lived on the land for years. The problems started in the 1880s, when the original Gist trustees died, leaving no money to pay the taxes. In the 1890s, the county foreclosed on the property and divided it into lots. People who lived on the land at the time were considered the legal owners. When they paid the taxes, the land was granted to them. But at some point, most people living in the settlement stopped paying taxes and the county stopped trying to collect them.

"This place isn't what it used to be," Turner said, waving his hand across the fields. "The old church has only two, three cars in the parking lot some Sundays. We're getting some younger people out here now, and it's a little like a ghetto. Trailer's falling apart. I'm not too proud of the way it looks. But I'm here, and I guess I'll stay."

Yet one thing is certain: the Gist Settlement, Paul Turner's memorable patch of green, will remain a community—so long as he pays the taxes and prays for rain.

10

Colors of Tranquility

> People are trapped in history, and history is trapped in them.
> —*James Baldwin, "Stranger in the Village"*

In the early 1900s, the blacksmith left town, followed by the undertaker and the postmaster. Decades began moving over Tranquility like evening shadows. After World War II, the state started buying land around the rural Adams County community to preserve it as it had been for centuries. A few farmers sold out; then a few more. When the grocery, Tranquility's limited-market market, closed in the 1980s, no one complained. Everyone knew that Fannie Bolender, friend and storekeeper, had to tend her farm. That's when everyone realized that Tranquility had changed from country town to Ohio wildlife preserve.

On one of my visits, on a warm and bright day in early October, leaves were already changing; the hillsides had become a kaleidoscope of gold and red and brown. I pulled into the parking lot of the original Tranquility Presbyterian Church, built in 1909, to eat my lunch. A peanut butter sandwich never tasted so good. I sat in the car and read a magazine story that showed pictures of a covered bridge that from 1864 to 1942 spanned Georges Creek at the bottom of Tranquility Valley. Another photograph captured a brass band in uniform. Members stood erect, proudly holding their horns. Printed on the front of the big drum were the words "Shelby's Cornet Band, Tranquility, O." In those days, Tranquility was still a tight community of farms and neighbors.

I decided to take a walk and ended up in front of a closed store, now all gray and weathered. It looked like something from Dust Bowl times. It had opened twenty-five years after Delbert Morrison's original store caught fire on this spot on September 6, 1912 (on Morrison's birthday, no less). Despite help from a bucket brigade, the store burned to the ground, and the Morrison family left for Kansas and a more hopeful future. The new store sold about anything a rural resident would ever want or need, including groceries, boots, dry goods, buttons, stockings, socks, pants and other apparel, coal oil and gasoline, eggs, antiques, tobacco, china dolls, silk hats, ladies gloves, laces, crackers, high-top shoes, peppermint lozenges, horehound, and jawbreakers. The post office also operated out of the store, where, it was said, "you could buy anything from needles to a mustache cup" for shaving.

Other business owners operated in town over the years, including Sanford A. McCullough, who during the Civil War served in Company G, 129th Regiment, Ohio Volunteer Infantry. He returned to Tranquility after the war and bought land and started making coffins for a living.

I thought of my paternal grandparents and how they were born in Cherry Fork, another small town in Adams County, in the late nineteenth century. They are buried there. After they were married, they moved to Cincinnati so that my grandfather could find factory work. When I was a young boy, I used to sit on their wide porch in the city and listen to them reminisce about small towns that I had never heard of—towns that have now declined or died. To me, Adams County seemed a strange and faraway world occupied by people who I would only know through my family's tales.

Like the neighboring ghost towns of Mineral Springs, Steam Furnace, and Marble Furnace, the unincorporated Tranquility continued to decline for many years. When other towns were dying because ideas and technologies had changed, Tranquility was losing the little momentum it once had because its people had continued to die or drift away. The town's postal cancellation stamp is now a collectible to Adams County residents who can still appreciate such things.

These days, Tranquility means one thing to me—the Underground Railroad. For it was here that runaway slaves appeared on hilltops and found refuge in John Thomas Wilson's house before heading north on their perilous run to freedom. Despite its soothing name, Tranquility was anything but tranquil in the mid-1800s. It would soon become a metaphor for the Union cause, serving as a sanctuary for blacks before the Civil War and later turning out more than its share of army volunteers once the fighting began. The colors of Tranquility are the colors of the forest—green, red, brown—and of the Union—red, white, and blue.

The community, sixteen miles southwest of Hillsboro on State Route 725, is now the destination of hikers and birdwatchers. To most people, the weathered place is known only for its state wildlife area, which contains one of Ohio's larger concentrations of wild turkeys. As I looked at Tranquility's lush green landscape, I wondered how its townspeople ever thought of leaving. The land was always filled with uncommon beauty. Early in the twentieth century, the Reverend Landon West of Pleasant Hill looked over the rolling countryside of northern Adams County and declared that God Himself built the Great Serpent Mound near there to mark the location of the Garden of Eden. Most people would chuckle at his logic, but not his sentiment, for Tranquility is like a tiny space station fixed on the edge of a galaxy of green.

The eye confirms only the old town's position: on State Route 770, in Scott Township, on the western fringes of Ohio's Appalachia. The ear tells more: In this secluded place, there is no familiar sound. No perceptible noise, the kind that reverberates in most people's heads throughout the day. When I first noticed this, it bothered me. I had been used to hearing unnatural sounds—airplanes overhead, trucks on the highways, sirens—for so many years that I thought something was wrong when there were none. True silence seemed strange.

Somehow, the woods around Tranquility have survived. When the pioneers in the late 1700s converged on the territory that is now Ohio, they brought axes and handsaws and went to work on the magnificent hardwood trees that nearly covered the state. The wood provided material for cabins and tools, boats and bowls. But in the valley of Tranquility, the pioneers were not so thorough or numerous. They did not cut down every tree they could find. Recent decades have brought no developers, no subdivisions, no apartment buildings. Out in the fertile hills in the early morning, a visitor can wake up and believe that he has been reborn, that he is the first man.

Tranquility's past is the past of every isolated hamlet: a town builds up and then either flourishes or dies. Although Tranquility dies a little more with each passing decade, it also manages to hold on. Through the years, the area's people have remained weak in number but strong in spirit. They've farmed the hillsides and worked in West Union, but they lived in the valley because they could see a sunset blocked by nothing but the hills.

The view is the main reason why John Thomas Wilson stopped here on a trip from his native Bell in Highland County. He stood on the hill, watched the sunset, and realized he had found his little piece of this earth. He built a log house right on that hill—front door facing the setting sun—and planned his future.

Scene looking into the valley at Tranquility in Adams County. (Photo by Randy McNutt)

John T. Wilson, abolitionist and congressman, as he appeared later in life. (Courtesy of Stephen Kelley)

Wilson was born on April 16, 1811, and reborn on his first trip here in 1832. Although he received a limited formal education, he was intelligent and hardworking. With an inheritance of several hundred dollars, the twenty-one-year-old Wilson bought staples and opened a general store in one of the rooms of his new house. A short time later, he traveled to Cincinnati to buy supplies. According to legend, the storekeeper figured up the charges and then asked where to ship any future goods. Wilson thought about the valley and replied, "Send them to Tranquility."

The word carried a special ring to him. It seemed to define the land, his life, and his hopes for the future. When he returned home, he named his estate Tranquility. The little community that eventually formed around the store took the same name. The store attracted people from every hollow within twenty miles. In 1840, the frugal businessman built a brick house onto the log one that he had built fifteen years earlier (both still stand today). He expanded his farm, buying land in every direction. (He later owned the land on which the Serpent Mound stood. He sold it in 1886 to the Peabody Fund of Harvard University.)

With a businessman's acumen, Wilson did everything by design. He suggested that the government open a post office in Tranquility, and in 1848 one did open under postmaster John McCreight. More people moved into the little town, and Wilson and a partner flourished with their business.

But Wilson was troubled by what he saw happening around him in the Ohio River country. Kentucky bounty hunters freely roamed the countryside looking for runaway slaves. The idea of hunting human beings disturbed Wilson greatly, and he vowed to stop it. He joined more than a dozen abolitionists, mainly Presbyterians (he was a Methodist), who helped start the Underground Railroad in Adams County, hiding escaping slaves. These local station keepers and sympathizers included prominent citizens such as Sam Baldwin, Benjamin Blackstone, Edward Cannon, Seth Gales, George Kirker, Joe Logan, and Peter Wickerham (likely a distant paternal ancestor of mine).

In the early 1850s, Wilson opened his house as a station on the Underground Railroad, helping fugitive slaves escape north. They crossed the Ohio River at Ripley in neighboring Brown County, at Portsmouth in neighboring Scioto County, or east on the Ohio River at Gallipolis. The network attracted sympathizers in the Ohio River counties, and Wilson didn't hesitate to offer his resources and support. Wilson usually hid slaves who followed the Ripley route. They entered the river town and stayed with the Reverend John Rankin and friends. For years, a rumor persisted about Wilson's house: When he built the brick mansion onto his old log house he ordered workers to install two staircases. One, a secret passageway from the attic, was used if bounty hunters charged up the main stairs. The fugitives could then escape as Wilson and his wife protested the intrusion.

(Today, a color photograph of his brick home is posted on the Internet site of the Friends of the Underground Railroad as an example of one of the few "stations" that have been identified and saved. Because many people involved with the group didn't discuss their former illegal activities, even after the Civil War ended, buildings connected with the Underground Railroad can be difficult to positively identify as havens for runaway slaves.)

The tiny town surely wasn't tranquil when southern bounty hunters arrived. After all, they had the law on their side; it was illegal—and dangerous—to hide fugitive slaves. Yet Wilson persisted. Several times, Kentucky bounty hunters forced their way into the Wilson home, despite protests from the family. The hunters nearly caught several runaways, who escaped through the secret stairway and into the night while the Wilsons delayed the intruders. One of the Wilson children once said that when she went to the basement to get something for her mother, she could see eyes staring at her from the root cellar. Sometimes the slaves stayed outdoors, for a faster escape. One story goes that when bounty hunters surrounded the house in later years, people from Tranquility came over and pleaded with the men to take the matter to court—or else. While they negotiated, the daring Wilson and some friends secretly escorted a group of slaves to safety.

At the beginning of the Civil War in 1861, at age fifty-one, Wilson joined the Union Army as an officer and military recruiter. He already walked with a limp from an old injury, and now he was organizing a unit of men from the Allison, Duffey, and Hamilton families, as well as other men from Tranquility, North Liberty, and Eckmansville. Wilson felt so strongly about the Northern cause that he invested his entire fortune in Union war bonds. He served as a first lieutenant in Company E of the 70th Regiment, Ohio Volunteer Infantry, under Colonel Joseph Cockerill, a West Union lawyer. They were a proud but green bunch of country boys when they gathered at the Adams County Fairgrounds that October. Most of them figured the war would last only a few months, that the Rebels would run at the sight of blue uniforms, and that the Union would be saved. While they drilled, their families and friends came by to watch and cheer and encourage the new recruits. They had no guns—wooden dummies had to do—until they left in February 1862, on their way to Paducah, Kentucky, and then farther south to a place called Pittsburg Landing, Tennessee—which, in the North, would be called Shiloh.

The first Adams County man killed there was William J. Ellis of Company H, on April 6, 1862. It was reported that near the landing, a southern voice yelled, "Halt! Who goes there?" Major John W. McFerran of Adams County replied confidently, "The advance guard of the Army of the United States." The man replied, "The hell you say!" The fatal skirmish occurred shortly after the first shots were fired.

John A. Cockerill was only sixteen when he enlisted as the 70th Regiment's musician. His father commanded the unit. On the day when the fighting started at Shiloh, young Cockerill was eating breakfast. He heard shots crackling in the distance. The sounds pulsed in his brain. He ran into his father's tent and found him buckling his sword. The man had no words for the boy. Not knowing what to do, the musician ran outside, grabbed an Enfield rifled musket and rushed over to the Shiloh church, where he saw "one of the most beautiful pageants . . .

ever beheld in war"—a sea of blue and gray uniforms moved across the rolling hills. The beauty and pageantry soon ended, however, when it transformed into what one surgeon later described as a cyclone of bullets and shell fragments, crashing down everywhere and ripping everything in their paths. Men rushed headlong into fire from rifles and cannons. Drops of blood blew across the land like rain. Observing the horror, Union colonel Issac C. Pugh of the 41st Illinois of Hulbert's First Brigade screamed, "Fill your canteens, boys! Some of you will be in hell before night and you'll need water!" The regiment left many of its own on the fields of Shiloh.

As the war continued, Wilson was promoted to captain. He lost a son, Spencer, in the fighting. His death haunted Wilson, who considered himself lucky to have survived. When he was discharged from the army on November 27, 1862, he returned to Adams County and tried to mend his broken life. Meanwhile, the 70th Ohio Volunteer Infantry fought on, with more soldiers dying every day. Its list of battles and engagements numbered more than thirty and included Missionary Ridge and Kennesaw Mountain.

In 1863, while the war still raged, Wilson's popularity helped elect him to the Ohio Senate. As evidence of this, one small Adams County community named Newport named its post office in his honor. Some residents went so far as to suggest that their town's name be changed to Wilson, but he didn't want the recognition.

While he served the public in Columbus, his regiment continued to fight in nearly every bloody campaign, including Memphis and Vicksburg, where the 70th and Colonel Cockerill are remembered with statues and plaques. From there, the unit rolled on to Chattanooga and Knoxville, and then to Atlanta with Ohio general William T. Sherman. In a cruel irony that war often reserves for the best, some members of the 70th were returning to Adams County on the crowded steamer *Argosy* on August 21, 1865, on the Ohio River at Perry County, Indiana. They had managed to survive the worst war in American history, but that night the packet's straining boilers exploded, scalding soldiers unlucky enough to be closest to the engines. The next day, ten members of the 70th were buried in a mass grave in another forgotten place called Rono Bottoms, Indiana.

Seeking more opportunity, Wilson successfully ran for Congress as a Republican and from 1867 to 1873 served in the Fortieth, Forty-first, and Forty-second Congresses. For better or worse, he helped shape—and punish—the defeated South as one of the northern Radical Republicans. Eventually defeated by a challenger, he returned to Tranquility, this time to work in the mortgage and loan business, where he enjoyed financial success despite his remote location. In addition, his war bonds paid off handsomely; he was a rich man. He wanted to give some of his fortune away. He later told the county commissioners, "It is sometimes better for a man to do in his lifetime that which he may contemplate [doing after his death]."

The owner of Tranquility's general store was the richest man in the county when he died in 1891, and he wasn't even a millionaire. He left the county $50,000 to build a home for orphans, many left alone by the war, and $5,000 to erect a monument to Civil War soldiers. Both still stand in West Union.

The Children's Home, built in 1883–84, is made of brick and limestone. The massive military monument, designed by architects Staniland, Merkle and Staniland of Dayton, is officially named the Wilson Soldiers Monument. It is the county's most important sculpture and one of its main landmarks. It stands to the right of the front entrance of the

The old gate at Tranquility Cemetery, where Adams County Civil War heroes are buried. (Photo by Randy McNutt)

The tomb of John T. Wilson and family in the Tranquility Cemetery. (Photo by Randy McNutt)

Wilson Children's Home. The sculpture, bronze with a granite base, stands more than fifty feet high and is ten feet, four inches wide. The large base supports a bust of Wilson. When the monument was dedicated on June 10, 1893, 600 Adams County Civil War veterans looked on, and an estimated 10,000 people attended the ceremony (the county's population was no more than 25,000 at the time). Speakers included Judge D. C. W. London, a Georgetown resident and a former colonel in the 70th Regiment, and Judge Samuel F. Hunt, a fine speaker. When they finished, another revered local military hero, John A. Cockerill, the former drummer boy and son of the regiment's organizer, unveiled the statue. At the time, Cockerill was a journalist.

The statue ensured that John T. Wilson would not be forgotten. In Tranquility Cemetery, Wilson's tombstone, once marked by an obelisk, has been updated. Now, a large rectangle of granite bears his name, as well as his wife's and son's. At the base of the monument is a Grand Army of the Republic star. As I walked around the cemetery, I saw the names of men who Wilson recruited to serve with him in the war. Among them was former postmaster John A. McCreight, who died September 12, 1904. (So many McCreights lie in the cemetery that they have their own section.)

Colors of Tranquility

As I stood before Wilson's marker again and considered his courage, I thought, Here lies a real American hero, unsung.

Few people recognize Tranquility when they see it. They drive past the community's sign and over the creek, never knowing they've just passed the place. Seeing the name on the town sign reminded me of a joke told by my friend Stephen Kelley. "We've got Unity, Harmony, and Tranquility in Adams County," he said wryly, "but not all the time."

These days, Tranquility isn't much: a few houses sprinkled across a green valley, a rotting former grocery store, a white frame church, and the century-old cemetery. Tranquility remains a place seemingly undiscovered. One autumn day when I visited, only the crowing of a big brown rooster pierced the silence.

Supported by a tax on sportsmen's ammunition, the Tranquility Wildlife Area was opened by the Ohio Department of Natural Resources in 1956. It consists of 3,818 acres of typical hill region. Forty percent is native woodlands: oak and hickory dominate the dry ridges and upper slopes; maple, beech, elm, and ash lie on the lower slopes and along the streams. Mixed brush with dense clumps of red cedar make up another 40 percent; grassland and fields fill out the remaining 20 percent of the preserve.

"We just let the country go back to nature," said Michael Toepfer of the Ohio Division of Wildlife. "We wanted people to be able to hike, watch birds, and to hunt and fish." They find a landscape filled with fox and gray squirrel, largemouth bass, bluegill, catfish, cottontail rabbit, bobwhite quail, woodchuck, raccoon, red and gray fox, opossum, deer, muskrat, skunk, and ruffed grouse. Wild turkey, not found in abundance in Tranquility since the early 1900s, have returned in strong numbers, as have a variety of both nesting and migrant birds.

Early on this balmy afternoon, Oren D. Mahanes and his wife, Virginia, stood by the front porch of their white Victorian house, speaking of the weather, gray partridge, and red-headed woodpeckers. They live in the old Presbyterian manse, between the preserve and the Tranquility Cemetery. Like John T. Wilson, they came from Highland County, loved the land, and couldn't leave. In retirement, they spend their days in the garden and in their lawn mower repair shop. Or they sit on the front porch, listening.

They have no idea of what happened here in 1861, and earlier. Ghosts of the slaves walked out of Tranquility long ago.

"The first thing of a mornin' you can hear the birds," Virginia said. "Late in the evenin' the whippoorwills start to callin'. Now, that may not mean much to some folks, but I love whippoorwills. Oh, that sad, wondrous call. We listen to the meadowlarks, brown thatches, bluejays. We put a crooked neck gourd out by the big oak tree, and the jays raised their young'uns in it. We'd hear them sing, then we'd hear the preacher ring the big bell of a mornin', callin' us to Sunday school. That bell rings out so clear, all across the hills."

Oren Mahanes just sat there and smiled.

"Oh, and when the leaves start to turn," Virginia went on, "we can sit here and see the rain a-comin' in, fallin' like sheets."

In silence, all three of us stared at the wooded hills in wonder.

I knew I would return.

11

The Legacy of Edward McClain

> With Full Confidence in the Generations yet to come. In behalf of Higher Education, Purer Morals and Broader and Better Citizenship. This Property is dedicated by the Donor.
> —E. L. McClain, 1915

In a time when most communities want to build new schools, McClain High School in Greenfield is straight out of the early 1900s and proud of it. I found a school building so old-fashioned, so stuck in the past, that it was truly a piece of vanishing Ohio. I was amazed that such an anachronism—a work of art in itself—could remain undefiled in a nation where many students fear and respect no one and the only tradition worth remembering is defiance.

Contrary to the times, students at Greenfield's McClain High receive a classical education—or at least a glimpse of one. The school's hallways are lined with marble sculptures of nameless nymphs—Joan of Arc, Demosthenes, Nike of Samothrace, sphinxes of the Nile, Athena, and George Washington. McClain is downright ethereal, one of those oddities of the Ohio countryside.

Built in 1914 by Greenfield manufacturer Edward Lee McClain and opened in 1915, the school features a rooftop garden (no longer in use), pergola walkways, a courtyard flanked by white pillars and fountains, frescoes, a massive swimming pool, a dining room, a library-study room, and an auditorium that seats 1,000 people. A 2,200-seat gymnasium was added in 1974. The school also contains valuable reproductions of paintings in every classroom, preserved by generations of self-disciplined students. Above green metal lockers runs a fifteen-panel reproduction of *The Quest of the Holy Grail,* an 1870 painting by Arthur Hughes. Students walk by, as oblivious to it as they are to the massive pipe organ built into the auditorium's 32-inch walls.

"You certainly don't see these kinds of things in other schools," said Jini Emerick, McClain's 1992 homecoming queen. "But I think a lot of the students don't fully appreciate their school until they graduate. Then they realize what an honor it was to attend McClain."

At the office, I met principal Dan Strain, who agreed to show me around the school. Perhaps the most unusual feature, he offered, is the respect for tradition and loyalty that it commands in an era that ignores such things. In fact, the school is so interwoven with Greenfield's social and cultural history that it's difficult for people to imagine life without the building.

The educational oddity was the idea of Edward Lee McClain and his wife, Lulu, who spent $750,000 to build and equip the city's high school in 1915. If it were built today, the school would cost multimillions. Although the building was a gift, the couple had definite ideas about how it should be operated. They wanted their hometown children to receive a worldly education.

That the school and its treasures have survived intact is a credit to the citizens of Greenfield. The McClains donated enough money to build the school, but they expected the city to pay for its operation and maintenance. With inflation and the aging process, that cost grows each year. The school has 15-foot ceilings and spans a city block, making it expensive to heat and maintain, especially for a small district that relies heavily on state funds.

"Money is tight," Strain said. "These days, we have to go a little longer without painting the walls. We figure that adding new stair treads in our school would cost $85,000. So we make do. The school becomes more difficult to maintain each year. Of course, we have things no other schools have to worry about. For example, we know that fluorescent lighting is the way to go, economically, but we don't want to take out the old hallway lights. The cost of their replacement bulbs goes through the ceiling, but those old lights are what make McClain different. We draw the line at changing the décor."

When the school needed new windows in the auditorium in 1995, school officials added a few double-pane ones to match the originals.

"The cost was unbelievable," Strain said. "We'd like to replace more windows in the school, but we have a tremendous number of large ones. Replacement costs would be astronomical and take us thirty years to complete the project." Administrators have compromised a little, however. In 1981, they converted the school's old steam heat to natural gas. Now, a computer controls the furnace.

Around Ohio, the McClain way is fading. In my hometown, Hamilton, the school district plans to tear down about eight schools—several of them were built in the early 1900s—and build new ones. Officials say keeping the old ones is simply too expensive. Other districts agree. All over the state, new schools are going up and old ones are coming down.

Strain, a 1974 McClain graduate, represents the generational link that keeps tradition alive. He is only the school's eighth principal. In Greenfield, McClain principals are treated like senators, with much respect. To Strain and others, McClain is not just a school; it is the soul of Greenfield, a farming community of 5,000 people. "It's such an honor to work here," he said. "Fourteen of our forty-plus teachers are alumni. Their pride in this building is directly transferred to the students. People from out of town sometimes ask me why we don't have vandalism. I tell them that all I'd have to do is publish the culprits' names in the paper and the community would take care of the problem."

Strain taught at an elementary school in the district and earned a doctorate in education from Miami University. He said he never seriously thought he would one day become the principal of his hometown high school. McClain is that special. As we walked down its halls, Strain pointed to a painting of F. R. Harris, the school's first principal: "How many other schools have a principal's portrait? The joke among alumni is that his eyes follow you as you walk down the hall. That's another tradition."

The traditions started with Edward McClain, who died in 1934. He never had much chance to receive an education; at thirteen he began working in his father's harness shop. There he made one of his earlier and more lucrative inventions: a horse collar pad fastened by an elastic steel hook, permitting the pad to be readily attached to and detached from the horse collar. It made him rich. From that one invention he built a company, E. L. McClain Manufacturing, in Greenfield. It was incorporated in 1930 as the American Pad and Textile Company. McClain invested in other things and started other companies, but his fame came from the horse pad.

In 1912, wealthy McClain announced that he would build for his town a campus school, something to inspire students and establish educational tradition. He wanted Greenfield students to learn the classics, among other things, so he insisted on a building that embodied those ideals. He wanted a school building that would last. He ordered the ultimate academic décor—busts, murals, and statues—to be placed throughout the school. Ever vigilant, McClain personally inspected the school on weekends, looking for dust on the statues. He demanded a spotless building, and school officials complied. Even today, the administration tries to meet his demands as much as possible.

The school was dedicated in 1915. In 1923, the McClains donated more money to erect a vocational building, three custodians' cottages, and the Greenfield Athletic Field. Voters approved a bond issue of $450,000 for a new elementary building.

A 1928 catalog writer described McClain as "The Complete School at Greenfield, Ohio, an illuminating example of beauty, efficiency, and economy in schoolhouse planning." Its grandeur attracted numerous national visitors in education, including Dr. William McAndrew, superintendent of Chicago's schools. On a tour of the school in 1928, he said:

> All the things which the state of Ohio says a public school should do are being done. Around them and in them is an influence of enjoyment, refinement, courtesy, and cheer that makes one want to linger. Think of an art gallery of 165 masterpieces in a public school in a town of 5,000! The art motif does not end with the collection. The grounds disclose it as do the greeneries in the corridors, the decorated tile at the drinking fountains, the beautiful panels on the outside walls. The silent tuition of beauty has been secured everywhere.

Now, despite the classical surroundings, 660 students wear typical high school letterman jackets and attend the usual sporting events. They file noisily through the halls, seeming unaware of their rich surroundings.

With Rookwood tiles gracing the area around each water fountain, McClain is a reminder of a more cultured time. Its large library looks like an old city library. Glass cases hold several Edward McClain inventions, including a geared pencil-sharpener, photographs of long-forgotten classmates, monogrammed school china, assorted student memorabilia, and sets of bound student essay books. "Until the 1930s,

The Legacy of Edward McClain

the school required students to give an oration in front of a committee before they could graduate," Strain said. "The reports are in those books. We've got them all."

The library displays a cartoon layout by Milton Caniff, the creator of the *Steve Canyon* comic strip, who was born nearby. Other paintings and pictures hang in the library, each with a moral or an allegory. The school also contains sculptor Hiram Powers's original bust *Ginevra*, probably the school's most valuable artwork. Donated in 1928 by former Greenfield superintendent William G. Molder in memory of his wife, the bust sits in an enclosed glass case at the school's main entrance.

A marble stairway rises just inside the front doors. It is the most convenient way to walk to the second floor, but students don't use it. We stood in the hall, looking up at the grand stairway. "Only alumni use our marble stairway," Strain told me. "The only time students can use it is at the baccalaureate service a week before graduation."

That night, parents take pictures and shoot videos of their kids walking down the stairs, clad in their caps and gowns. Boys walk down the side where Mr. McClain's picture hangs; the girls come down the other side, past Mrs. McClain's painting. "We have to pass the Kleenex that night," he said. "It's tradition."

12

Ghosts of Rogues' Hollow

> Rogues' Hollow had its fights. With a large group of miners frequenting different saloons, anything was apt to happen, and did.
> —*Russell Frey*

In northeastern Ohio there is a place—filled with as much legend as reality—called Rogues' Hollow. Once known as Ohio's Sleepy Hollow, it is considered one of the state's most haunted ghost towns and, in its day, one of the toughest mining towns anywhere.

With an estimated 103 coal mines operated around it, I suppose Rogues' Hollow is what San Toy, Perry County's raucous old mining ghost town, would have been if it were haunted. I imagine Rogues' Hollow looking something like Deadwood.

Of course I had to see it. So I followed State Route 21 through Wayne County and over into Chippewa Township, just south of Doylestown. When I finally got close to Rogues' Hollow, however, I wandered into a heavily wooded area and became confused. (This is not unusual, considering that I was looking for a ghost town.) Finally, I saw the Rogues' Hollow Historical Society building, a wooden replica of an old woolen mill that stands near where the town once stood. The society, one of those unsung museums dedicated to saving local history and culture, dutifully keeps everything from old school class photographs to maps to a bucket of human teeth. The building lies in the Chippewa–Rogues' Hollow Nature Preserve and Historical Park.

After I visited a decade ago (since then, the place has become a public park, open only during the day), I read the historical society's newsletter and saw a good line penned by Charlie Cummings, who was then the president: "There isn't much news right now but there will be." Fitting commentary for a ghost town.

After driving around the rural area just before dusk, unaware that much of the property was privately owned, I saw an older man. So I stopped. Just as I was ready to say hello, he yelled, "Hey, you—get out now!" Ever since, I have regretted not staying longer. Since then, other ghost town hunters have told me they have tried unsuccessfully to find the exact location of Rogues' Hollow. To me, this added to the allure of the town—a wild, untamed place of legend that eludes those who stalked it.

Most of what is known about the community's past comes from newspaperman Russell W. Frey, publisher of the *Rittman Press* in neighboring Rittman. For years he collected Rogues' Hollow memorabilia and interviewed its older residents. In 1958, he wrote *Rogues' Hollow: History and Legends,* which went into a third printing. Intriguing chapters include "Was the Nation's Toughest Spot," "Hides a Real, Dangerous Past," "Gang Fights Common in the Hollow," "Killers Terrorize as People Arm," "The Ghost of Chidester's Mill," and "Big Snake Legend Verified." The titles filled my mind with scenes of shootouts, bootleggers, and hauntings, and the big snake reminded me of the nineteenth-century snake creature in Warren County.

In the early 1960s, Frey helped establish the Rogues' Hollow Historical Society, which in 1973 purchased property and built the replica of old Chidester woolen mill that houses the group.

The area's earliest white inhabitant, Samuel Chidester, came from Akron in the 1820s. A community slowly developed. Rogues' Hollow hit its heyday in the 1860s and began to die in the late 1800s. As late as the 1920s, some residents remained. In the 1950s, the town's oldest native, Walter "Turp" Collier, told Frey, "Rogues' Hollow was the toughest damn spot in the whole United States." Frey added: "The Hollow had a reputation. It was bad and it was disagreeable. People avoided going near it. Traveling men making the trip from Clinton to Doylestown always went by the roundabout way of Johnsons Corners instead of going the shorter road through the Hollow. People all over northeastern Ohio talked about it."

Perhaps that was because it was always a disagreeable place. Editor C. W. Linter of the *Doylestown News* wrote on April 21, 1922, that Rogues' Hollow was a lively town in its day, "but the old times have changed. It is only a shadow of the days gone by." A few months earlier he'd written:

> Pioneer Hatfield is the authority for the statement that Rogues' Hollow was named by a Doctor Crosby who owned the ground and had it laid out. What was meant by "laid out" this writer cannot understand. Had he said, "cast out and forgotten to civilization," it would have been more in keeping with this once memorable place. . . . At one time Rogues' Hollow . . . had distilleries. The whiskies, however, were of the kind that the different brands were harmless when taken singly, but when mixed were full of fight and general disturbances as the court records of the early days still bear witness thereto.

The town went by different names at different times. The Indians called the area Nibrara, or Beautiful Valley. Early white residents wanted to name it in honor of Peter Angfang, a gristmill owner. Still others wanted to call it Rogue. Later, it was called Peacock, for the rainbow-colored coal found in the area. The coal miners, who had helped build the Ohio Canal, drank hard liquor and fought every Saturday night. In time, the town reverted to a derivative of its original name, calling itself Rogues' Hollow.

In the 1850s, stagecoaches stopped at Walsh's Saloon, a haven for counterfeiters. Each man at the bar carried money in his boots. When one of them got drunk and passed out, the others would remove his boots and steal his money. For years the frame building was used as a house. It was still standing when Frey wrote his book. Mike Walsh, a former miner who weighed over 300 pounds, owned the saloon and operated it with his four sons. He had a special chair—large enough to accommodate his wide girth—in one corner. The family lived above the saloon.

In time, six more saloons opened to serve the unlucky stagecoach travelers and the area's thirsty coal miners. Their names are reminiscent of Wild West bars: Hole-in-the-Wall Saloon, Mrs. Ducey's Saloon, the Devil's Den. Miners got paid once a month, and many of them immediately headed to the saloons to spend their entire paychecks. They might not return to the mines for days and weeks—or until their paychecks finally had been spent. Other times, when miners ran out of alcohol money, they'd stand out by the road and surround an oncoming farmer or traveler and demand a dollar for a keg of beer. If they didn't get the money, they would intimidate the poor travelers.

They made their legitimate money in the mines, which in the late 1800s and early 1900s were called many different names, including the Boak Mine, the Ruth Mine, the Wagner Mine, the Messenger Mine, the Landis Mine, the Billman Mine, the California Mine, the Chippewa Mine, the Woods Mine, and the Simonds Mine.

Some of Rogues' Hollow's women—who were just as tough as the men—worked in private mines. A woman named Rebecca Gillespie, who lived east of the Hollow, near the Volcano Mine, used to dig coal with another woman to earn additional money when their husbands were out on drinking binges. Her miner husband, Jim, used to drink hard. Often she would wait for him outside the mine to get off work so that she could take his pay. She knew that if she missed him, he would buy drinks for everyone in his favorite saloon.

One story goes that Rebecca owned a pet monkey. On chilly nights, she would place the monkey in an oven to keep warm. The door was left ajar so the monkey could breathe. Once, when she was out digging coal or doing some other manly task, some men lit a fire under the stove to get warm. When she arrived home and opened the oven, the monkey had been roasted alive. Rebecca cried for days.

The high times didn't make for all the legends in Rogues' Hollow. The strange times did, too. Most of them occurred in the nineteenth century, when the countryside was rural and the population believed in ghosts, monsters, and evil spirits. One night a farmer was driving his wagon up a hill when he stopped to look at a big oak tree. He claimed he saw something ugly on a low branch, something that he was certain was the Devil. The creature had glowing red eyes. Later, the farmer returned with some friends, and they saw the same creature riding a headless horse. Other people also reported seeing such a creature and a headless horse—an interesting twist on the headless horseman story.

Another time, while a miner named Frank Herwick was shoveling coal in a mine that he leased, a vicious thunderstorm hit. He saw a lightning bolt strike something just outside the mine entrance; the powerful electric charge followed the iron tracks that led into the mine. It was at this point when Herwick said he saw a ghost, walking around the interior of the mine. As thunder boomed outside, unseen hands grabbed picks and shovels and waved them like a conductor's batons. Then, in the light of a kerosene lantern, the ghostly figure appeared again. Herwick became so frightened that he bolted from the mine and ran all the way to his home, which, of course, doubled as a saloon. There he recounted his ghost story to other miners. He never did get over the sight. He subleased the mine to concentrate solely on running his bar, where hallucinations from strong drink were only that—the wild dreams of bored miners.

Throughout the 1800s and early 1900s, apparition sightings were common in the Hollow. Every family had its own peculiar tale. Ghost stories became an important part of local lore and legend. One ghost supposedly haunted a place that the locals called Ghost Town, where thirty-six old, abandoned miners' shacks stood. The ghost often made itself visible to people as they were walking by the old place. The story persisted for generations.

When Frey was writing his book on Rogues' Hollow in the late 1950s, he interviewed a number of elderly people who clearly recalled the late 1800s and the superstitions that plagued that era. "After you talk to these old-timers," he wrote, "then you begin to understand how people become acquainted with pixies, elfs, dwarfs, spirits, and ghosts. In sifting out the tales which border on the land of exaggeration, sometimes it is difficult to know fact from fiction."

Frey reported that ghosts were most often observed in the Hollow on moonlit nights. He wrote, "Then the Hollow fairly comes alive with the residents of the spirit world, those who had a hand in making Rogues' Hollow a wild and dangerous place scores of years ago."

But dangerous ghosts didn't cause all the trouble. Roughnecks, gunslingers, and criminals abounded in the Hollow. According to one legend, Blinky Morgan, a nationally known horse thief, frequented Rogues' Hollow. He stole horses in Virginia and sold them in Michigan. Morgan hid some of his illegal horses in a Rogues' Hollow coal mine that was connected by tunnel to a brick building that had been used as a stagecoach stop. In 1887, authorities finally caught him when he robbed a store in Ravenna in Portage County. He was later convicted of theft and never returned. No one knew his fate.

Sherri Brake, who conducts the popular Haunted Heartland Tours, has held seminars in the Rogues' Hollow museum, providing two hours of classroom work and two hours of investigation time for each session. She considers it a fitting place. Her topics have included "Ghosts vs. Spirits," "History and Hauntings of Rogues' Hollow," "Ghosts on Tape," "Science and the Skeptic," and "Bigfoot Sightings and Ghost Sightings in the Area."

"It has been said that Rogues' Hollow has a special type of energy that draws people into its center. Perhaps it is attributed to the power of natural energy," Brake observed. "Perhaps all the energy from the Hollow's rowdy days in the 1860s and 1870s still resonates through the air. Or maybe it's our imagination."

Brake, who serves on the historical society's board, said the ghost town is made of legends, which attracts people from across the state and nation. "There is a spot called Cry Baby Bridge," she said. "It is one of twenty-four Cry Baby Bridges in Ohio. But this is the real thing. When I was giving a tour there a few years ago, some people from out of state tried to crash the event. The place is quite legendary. There are two stories as to how it got its name. Both occurred in the 1800s. One is about a local woman, reportedly a witch who became pregnant. But she didn't want the baby, so she took him to the bridge and drowned her child in Silver Creek below. The second explanation for the name, also from the 1800s, comes from a tragic incident in which a family was riding in a wagon that was descending the hill above the bridge. Well, something scared the horses, and the wagon ended up being thrown into the creek. A child perished. Now, for whichever reason, people claim they can hear a child crying at night along the bridge. I tell people this is legend; there is no documentation. The story has been passed from decade to decade."

Brake said the crying baby legend is one of several prominent tales that attract people to Rogues' Hollow. Another reason is that the ghost town is strange. Brake said it was such a tough town that in the late 1800s, county sheriff deputies refused to enter. "They'd look down on it from a hill," she said. "That was close enough for them."

A few years ago, Brake said she escorted a psychic to Rogues' Hollow. "She looked up toward a clearing and said, 'Do you see those three men standing over there?'"

"'No. I don't see anything,' I said."

The psychic said only their legs were visible to her, and they wore gray pants, like workers' pants. What she didn't know was that this town used to be a big coal-mining community, and some miners were killed when they were run over by coal cars on tracks that came rushing along in the dark. That could account for the "men" she saw. Perhaps they had been cut in half. "Rogues' Hollow had a lot of mining tragedies," Brake said. "There were so many accidents involving explosives. Miners had to light their fuses by hand, then run away. Sometimes the fuse malfunctioned and blew up [the dynamite] before the men could run off. Every now and then we hear about someone seeing a miner. One woman in our group looked up on a ridge and said she saw a man standing there, hands on his hips, as though he disapproved of us being there. Then he vanished. A member of the group took a picture, and when we looked at it we found a large, brightly colored orb."

Writer Katie Young knows that something about the Hollow is different. One night near Halloween in 2008, she participated in one of the tours in Rogues' Hollow, and she came away impressed. In a story published by AkronNewsNow.com, she said she asked questions out loud and then picked up electronic voice phenomena (EVP)—sounds inaudible to humans but capable of appearing on audio recordings.

"After the crowd [of visitors] broke apart to hunt the Hollow for ghosts, I decided to go back to the foundation of the McCullough house and try to record some EVP," she wrote. "While standing there asking questions I did not hear any children's voices, that is until I listened to what I [had] recorded."

Brake placed the audio on her website. I listened to it one quiet afternoon in my home office. There definitely was some strange background noise on Young's tape. But what was it? Squirrels scolding her? Birds shrieking? Or was it children—children still present in that past, wild place?

Rogues' Hollow lives!

13

Confederates on the Island

> I had rather lose a limb & be free.
> —*Lt. John Taylor, 7th South Carolina Cavalry,*
> *on being imprisoned on Johnson's Island*

Far upstate, deep inside old Yankee country, I drove along Lake Erie's rocky coast until I reached Marblehead, a busy tourist town in Ottawa County. On that sunny August afternoon, while young tourists shopped for flip-flops and middle-aged men in brightly colored shorts rented fishing boats, I came searching for Confederates.

For years I'd heard the legend of Johnson's Island, a little chunk of beauty in Sandusky Bay, three miles north of Sandusky. There, the Union War Department operated a prisoner-of-war camp from April 1862 to September 1865, nearly six months after the Civil War had ended. Most Ohioans don't know that such a camp ever existed on Lake Erie, or that its roster also included some northern citizens who were plucked from their homes for criticizing Abraham Lincoln's war policies.

One of them, an outspoken Hamilton physician and politician named John McElwee, intrigued me because he was from my hometown. I wanted to see where the antiwar Copperhead newspaper editor served his prison term for treason. Of course, the island's Confederates, most of them Rebel officers, fascinated me, too. Of the nearly 10,000 prisoners who served time on the island during the war, twenty-six were generals—or they became generals after they left the camp. Major General Issac Trimble stayed the longest, fourteen months; Major General "Allegheny" Ed Johnson the shortest, just two weeks. Many of their soldiers remained there for years—and some are still buried there.

The island lies off a piece of land that juts into Lake Erie. To the north, the strip is flanked by small islands; to the south are Sandusky and Cedar Point. The Federals chose the island for a prison site because it was nearly inaccessible country that contained plenty of timber for building prisoner housing and the small fort that would be erected in the middle of the island.

After walking around Marblehead for a short time, and wondering how to get over to the island, I spotted a white frame building on West Main Street and a sign for the Johnson's Island Museum. When I walked up to the small single room on the second floor, two other visitors were looking around at exhibits. A docent, a man in his sixties, was answering questions.

"Who was sent here?" a young woman asked.

"At first, the Confederates came from the Battles of Fort Henry and Fort Donelson," the docent replied, as if he'd heard the question before. "As the war continued, they came from other battles. The winters were harsh for southern boys used to warmer weather."

The woman grimaced.

The museum, operated by the Johnson's Island Preservation Association, features a model of Prisoners' Barracks Block 10 (typical of the eight barracks), period photographs of the camp, and artifacts discovered on the island over the years, including rusted gun parts, utensils, bullets, uniform buttons, and other things common to prison life. The group wants to make certain that the island's history survives the dual attacks of time and development. The prison—and its fifteen-foot wooden walls—was destroyed by limestone quarrying in the early 1900s and encroaching housing developments since the 1950s. Since 1989, David Bush, an archaeologist at Heidelberg University, has been studying the grounds. His mission: to ensure that the remains will always be available to help future generations understand, interpret, and experience the Civil War.

The museum's docent identified himself as Robert Ibos, an officer of the Preservation Association and a resident of Johnson's Island. He told me, "I'm originally from Cleveland. I liked Johnson's Island so much that I retired here. Some local people know all about the island; others are too busy making a living to know about it. Whenever I see young people at the prisoners' cemetery, I feel good—even if their parents must have dragged them there. At least we can expose them to the island and its past."

He said island residents often dig up things in their yards. "I found a whiskey bottle once; I was amazed it hadn't broken. I also found a lice comb, a belt buckle, and an ink well. I was just digging in my garden on the island."

A local man, Epaproditas Bull, bought the island in 1813. Trees covered the rugged island, which for years had been considered a favorite Indian locale—where they fished, held festivals, and brought their captives for torture. After Bull's death, his family sold the island in 1852 to Leonard B. Johnson, who in 1861 leased forty cleared acres to the federal government for the prison. By late 1862, newly captured Confederates were pouring onto the island.

"I've studied the prisoners," Ibos said. "Charles Pierce of Louisiana, I believe he was a captain, is my favorite. He reminds me of Steve McQueen's character in *The Great Escape*. Seven times he tried to escape. Once, he ran away on the ice and they fired cannons at him. On the shore, a bunch of farmers gathered, after hearing the booms, and they caught him. There was a fifty-dollar gold reward for the capture of any prisoner."

At first, life wasn't excessively harsh. Food was adequate. There were 600 books in the prison library, and prisoners formed a debating team and took the opportunity to learn German and French from their fellow prisoners. They also could buy newspapers, food, clothing, ink, and paper from the prison sutler. They spent their useless Confederate money in poker games. They even acted in the Rebel Thespians group. Because most Confederate officers came from the upper class, their families had money to send to their captured sons. As the fighting continued and Southern treatment of Union prisoners deteriorated, however, the War Department reduced the prisoners' rations by half and severely limited what items could be purchased from camp stores. When Union and Confederate governments cut back on their prisoner exchanges halfway through the war, the prison became overcrowded. Life became harsh on the island.

In its nearly four years of operation, Johnson Island's prison commanders counted only ten known successful escapes, most of them cases of prisoners dressing like guards and leaving, or Rebels running from the prison and somehow finding a way to float or paddle to Sandusky. Some of them took trains and headed east and, from there, south.

After the war ended, the Johnsons resumed farming on the island. But later, the family developed bigger plans. In 1894, the owners founded the Johnson's Island Pleasure Resort, which went bankrupt in 1897. In 1904, a second and larger incarnation of the resort opened, with a dance hall, pavilion, restaurant, hotel, and outdoor dining center. But after only a couple of years, it also went out of business. Cedar Point's pleasure resort was too much competition.

The irony of a "pleasure resort" on the site of a Civil War prison was not lost on me.

That afternoon I took State Route 163 past the Marblehead lighthouse and over to Gaydos Drive, where I paid a dollar to take the causeway to Johnson's Island. Most of it is privately owned; the only public place is the prison cemetery. On first entering the island, I noticed that everything looked green, like some lush park from long ago. I could see Cedar Point's roller coasters and ferris wheel from my car window. Nothing else remained of the prison, which at its peak consisted of 100 buildings scattered across fifteen acres. No one knows exactly how many soldiers were buried there. When the neglected cemetery was improved in May 1890, 206 marble grave markers replaced the cemetery's original worn-out wooden markers. It is estimated that 300 prisoners died on the island. A granite marker read: "Dead but sceptered sovereigns who still rule us from the dust."

I remembered the stories I'd heard about the ghosts of Johnson's Island—the same kind of tales you hear about all Civil War battlefields. The best story might be apocryphal. In the early 1900s, Italian workers were quarrying stone near the cemetery when they heard men's voices singing an unfamiliar melody. As the voices grew louder, the workers turned and saw ghostly figures rising from the graves. The dead formed a group and marched across the bay. The Italians had never heard the song before. When they returned to shore, they hummed it for their bosses, who recognized it immediately. It was "Dixie."

To me, the cemetery seemed a lonely place, even on that summer day in tourist season. A few other people walked around, looking at the graves and the historical markers and three monuments. A refreshing breeze blew across my face. Except for the distant roar of a lawnmower, the island was quiet. I stood there for a few minutes, trying to understand what life must have been like there in 1864. My mind wandered like scenes from a silent movie. I imagined a windy winter's day, with deep snow covering everything and the whole camp firing snowballs in what prisoners called "the only snowball fight in hell." Quickly my mind changed seasons, imagining the day when several guards—local men hired by the camp commander—were accused of selling whiskey to prisoners. (Surely a bottle was a prized commodity in any war camp.) As soldiers escorted the accused civilian guards from the stockade, the prisoners hooted, howled, and jeered. One guard, his hands tied behind his back, left at bayonet point. A placard hung from his neck: "I Sold Whiskey to the Rebels." Then I imagined another cold day, January 1, 1864, when the old camp commander, William Pierson, the former mayor of Sandusky, walked out for the last time, replaced for mistreating prisoners. I could almost hear them cheering "Hurrah!"

I entered the cemetery through a century-old iron arch that displayed, in big white letters, "Confederate Soldiers 1861–1912." I wanted to visit the graves, each one marked by a white Georgia marble headstone. Nearby stood an old memorial statue, sculpted by Confederate veteran Sir Moses Ezekiel, a Virginia Military Institute cadet who served in combat. When the memorial was dedicated in 1910, 4,000 people attended the ceremony. To me, 4,000 people seemed an amazingly large number for such a rural place, but in those times people took their veterans seriously. Some Civil War vets were still alive, and the war's impact—emotionally and economically—could still be felt throughout the North and the South.

As I looked around the clean and attractive cemetery, trying to conceive of the divisiveness of the times, I wondered whether the families of the 200-some ever knew what happened to their soldiers. If so, I also wondered whether those families felt another kind of sorrow, knowing that their sons, fathers, and nephews were buried on Union soil.

That soil, that hunk of land nearly a mile long and half a mile wide, held at its peak operational period about 3,000 Confederates, who must have felt frustrated living behind prison walls on an isolated island in the chilly North. Did they hear of Grant's victory at Vicksburg in 1863? Did they know of Lee's defeat at Gettysburg? Did they hear news of the killing fields—Antietam, Second Bull Run, Shiloh, and Franklin, Tennessee? Did they write faithfully to their mothers, sisters, and wives? How many soldiers thought, *I wish I could swim*?

. . .

The monument to Southern soldiers at Johnson's Island. (Photo by Randy McNutt)

In 1864, while prisoners' rations dwindled, Rebel armies were pinned down across the South. What the Confederacy needed was a diversion—something that might force the Union to send its soldiers in the other direction. To Jacob Thompson, the Confederate commissioner in Canada, the answer was the Northwest Conspiracy, his long-shot plan to liberate two Ohio prisons, Johnson's Island and Camp Chase in Columbus. He also hoped to liberate prisoners at camps in Indiana and Illinois, arm them, and start a rebellion against Lincoln's government with the aid of the Copperheads—the peace Democrats who counted substantial support in Ohio, Indiana, and Illinois.

Thompson's problem was keeping his bold plan secret, for a large number of Union spies worked out of southern Canada. Their ears were always cocked. Yet Thompson, who had served in the United States Congress for twelve years and later as President Buchanan's secretary of the interior, knew about political intrigue. Although he had doubts about his chance for success, he decided to act on his plan. He chose Captain Charles H. Cole, a former cavalry officer who had escaped from another Union prison. Cole's part in the plan was to capture the USS *Michigan*, a side-wheel steamer and the Union's only military vessel in the area. It guarded the island.

Following orders, Cole traveled along the Great Lakes, claiming he was a wealthy oil speculator. He was to devise a plan to liberate Johnson's Island and find the location of the *Michigan*. That August, Cole, flush with $60,000 from Thompson, moved into Sandusky's West House with Annie Brown, whom he had met along the way. She told people that she was his wife. As weeks went by, Cole introduced himself to the *Michigan*'s officers and started compiling information on the ship's activities.

Then, just days before the raid was to start in mid-September, the plan began to unravel. A man claiming to be a former Confederate soldier now living in Canada approached Union authorities in Detroit and told them of the Rebels' plans to capture the commercial steamer *Philo Parsons* and use it to board and capture the *Michigan*. He said a man named Cole would drug the warship's officers while a second group would board and capture the *Michigan* from the *Parsons*. The *Michigan* was alerted. Union troops captured Cole and took him on board for questioning.

Meanwhile, on September 19, 1864, the other half of the conspiracy began at Sandwich, Canada, near Detroit. Four Rebels boarded the

Parsons. As it stopped at various islands near the Ohio shore, twenty more raiders boarded the steamer, lugging a big trunk. When the boat finally left Kelleys Island, the raiders pulled out revolvers and captured the *Parsons,* then opened the trunk and removed a cache of weapons. The group's leader, Captain John Yates Beall, forever to be called the Pirate of Lake Erie, took command. His raiders discussed their plans to liberate the prisoners on Johnson's Island. They waited for a message from Cole, who by this time should have captured the *Michigan.*

When Cole failed to send a prearranged signal to Beall on the *Parsons,* Beall knew something had gone wrong with the plan. He worried that if he continued toward the warship, the *Michigan*'s fourteen cannons could be trained on the *Parsons*. So he and his men turned and headed for Canada. Back at Sandwich, they pulled into a harbor and sank the boat. Then they fled. Months later, Union authorities captured Beall in New York and hung him for spying and piracy. Already in custody, Cole spent the rest of the war in prison.

The prisoners on Johnson's Island probably never heard of the Confederacy's failed plan. On that day, September 20, they might have heard less exciting news from eight-year-old Leonard Johnson, son of the island's owner, who visited the camp regularly to cheer up the prisoners. They enjoyed joking with Leonard and his friends. Also on that day, the prisoners might have staged another play, or a sporting event, to pass the time.

For them and everyone else, the Northwest Conspiracy ended before it began.

Later in the war, the prisoners on Johnson's Island included some "traitors"—Ohio Copperheads convicted by military tribunals for violating General Ambrose Burnside's General Order No. 38, which forbade anyone from publicly denouncing the United States government and the war. (The tribunals were similar to the ones that try terrorists today.) Burnside, a Hoosier who was considered a fair and kind man, had been through many bloody battles; he could not tolerate war opponents. His tribunals sentenced the citizens to hard labor at the direction of the camp commander. Nowadays, civil liberties lawyers and libertarians would challenge the tribunals as unconstitutional.

In 1864, two of the prison's newcomers were from Hamilton, a stronghold of Peace Democrats, spies, and antiwar protestors. On April 18, authorities arrested George Donges for yelling "Hurrah for Jeff Davis!" in a public place in town. Obviously, Donges was something more than a Peace Democrat; he was a downright Rebel sympathizer with a penchant for self-destruction. When an angry citizen—Union supporter Peter Kregenhofer—complained about Donges's remark, Donges went wild. According to a federal indictment written by Assistant Adjutant General Lewis Richmond, Donges "did violently assault" the victim, "strike him in the face with his fists, knock him down with a slung-shot, and kick him in the face, seriously wounding and bruising him." As a result, Donges was ordered to serve a prison sentence on the island.

Then there was Dr. John McElwee, who dared write and publish antiwar editorials in his weekly newspaper, the *Hamilton True Telegraph*. By this time he had given up practicing medicine in favor of newspaper work and politics. He was the *True Telegraph*'s editor and part owner and the Butler County clerk of courts. His first indictment came for writing these words: "It is our subtle conviction that the war, if protracted, will bring anarchy upon the North, and ultimately some form of despotic government."

Authorities knew that he had long been an unofficial adviser to former congressman Clement Vallandigham, the nation's most vocal Peace Democrat. In April 1863, Union soldiers arrested McElwee on a charge of treason, just as they had Vallandigham. Soon after, both men were freed. Vallandigham was kicked out of the country. McElwee, who had returned home, went to Canada with three other Copperheads to personally escort Vallandigham back to Hamilton, where he would start a campaign for governor, which he lost.

But McElwee had just begun to agitate. In November 1864, the government arrested him again, for writing stories critical of the draft and Lincoln's administration. This time, the Federals wanted to stop him from writing editorials, period. So they convicted him by a military court's ruling and sent him—a private citizen, mind you—to Johnson's Island, where he could swap stories with Confederates when he wasn't washing floors and splitting logs for firewood.

Before leaving the island cemetery, I glanced around one last time, just to make sure that the doctor did not end up in the cemetery for practicing freedom of the press. I learned that he did not. While browsing the Johnson's Island Preservation Association's website when I returned home, I read that after the war had ended, all the Confederates were released in September 1865. "The last prisoners included two die-hards who refused to take the oath of allegiance" to the United States. They were finally released on September 5. I chuckled at the thought of the two "die-hards" and wondered if they were Donges and McElwee, still smarting from their high-handed convictions and refusing to take any oath to the Federals.

As for Donges, I know nothing of him after his conviction, but I do know that McElwee returned to Hamilton, where he continued his writing, often on the subject of medicine. By 1870, he disappeared from public view. It was as if history swallowed him whole.

Dr. John McElwee, rabble-rouser and a prisoner at Johnson's Island, was never heard from again.

Ghosts of the Stage Lines

14

The Wickerham Secret

> The mystery of who perpetrated this ghastly malefaction remains today.
> —Stephen Kelley

For me, discovering historic inns—dead or alive—is as interesting as finding ghost towns. They are similar because their stories often intertwine. In the early days of the nation, taverns and inns dotted the landscape. Inns helped support communities by hiring local people; owners also took on the role of postal clerks and opened their doors for community meetings.

Before inns operated in remote parts of Ohio, families pinned notes on their cabin doors when they had to leave, welcoming travelers who needed a place to stay for the night. (Pioneers assumed that Indians couldn't read.) Some of these generous homeowners later decided to start charging for their hospitality and thus created the early pioneer inns. Families with larger houses kept a spare bedroom for the exclusive use of travelers. When stagecoaches started stopping, innkeepers earned a steady income. But country travelers did not receive what I'd consider first-class accommodations. The early inns used sleeping lofts filled with straw; several guests slept in the same bed. Only the fancier inns offered feather beds. Innkeepers cultivated large gardens—and often a patch of corn—for use in their cooking. They served fried rabbit, groundhog, turkey, venison, squirrel stew, and opossum with sweet potatoes. Inns included handsome log ones such as the two-story inn built about 1810 on the Andersonville Road (now U.S. Route 50) in Brown County's

Perry Township, and which is now on the National Register of Historic Places. In Highland County, Greenfield's Travellers Rest, built about 1812, was made of native stone (it's now a museum).

Before railroads connected small towns, stagecoach lines delivered mail and passengers on rocky dirt roads. It was a jarring ride for drivers and passengers, but even important people—Andrew Jackson included—had to take the bumpy stages if they wanted to travel.

And coach drivers—rough-talking men dressed in flannel—commanded the vehicle. After taking many rides on stagecoaches during a tour of the states, Charles Dickens described one such American frontier driver: "He is always dirty, sullen, and taciturn. He always chews and always spits, and never encumbers himself with a pocket-handkerchief. The consequence to the box passenger, especially when the wind blows toward him, are not agreeable."

Stagecoaches—"the box," as Dickens called it—varied in design and luxury (or lack of it). Some coaches, like the Concord, were painted in gold and red and other colors. They cost $1,000–3,000, a large sum back then. When arriving at rural inns, the coach driver blew a horn to alert the innkeeper.

Today, all that remains of the stagecoach system is an occasional house or inn where the stages stopped. Many towns that were once served by the stagecoach lines are now ghost towns. They survived only a few decades after the once-profitable stage business finally died in the early twentieth century due to expansion of the railroads.

On this trip, I read a stagecoach traveler's account of his 1807 journey from Adams County to Chillicothe in Ross County. Much of that countryside is still wild and rural; I can't imagine how dangerously rugged it was back then. The writer, a Dr. F. Cumming, shared a stage with a poor, older man named Lashley. Inns were about four to eight miles apart—a good ride in a stage. Cumming wrote later:

> Old Lashley complaining of fatigue, [so] we stopped at Marshon's farmhouse, ten miles from Brush Creek, where finding that we could be accommodated for the night, we agreed to stay, and were regaled with boiled corn, wheaten griddle cakes, butter and milk for supper, which our exercise through the day gave us a good appetite for; but I did not enjoy my bed so much as my supper, notwithstanding it was the second best in the house, for besides it was not remarkable for its

cleanliness [and] I was obliged to share it with my old companion; fatigue, however, soon reconciled me to it, and I slept as well as if I had lain down between lawn sheets.

Cumming noted that Mr. Marshon, a New Jersey native, was building "a large log house in which he means to keep a tavern." The Marshons tried to provide entertainment. As Cumming observed, "Three of his sons play the violin by ear—they had two shocking bad violins, one of which was of their own manufacture, on which they scraped away with mercy to entertain us, which I would have most gladly excused, though I attempted to seem pleased and believe I succeeded in making them think I was so."

Neither violins nor vibrating coach wheels serenaded me on my journey. For hours all I heard was the Jeep's canvas top smacking like a bullwhip as I traveled alone to rural Adams County. I was headed to my friend Stephen Kelley, a Buckeye historian and archaeologist who had once guided me to local ghost towns. This time, I wanted him to escort me to his county's old inns. Obviously pleased with my latest idea, he suggested that we start on Old State Route 41, the original Zane's Trace. Ebenezer Zane started it by using an Indian path named the Coshocton Trail, which ran northeast to Lancaster as a part of his trace that ran from Wheeling to Maysville. In time, the Trace grew into a popular route.

Kelley described how Adams County looked when the settlers arrived in the late 1700s. "This area was a fantastic place to hunt because of the salt licks that attracted animals," he said. "They migrated from salt lick to salt lick. Elk, buffalo, deer, and other animals that needed salt all went to the licks. Roaming by instinct, they eventually figured out the easiest routes between licks, and migrated from grassland to grassland. By the time the Indians came here, the routes were already laid out. Zane's Trace, now Old Route 41, was once a buffalo trace." He went on, "For years, historians believed that Ohio was once 90 percent forest. Not true. There were great grassy areas among the vast woods. Can you imagine seeing a large herd of buffalo crossing the Ohio River? They had to cross; they had no choice if they wanted to get to the Kentucky side. In time, the buffalo were hunted to extinction here. These days a buffalo herd is kept next to Route 41. Willing or not, they have returned to the land of their ancestors."

I explained my interest in the inns, and Kelley noted that Manchester, on the Ohio River, had the county's first tavern—a crude inn. Kelley said a traveler named George Sample, who would settle on Ohio Brush Creek at Soldier's Run, stayed at the tavern in 1797. The experience must have impressed Sample, for forty-five years later he recalled it in an article in the *Western Pioneer:*

> There were fifteen to twenty cabins at Manchester, one of which was called a tavern. It was at least a grogshop. There were about a dozen visitors at the tavern, and . . . they appointed me to assist the landlady in making eggnog. I was inexperienced in the art, but I made out to suit them very well. I put about a dozen eggs in a large bowl, and after beating, or rather stirring the eggs up a little, I added about a pound of sugar and a little milk to this mass; I then filled the bowl up with whiskey, and set it on the table; and they sat about the table and sipped it with spoons. Tumblers or glasses of any sort had not then come into fashion.

Sample said the inn's owners, an Irishman named John McGate and his wife Katy, participated in "many broils and fisticuffs" that usually involved an often-indicted schoolmaster, James Dunbar. Apparently no parent in Manchester worried about Dunbar's reputation. Perhaps the bottle was his only escape from a dreary life of teaching pioneer children, who suffered from colds, bowel problems, and worms.

Despite rural Adams County's sparse population and hilly terrain, many inns operated there in the late 1700s and early 1800s. Location was the attraction—on Zane's Trace. Some inns—the Bradford Hotel in West Union, the Stone House on Lick Fork, and Horn's Hotel at Locust Grove—had official names. Others did not. (These days, only the Bradford remains in business, only on weekends, as the Ole Wayside Inn.) Inns also opened in now-forgotten communities named Alexandria; Adamsburg, better known as Killinstown; Waterford, at the mouth of Lick Fork; and Palestine, on the Limestone Road (a later name for Zane's Trace), between Peebles and Locust Grove. Kelley said most of the old inns were interchangeably called taverns. They offered whiskey, lodging, and brawls.

From Kelley's home in Seaman we drove over to Route 41, the way Morgan's Raiders headed after leaving Harshaville in July 1863. I imagined them riding along the dusty road, the Stars and Bars flowing and one stubborn cavalryman clinging to an unwieldy gilded birdcage that he had taken from a local farmer. "Morgan's men camped for the night right over there," Kelley said, pointing to a spot in fields and woods. We pulled over and looked around. "Their camps stretched for seven miles. Morgan himself stayed the night in the comfort of the Kilpatrick Tavern, an inn over in Jacksonville, which we call Jacktown. A few others stayed at the Wickerham. We know this because a grandson of the inn's founder saw the Rebels that night. He later reported that some of them slept on the floor of his grandfather's 'old tenement'—the inn."

Kelley had been researching the Confederates' raid through Adams for five years and has compiled information for use in a multicounty program that will identify stops on Morgan's Raid with historical markers. One of the markers will be placed at the Wickerham, which operated as an inn from 1800 to 1850, when it also reportedly served as a stop on the Underground Railroad.

To make conversation, I mentioned that my paternal grandmother's maiden name was Wickerham. I told Kelley that after they married, my grandparents left Adams County for Cincinnati to look for work.

"Did you say Wickerham?" He flashed a grim smile that left me wondering what he was thinking. Shaking his head, he said, "Yes, well, just up ahead you will see the actual Wickerham Inn, built by Peter Wickerham when this area was nothing but a wilderness."

A mile south of Locust Grove, on the east side of Route 41, Kelley pointed to a sturdy building, painted white, with traces of weathered brick showing. It was once the Wickerham Inn—the oldest brick building in the county and one of Ohio's oldest. In front stood a metal Ohio historical marker that told a brief history of the place, as written by Kelley.

In 1801, Peter Wickerham received a license to operate a tavern in his home. He also planned to use it as a stagecoach stop on the Trace, which bisected the family property. Four years earlier, the Revolutionary War veteran had purchased the land after arriving from Pennsylvania. In granting his petition for a tavern, the local court noted that Wickerham was a "civil citizen and very worthy of the character of innkeeper." Business increased steadily as more travelers discovered the Trace. Nationally prominent figures, including Henry Clay and Andrew Jackson, reportedly stayed at the Wickerham Inn on their way from Kentucky and Tennessee to Washington, D.C.

This intrigued me. "No one ever mentioned that my grandmother's people once owned an inn," I said.

Kelley laughed loudly. "Well," he said, "I'm not surprised." Flashing a smirk, he turned to get a better look at me. "Let me tell you a little something about your stock. One night in the early 1800s, a coach stopped at the inn. It was rumored that the new driver carried a large amount of money. Hours later, lodgers heard a commotion coming from the driver's room on the second floor, but nobody bothered to go see what was happening. In those times, a lot of the old wayside taverns had special rooms for coachmen. When the man didn't come down for breakfast the next morning, a boy went up to get him. He found blood all over the floor."

I grimaced. "Oh, no . . ."

"Oh, yes! It was widely rumored that the inn's owners killed the driver for his money," Kelley explained, "but his body was never found. Soon after the disappearance, people started claiming they saw a ghost on the second floor—the ghost of a headless man. Many years later, when descendants tore up the basement floor to install a furnace, they found a well-preserved human skeleton—minus the head. We presume it was the dear, old coachman buried there. I believe the family had to do something with the body, so they dug a hole in the basement, threw the body in it, and tossed in some lime to mask the odor. They got away with murder."

"Perhaps a guest did it," I offered sheepishly.

"Oh, please!" he said. "Wouldn't you know if somebody were digging a grave in your basement?"

"Well, I've heard there were people named Wickersham around here back then," I said. "Maybe they did it."

"They're all the same family anyway," he said. "Spelling was pretty loose then, that's all. I've boldly surmised that more than one person was involved in the crime. Maybe Wickerham and his family worked together. It was rumored that they cut off the guy's head and tossed it in a pond. But neither head nor money was ever recovered. When I lectured at a historical group one evening, my theory upset some of the Wickerhams in the audience. They said old Peter Wickerham was a staunch Methodist. One of them said, 'How dare you suggest that of a Methodist!' Well, I'm a Methodist, too, but that designation doesn't mean somebody is above committing murder."

He smiled and shook his head knowingly. I was too shocked to talk.

"We don't know a lot about Mr. Wickerham," Kelley said, "but he was a prominent citizen and rather prosperous, so no one would have questioned him. He died at age eighty-five. Now, some people claim the coachman incident happened in 1804, but it had to be later. Stagecoach travel on Zane's Trace in Adams County didn't start until after 1806, and it was stopped before 1842. So sometime between those years, the Wickerhams must have, well . . ."

He smiled devilishly. I couldn't tell if he was having fun with me or trying to make a point. I suppose he was doing both.

"In the 1970s," he went on, "I went over to the house and spoke with an old woman—a Wickerham descendant—who lived there. I asked her about the bones. She told me, 'I keep them in a box under my bed.' Of course, I thought she was joking. Then she left the room and returned with a box. She sat down, opened it, and pulled out a couple of leg bones and some other kinds. But she didn't have the skull. Too bad."

"Stephen, are you making all this up?"

He looked offended. "Absolutely not! This legend of Old Adams is one of the few area ghost stories of which I'm aware and is based on historical facts. Many people have claimed to have personally seen the ghost—specter—whatever he is—but most witnesses ask for anonymity. I will admit, however, that there are multiple versions of the phantom story, including one involving a dog. Over time, it has become increasingly difficult for me to separate fact from fiction."

"No kidding," I said. I sat silently for a few minutes to ponder the situation. "But why would they bother to cut off the guy's head?" I asked finally. "Why wouldn't they just stab him and be done with it?"

Kelley looked perplexed. "Questions, questions," he said. "I don't know all the answers."

"Well, how did the old woman respond to your questions?"

"Oh, she was a good sport about it," Kelley said, grinning. "But I think the whole thing is, uh, macabre. Don't you?" He studied me, perhaps trying to determine which side I would take. Then he went on, "You see, she had returned to live in the house after living elsewhere for years, and she slept over a box of bones—yes, those bones. She stayed there, the last of the Wickerhams, until the place was sold later in the '70s." He smiled at me mischievously. "Your people, mind you."

I groaned and drove on.

The Wickerham Secret

In recent years, the inn's headless ghost has gained a following on the Internet. Several websites discuss the coachman. They say that hundreds of people have reported seeing the ghost over the years. Kelley said the ghost has become one of the county's most popular legends.

"Within a short time of the murder," he said, "many people in the area started claiming to see an apparition in the upstairs window of the inn. It was a distinct outline of a headless man. Perhaps he was seeking his severed head. As the years passed, many other people reported seeing the phantom. In the 1910s, a version of the story went that a little white dog accompanied the ghost. Since then, with all the rumors, it has become difficult to know what really happened all those years ago at the Wickerham Inn."

He held up an index finger and said, "Ah-ha. That brings up another headless story—this one from the Treber Inn."

"Were my ancestors involved again? Any Methodists?"

"Oh no," he said, sighing for effect. "They were busy enough."

We drove around looking for the inn built on Zane's Trace in 1798 by a pioneer named John Treber. As the road developed a few years later, it offered transportation by coach from Maysville, Kentucky, to Chillicothe, Ohio, and on to Wheeling, then in Virginia. Located four miles north of West Union on Route 41, the inn—one of the oldest hewed-log buildings in Ohio—was covered with weatherboard. (The building is now on the National Register of Historic Places.) Its long second-story wooden porch with a railing allowed guests to catch summer breezes. The large kitchen and dining room to the rear were made of stone quarried in the area. In the Treber's prime, a large wooden sign that read "Traveller's Entertainment" welcomed visitors to the inn. Prominent politicians stayed at the Treber, including Andrew Jackson, Senator Thomas Benton, and Henry Clay. When Jackson stopped in late 1828, he and a party of followers were on their way to his presidential inauguration on March 4, 1829. They sipped coffee and ate biscuits prepared by Mother Treber, the wife of Jacob Treber, a son of the founder. She was proud of her work. She once told an impudent guest, "You never tasted finer coffee nor eat better biscuits, for I prepared them myself."

Kelley motioned for me to turn onto another road and then said, mocking a tour guide, "To your left you'll see the tree that once held the head of Ashael Edgington. He and brother John were caught up here by a group of Shawnee in pioneer days. John managed to outrun the Indians—a major feat—but Ashael was shot and killed. The Indians cut off his head, broke a baby white cedar, and rammed the head down on it, arranging it in just the right position so the search party could see it from a distance. This was a scare tactic that they used back then. The tree mended itself, and today you can see it's got a fat 'S' shape to it, where it grew back together. See it hanging there, right over State Route 41? I have this fear that someday I'll drive by and find the Ohio Department of Transportation chopping it down."

"Let's get out of here," I said. "Too many people lose their heads in your county."

He seemed to not hear me. "Well, there's a gruesome sequel to the story. The family buried his remains near Lick Fork. They thought they put him a sufficient distance from the stream, but the water came up and started washing away at his grave. He was reinterred without his head. Meanwhile, the owner of the Treber Inn kept Ashael's skull on his mantel for years, as a conversation piece. Sensitive guy, wasn't he? I told that story to an older woman in the community who is a descendant of the Treber owners, and she said, 'Oh my, no! No relatives of mine would ever do anything so grotesque.' I said, 'Well, they did.' And one night, after peace came years later, three Indians stopped at the inn and drank heavily. They bragged about killing Ashael years before. Later that night, as they left, somebody shot them. Johnny got them, I think. But the head never did join the body in the grave. One day somebody came to visit the inn, and claimed he was a relative of Ashael. The Treber owner gave him the skull as a keepsake. My guess is that the visitor wasn't a relative at all. He probably only wanted to use the skull to scare people at Halloween."

"One skull accounted for, Mr. Kelley," I said, "and another missing in action."

I dropped Kelley off at home and headed farther west along more Ohio stagecoach routes in the minimal comfort of my Jeep Wrangler, which at times felt as bumpy as a stagecoach. In Ohio's southwest tip, I entered Hamilton County's Colerain Township, where, at one time, every few miles a tavern or inn operated on the old Colerain Pike. (It is now four-lane Colerain Avenue, a congested route on which cars sometimes move slower than horse- and oxen-pulled wagons.) Across the state and nation, many such country inns—I call them ghost inns—operated for a few years, encouraged small communities to grow, which slowly faded into nothingness. I set out to find the stories behind them.

Because I knew little about Colerain Township's past, I needed a native guide—someone who could see past and present. So in Hamilton I picked up an elderly uncle, Vernon Hornung, who grew up in a small town called Dunlap during the years after World War I. Now a ghost town, Dunlap is a direct descendant of Dunlap Station, founded by the pioneers. By the time my uncle was born, stagecoaches had given way to automobiles and Dunlap had started to decline. Now, it is a good example of a rural village swallowed by one of Cincinnati's larger suburbs.

Farms surrounded Dunlap until the 1940s, when soldiers returned from World War II, married, and headed to newly built subdivisions. Since then, most of the township's original villages have vanished in a wave of development; their transient residents are unaware that towns once sat on their lots. Now, only the town names survive—vague reference points that few people understand—and the ghosts of towns linger among the chain stores. But people who grew up around Cincinnati can still recall the names Dry Ridge, Groesbeck, Northbrook, and even the more obscure Barnesburgh (later Barnsburg).

We started counting other forgotten towns as we took back routes and ended up on Hughes Road, in a little valley below "Mount Rumpke," a huge commercial landfill. Signs welcomed us to the Handle Bar Ranch. It opened in 1937 and still operates, but on the day we visited it was closed for the season. A log cabin stood at the bottom of the hill. The site's architecture was an oddball buffet—Tudor, Wild West, Prairie, and Spanish. "You build on as necessity arises," owner Anna Gay Ritter said. A red tile roof covered one building. Dark-brown cabins contrasted sharply with a light covering of snow. Big stone fireplaces and picnic shelters gave the place the appearance of a pioneer settlement.

At Bevis, across from the Colerain Towne Centre near Interstate 275 and Colerain Avenue, we found the conjunction of Wal-Mart and Lowe's and American marketing gone wild. No one would suspect that in the 1800s Bevis thrived here—a small town known for the Bevis Hotel. Jesse Bevis used his earnings from a flatboat business to buy land and build the inn, which opened on New Year's Eve 1855. The town was a coach stop when taverns and inns supplied the needs of bone-weary travelers whose entire bodies must have ached from thumping rides on the coaches. In time, however, development caught up with Bevis and the township.

When the suburban boom hit in 1950–60, Bevis and Dunlap and other small towns were covered over like ancient shale beds.

"I wonder what the Bevis Hotel was like," I mused.

My uncle smiled mischievously. "You know the old saying: 'Sleep tight and don't let the bedbugs bite.' Back then, bedbugs were a part of life in the country hotels. The beds were pretty uncomfortable, too. There weren't any harsh chemicals around to kill the bugs, so they became a part of the traveling life. If you stayed in the old inns, I always heard, the chances were good that you'd bring home some company."

At age ninety-two, he remembered these kinds of towns vividly.

"Dunlap had a butcher, a saloon, and a general store that sold everything from farm machinery to kerosene lanterns. But we always called the place Georgetown. I know the map said Dunlap, but we knew it different. Post office people made the change because there was already another Georgetown. But that didn't matter. To us, Dunlap would always be Georgetown. We could always tell when somebody was an outsider because he would refer to the town as Dunlap." He looked around, trying to determine exactly where we were headed, and added, "Rural Route 1, Pleasant Run. Address, long gone."

We sat silently as I navigated the traffic and passed through a place where a road exited onto busy Colerain.

"Where was Dunlap?" I inquired.

He smiled. "You mean Georgetown?" He went on, "There was ten to twelve men around town named George. My granddad was a George. The butcher was a George. Oh, there was Georges all over town, you see, so to us the village was Georgetown."

"Georgetown—Dunlap—whatever it is. It's a ghost town now," I said.

"A what?" He laughed. "I'm not sure the place ever was too lively."

As I drove south, he yelled, "Pull over!" He pointed to a vacant lot, and then looked at a few retail buildings that surrounded it. "We're in it," he announced. He said he had not seen the place in years. He climbed out of the Jeep to look around.

"The 1913 flood washed away some of the buildings," he said. "I was a child then. I was always told that a fire ripped through town in 1887. Burned up a house, saloon, and stable. Fires destroyed a lot of old towns back then. My family's store and slaughterhouse were saved, though. A neighbor, Ralph Struble, wrapped his head in wet clothes, laid flat down upon the cone of the roof, about twenty feet away from the fire, and tossed water over the back end of the store until the fire died out."

The Wickerham Secret

By the early 1900s, Vernon said, Dunlap had the best of the old and the new: a blacksmith shop and a mechanic's shop that specialized in Overland automobiles. He could still "see" them; I could not.

Driving around the area, we passed the ultimate general store, Northgate Mall. These days, Colerain Avenue is lined with cars for miles at rush hour, and every conceivable brand-name store lines both sides of the highway.

"A few years ago," I said, "I read that 55,000 cars pass this place every day."

He shook his head in either disgust or amazement. "Where in the deuce do they all come from?" He pointed to something up ahead. "Right over there, in back of the mall, was the old Mount Healthy Airport. A big pond sat where the mall sits now. People used to drive cattle down Colerain Avenue—it was a gravel road then, like gravel from a creek—on their way to slaughterhouses in Cincinnati. They'd stop to let the livestock drink from the pond."

All I could see was a big gray ribbon overflowing with cars.

Busy Dunlap was a stagecoach town in the 1800s, when another George, George Struble, opened a hotel on the old Colerain Turnpike. He owned a farm along the highway, too. Many other stagecoach hotels operated on or near the pike, including the Six Mile House (the building still stands) and the Glen Airy House, near West Fork Road. A newspaper reporter once wrote, "All farmers who have occasion to travel to and fro along this pike are sure to stop at the Glen Airy for refreshments of all kinds. Meals are served in first class style, comprising both the delicacies of the season and good common country fare."

When we finally arrived in Dunlap, we found little left from my uncle's days. He stood along the road and recited the names of every resident he knew as a boy. "They weren't all Georges," he said with a laugh. He recalled the town's lore, its school days, and its lost legends—even the town's ghost.

He pulled out a yellowed *Cincinnati Enquirer* clipping, "A Scary Tale from Dunlap History," written by reporter Robert Mulford. My uncle had saved this brittle piece of history for probably fifty years. As he read it aloud, squinting to see the small type, his hometown lived again—if only in his mind:

> Dunlap is "real country." Off of all lines of railroad, it is four hours ride by stage from Cincinnati. . . . Dunlap, like all other towns, has

its romance. There is a legend of [a ghost] who appeared nightly on a prominade [sic] on the road. Early, a man named Stimson cleared off a section of land and cultivated it. By some provision of the law it was required that a certain corner of a claim be cleared and it was the bad fortune of Stimson to get into the end of another man's claim and he [Stimson] had to move. . . . There was a story that Stimson had killed the man responsible for his removal from the clearing, and threw his body in [a] well. It was in this well that the headless man made his abode. . . . [For years] the headless man of mystery patrolled the dusty pike. Long ago did he reign [as] the bugaboo of the hamlet, and children would not venture out after night past the abandoned well for neither love nor money. But his day is over, and the old well is so stopped up with ground and debris that the headless man is pinned in his grave.

Vernon Hornung sat there smiling at the thought of the Overland garage, the ghost, and his childhood.
Dunlap — Georgetown — small town.
R.I.P.

15

Riding the Line

> If only a man could have lived long enough, he could have sat here, in the front room of the Golden Lamb, and—glancing up once in awhile—watched the whole history of Ohio pass by.
> —*Charles Kuralt, CBS* Sunday Morning

In Lebanon, Broadway was built wide for a good reason—to accommodate stagecoaches that needed to make wide turns. They rolled through town in the 1800s, stopping at several hotels, including the Golden Lamb, "Ohio's Oldest Inn."

The icon of Broadway began in 1803, when Jonas Seaman acquired a lot from Ichabod Corwin ("the Donald Trump of his day," joked former inn employee Fred Compton) and opened a log tavern on the site of what is now one of the Golden Lamb's dining rooms. In 1815, a two-story brick building was erected; a third floor and an addition were added over the next fifteen years and then a fourth floor in 1874. Early innkeeper Henry Share advertised his inn as "handsome accommodations not excelled by many in the west." As the hotel evolved, it took on the various names of its owners, including the Bradley House and the Lebanon House. But the inn's sign—a golden lamb—remained. Many old inns adopted such catchy names, like early logos that were painted on signs and hung out front for the use of illiterate stagecoach drivers. (Another inn, at Blue Ball, once featured a sizeable blue ball, which drivers could not forget.)

Over the years, Lebanon and the Golden Lamb Inn became popular destinations of several stagecoach companies, including the Accommodation Line, a Springfield company that ran a Cincinnati-to-Springfield

This postcard from the 1960s shows the early sign of the Golden Lamb in Lebanon. (Author's collection)

route via U.S. Route 42. Lebanon also was a nightly stop of the Ohio Stage Company, which ran from Cincinnati to Eaton and on to Richmond, Indiana. Its passengers stayed on the road two nights—first at the Golden Lamb and then at the Madison House, a fine inn at Front Street and State Route 122 in West Middletown. Another Cincinnati company, the Western Stage, ran to Dayton, stopping at the Madison and then on to Carlisle. The Madison, built in 1846, customarily stocked twelve gallons of whiskey, fifteen bottles of brandy, ten gallons of white whiskey, as well as various other alcoholic beverages. In the early 1850s, customers paid fifteen cents for a meal.

Of all the inns that operated on stagecoach routes in southwestern Ohio, the Golden Lamb is the most notable survivor—an original county seat hotel. The Lamb consistently draws diners and travelers and continues to promote its history. Of course, other historic inns still entertain guests across Ohio—the Red Brick Tavern in Lafayette, for instance, and the Rider Inn in Painesville. But the Golden Lamb is one of the larger of the old inns. In the 1800s, it was known chiefly for its accommodations; throughout most of the twentieth century, and still today, it is known for its restaurant. (My meal of choice is the Butler County Tom Turkey.)

One early winter afternoon I stopped in Lebanon to explore the sprawling inn, which is now owned by U.S. Senator Rob Portman and his brother and sister. Their grandfather, Robert H. Jones, bought the inn in 1926, when its plaster was cracking and the place was looking threadbare. Jones, a visionary entrepreneur, believed he could restore the Golden Lamb and take it to a new level of service. Ably assisted by his wife, Virginia, he managed to keep the inn through the Great Depression. They flourished behind the stately brick walls for forty-some years, bringing the place character, establishing a popular menu, and featuring Shaker furniture that reflected the area's heritage.

In a hallway on the first floor, I found a half-dozen framed documents, including a contract for an indentured servant and an old advertising handbill for a stagecoach company called the Dayton and Lancaster Lines, which connected at Lebanon for its Cincinnati route. The handbill, dated 1883, featured an engraving of a fancy stagecoach and team of horses. An inn supervisor, De-De Bailey, walked up behind me and noticed my interest. She read aloud: "This coach is furnished with safe, substantial horses, and with an attentive, sober and honest driver, stopping at Sharonville for exchange of horses." She laughed and added, "We think of impaired drivers as being a modern problem, but people back then must have had some trouble, too."

I was fascinated with the Golden Lamb—all old inns—because I could eat, sleep, and hang out where great people and many everyday people of the nineteenth and twentieth centuries once stayed. I could occupy their space. For a moment I imagined them pulling up out on Broadway in a stagecoach and marching inside without fanfare; even great writers such as Charles Dickens and Mark Twain and men who would become United States presidents. They must have been grateful to see the lobby's welcoming benches and warm fireplace. While I stood in there, looking out on Broadway, I asked myself, How did Dickens act on a day in April when he visited the inn? Was he arrogant? Was he cheap? Was he irritable from the long, hard ride? I can imagine he was every bit the curmudgeon when he was cross.

At 1:00 P.M. April 20, 1842, Dickens arrived by mail coach with his wife, a maid, and his personal secretary. When he stepped onto the dirt street, Dickens found neither brass band nor solicitous politician. His party entered the inn (then named the Bradley House) for food and refreshments. The local water and tea tasted foul, so Dickens asked proprietor Calvin Bradley for brandy. Bradley replied that he operated a temperance hotel. By the time Dickens and his entourage departed on a stage a short time later, he was still frustrated and thirsty. Writer Fred Compton explained in his book *The Golden Lamb: Tales from the Innside:* "Charles Dickens is the only guest of the Golden Lamb to have both a bedroom and a dining room [named in his honor].... The irony of this situation is that Charles Dickens hated the Golden Lamb. He wrote terrible things about the inn in his book *American Notes,* which was published shortly after his visit. Dickens probably gave the Golden Lamb its first bad review."

Lebanon's *Western Star* was not impressed by the famous author's visit: "Mr. Dickens and lady passed through this place on Wednesday ... and we have been gratified to observe the total absence of all that parade and sycophancy which characterized his reception in the Eastern cities. It will give us a better opinion of ourselves, if even Mr. Dickens should not think the better of us for it." Of course, Dickens did not.

Chuckling at the sight of so many framed prints of Dickens and his characters hanging on the walls (including a large painting of Dickens arriving at the inn), I stepped outside to get a better view of the front of the Golden Lamb. On my way out the door, I noticed with certain amusement a poster that was promoting a December Youth Symphony and Chorus performance called "A Dickens of a Concert." Feeling restless, I walked two doors up Broadway to an antiques mall. Browsing there, I spotted a bright-yellow brochure titled, in black, "Ohio's Stagecoach Taverns," published in 1979 by the Ohio Department of Economic and Community Development. It listed fifteen former stagecoach inns that were then still doing well as restaurants and hotels. I noted sadly that one of the inns listed, the Symmes Tavern in Fairfield, no longer served diners and travelers. It now served the financial needs of clients as a branch of Chase Bank. Others that I had visited included Malabar Inn, built in 1820 on the Marietta–Cleveland stage route; the Twenty-Mile House, built in 1802 and commissioned as a stage inn in 1810 (Cincinnati's public landing was only a day's ride by coach); the Old Worthington Inn, which opened in 1831 as a stage stop under the name the Central House, a ten-mile stop out of Columbus; and the Columbian House in Waterville, built in 1828 as an Indian trading post and tavern on the Detroit–Defiance coach route. Of all the inns I've visited, however, the Golden Lamb intrigues me the most. This is because of its important guests, visitors, and quirks. Twelve presidents visited, including U. S. Grant and William McKinley. Their names are painted on room doors. Some guests stayed during the primes of their fame; others before or after. One of the most controversial was former congressman Clement Laird Vallandigham, who died at the Golden Lamb in 1871. He was either loved or hated as the nation's chief Peace Democrat. He has fascinated me because he risked his life and career for principles.

Son of a Presbyterian minister, Vallandigham was born in 1820 in Lisbon in Columbiana County. He taught school before becoming a lawyer in Dayton, and in the 1840s he served in the Ohio House of Representatives. After losing three consecutive congressional elections, 1852–56, he narrowly won the contested election of 1858. The Jacksonian Democrat—one of a faction that called themselves "Copperheads"—believed in low tariffs, states' rights, and a strict interpretation of the constitution. Although he did not advocate secession, he believed that states had the right to secede. When the Confederacy was formed and war began in April 1861, he opposed it on the floor of the House. State Republicans soon gerrymandered his Third District, which ran from Dayton south to Butler County. As a result, he lost the next election, but he continued to speak out against the war. In Cincinnati in 1863, General Ambrose Burnside, the area's military governor, ordered Vallandigham arrested for publicly criticizing the war and the president. A military tribunal convicted him; the sentence was upheld by a federal judge. But Lincoln realized a prison term for Vallandigham would only strengthen his Copperhead followers' opposition to the war. The president ordered Vallandigham expelled to the South. The Confederates didn't want him either, however, so he ended up exiled in Canada. At the urging of his Butler County supporters in the fall of 1863, he ran for governor in absentia. He returned to Ohio to campaign, but Lincoln decided not to arrest him again. After losing the election, he returned to his life as an attorney in Dayton. He sought election to Congress again but failed.

In 1870, Vallandigham agreed to represent a Hamilton man accused of fatally shooting a man in a bar. He asked for a change of venue and ended up in a Warren County court in Lebanon. While staying at the Golden Lamb (then called the Lebanon House) during the trial, he tried to demonstrate for other attorneys how the victim could have shot himself accidentally. The complicated move required Vallandigham to use a gun as a prop. He didn't know it was loaded when he fired the gun at himself. A bullet entered his abdomen, and he died hours later.

John Zimcus, a retired Lebanon teacher whom the inn hired to mingle with guests and explain the inn's history, told me that the Vallandigham Dining Room was actually Room 15, where Vallandigham stayed—and died—at 9:45 A.M. on June 21, 1871. His name is painted in black letters on the room's white door.

As I was reading a framed magazine story about Vallandigham's last court trial, which hung on the wall, an older woman named Geri entered with a vacuum cleaner. She said, "He's around here somewhere."

She shot me a serious look. I said, "You mean Mr. Vallandigham?"

"Oh, yes," she said. "I've seen him—at least I think it's him, or his ghost."

A few weeks earlier, former inn manager Fred Compton warned me: "There aren't any ghosts in the Golden Lamb. Vallandigham doesn't walk the halls. I would know."

But Geri claimed people have seen ghosts. She said they see them more often on the fourth floor, but she has seen a Victorian man on the second. "I'm a born-again Christian," she said. "But I know what I've seen. When I came to work here two years ago, I didn't believe in spirits. Then I changed my mind. His spirit still wanders around here. He's also been spotted in Room 27 on the fourth floor, and in snapshots."

"Maybe the guy in 27 is someone other than Mr. V.," I said.

She paused thoughtfully, and said, "Well, that could be. Who knows?"

One night, a few years ago, my wife and I stayed all night at the Golden Lamb, in a room just down the hall from the Vallandigham Dining Room. I asked the manager if he had ever seen its namesake's ghost, and he said no, "but people come here just to see his room. His gun demonstration took place there, you know. It's historic."

I later spoke with De-De Bailey, who has worked at the Lamb for thirty-some years. She said she is a skeptic who has tried to "debunk much of what I've heard around here. I used to call myself a 'Geri Debunker.' Yet a few things I can't explain, and that includes the man I saw in the background of a photograph. Now he might be Vallandigham." She paused. "Would you like to see some photos?"

In the basement office, she turned on a computer and called up four different photos taken on June 12, 2006. I could see foggy patches on all four pictures. "I think this could be the image of a little girl," Bailey said, pointing to a corner of one picture.

I couldn't tell.

She pointed a pencil toward white spots. "These are orbs, I suppose," she said. "Balls of unexplained light." She admitted that she has seen some other unusual things at the inn and has heard more strange tales from regular guests and fellow employees.

"One Sunday," she said, "I stepped into the Buckeye Dining Room and took about ten to fifteen steps farther to look things over more closely. That's when I heard a heavy sigh let out right behind me—like it was almost against me. I turned; no one was there. My mind seemed to go into fast motion, and I thought, I did hear that sigh. It made the hair on the back of my neck stand up. I went straight to the front desk and told the woman who was working there that night. She said that sometime earlier that night, a couple of dozen glasses fell over and broke. Highly unlikely, yet it happened."

She said her guests have told her strange stories, too. One couple, who has stayed at the inn many times, claimed they heard a key enter the lock in the middle of the night, yet every time they opened the door, no one was in the long hallway. Another guest told Bailey that an unseen force tried to push her over a railing on the fourth floor. "Her husband had to pull her back," she said. "He felt it, too."

I must have looked interested, for she asked me to accompany her to Room 15, on the second floor. There I saw two framed stories about Vallandigham hanging on the walls along with an oval-framed color portrait of the man himself. Bailey sat directly under the portrait. She looked up and said, "Someone took a photograph of Room 27 on the fourth floor, and it was placed on our first website, back in the 1990s. There was a face in the picture, and it looked like Vallandigham's, especially his goatee. The resemblance was bizarre—it was the first thing I thought of when I saw the picture. A customer looked at it on the website and called us and said he could see a part of a man in the photo. I believe it was that caller who first speculated that it was Vallandigham."

Unfortunately, the claim is difficult to substantiate, even for paranormal researchers, for visitors have claimed to see more than one Victorian man roaming the halls of the Golden Lamb.

Bailey recalled a time in the early 1970s when the descendants of a Dr. Reeve, a physician involved in Vallandigham's Hamilton murder case in 1870, met annually for a dinner at the Golden Lamb. Walking to the west wall, she glanced at the story that mentioned the doctor. "They came here to the [Vallandigham] dining room," she said. "They did this regularly for some years. Maybe they were drawn here because Vallandigham is here." She smiled mischievously. "Who really knows?"

Heading north to Waynesville on U.S. Route 42, I saw highway signs for the old Accommodation Line, designated an Ohio Scenic Byway in 2000. (A byway differs from a state Scenic Highway in that it takes into consideration local culture and history as well as scenery.) It featured interpretative centers and road signs with a stagecoach logo. The Scenic Byway designation—twelve miles from Waynesville north to the village of Spring Valley in Greene County—honors the route of the old stagecoach company.

The Accommodation Line peaked in the 1820s and 1830s, operating in Butler, Clark, Hamilton, Greene, and Warren counties. Today, the old routes encompass Old Clifton Road and U.S. Routes 42 and 68, running through Cincinnati, Reading, Sharonville, Mason, Lebanon, Spring Valley, Xenia, and Springfield.

On this drive, I brought my friend Dennis Dalton and a fancy brochure I'd picked up titled "A Self-Guided Walking Tour of Historic Waynesville." "You won't need it," Dennis said as we set out on foot to explore his hometown and the ghosts of the Accommodation Line. The company's founders also operated their own inns—John Satterthwaite ran the Halfway House in Waynesville and Colonel Billy Werden the National Hotel in Springfield. The 10.4-mile byway starts at State Route 73 and Main Street, at the southern edge of Waynesville, and continues north on U.S. Route 42 to Spring Valley Road, at the northeastern edge of Spring Valley.

The byway idea began in the late 1990s, when Ed and Adah Andres of Waynesville published a booklet about the Accommodation Line. "If the stagecoaches got stuck, passengers had to get out and push," Ed told me. "It was a tough way to travel, but it was all they had." In 1962, the couple bought Satterthwaite's house and lived in it until 1992. They restored it and placed it on the National Register of Historic Places.

Soon after they published their booklet, Waynesville village manager R. Kevin Harper suggested making the Accommodation route an attraction—a Scenic Byway. Originally, the route was a dirt road with log bridges. In Waynesville, stage travelers stopped for the night at the

Riding the Line 181

Holloway Tavern. Although few other stagecoach sites remain in town, there are historic places along the way, including Waynesville's old lockup, which the village has rehabilitated into an Ohio Scenic Byway interpretative center.

At 195 South Third Street, Dalton and I stopped at the historic Holloway Tavern, a stagecoach stop that David Holloway built in 1805. For years the inn hosted many prominent people, including statesman and orator Henry Clay in 1825 and Charles Dickens in 1842. "It's a private home now," Dalton said, looking at the long front porch on the white frame house. "But in the 1830s, when the Accommodation Line ran through Waynesville, stagecoaches dropped off passengers here nearly every day."

The town was a convenient stopping point in the days before railroads—the halfway point between Springfield and Cincinnati. Dalton said, "The big story at the Holloway was Charles Dickens. After leaving the Golden Lamb, he stopped here—on April 21, 1842—and asked for brandy while his coach was changing horses. Again, he didn't get it. The inn operator tried to explain the no-alcohol policy, but, by this time, Dickens was livid. He went on to Xenia and then to Columbus on his American tour. When he returned to England, he wrote *A Christmas Carol* to pay off some debts. He also managed to write a travelogue of his tour of the United States, in which he paid back that small Ohio community and the dry Quaker tavern host by describing an unnamed town of 'squalid mud huts,' presumably Waynesville."

We walked past the old John Satterthwaite House, which is also called, for one obvious reason, the Halfway House. The Ohio federal-style farmhouse with Flemish bond design, at 498 North Third, still has its original arched doorway. Satterthwaite built the place in 1812, and in 1827 he converted it into an inn for his stage line.

"Third Street was our major street back then, so the stages came through here," Dalton said. "Satterthwaite's inn became quite the busy place. Being a Quaker, he is said to have used it as a stop on the Underground Railroad. Of course, many buildings are alleged to have been stops on the Railroad."

In Waynesville, most of the Accommodation Line's passengers stayed the night at the Holloway Tavern, leaving the John Satterthwaite House to the weary stage drivers. When Satterthwaite died in 1837, the company began to decline. And then the railroads arrived in the 1840s.

As I walked around town, I was amazed to see a village that today could almost pass for a town of stagecoach times. Waynesville has stood proudly on its English heritage and since the early 1980s has promoted itself as "the Antiques Capital of the Midwest"—"Park your car, step back in time, and enjoy shopping in our quaint historic village." Yet, the German legacy of homemade sauerkraut continues to drift into the public consciousness. Thirty-five years of Ohio Sauerkraut Festival tradition will do that, even to a small English town. The annual October event, attracting several hundred thousand visitors, is followed by Halloween and a much closer approximation of Waynesville's true self: "the Most Haunted Town in Ohio." A writer gave the town this title in the 1990s, and nobody here has bothered to dispute it. In fact, in some quarters it is encouraged, in sort of an underground way so that it won't scare off the middle-aged tourists who come to purchase antiques during the daylight hours.

Actually, Waynesville's ghostly reputation is enhanced by its postcard-perfect appearance. Most of the buildings downtown were built in the mid-to-late 1800s and are now refurbished. ("Main Street hasn't looked this good since 1797," antiques dealer Bill Stubbs said.) Having reinvented itself with a coalition of local government, business, and residents, Waynesville promotes itself heavily as a regional antiques center. In the late 1970s, the antiques business provided a failing, out-of-the-way town with a means to compete. "We capitalized on our own history," said R. Kevin Harper, the village administrator who helped the town promote its past. "It helps that we have many historic buildings left, and that the town is very attractive. But this was all possible because of cheap storefront space and entrepreneurs."

The village was the vision of founder Samuel Heighway, who purchased land on the west bank of the Little Miami River from real estate speculator John Cleves Symmes. Heighway laid out Waynesville in right angles, like an old English village, with eleven squares of four acres each and a square in the middle. Today, the middle square is gone, but the others have kept their original names, marked by signposts on each street corner. The Miami Monthly Meeting, the first Quaker group established in southwestern Ohio, still meets here. Before the Civil War, the town had its share of abolitionists, who hid slaves on the Underground Railroad. A network of tunnels connected safe homes to the river so that slaves could elude bounty hunters and continue on their journey to

Canada. In those days, Waynesville was the hub of rural Wayne Township and northern Warren County. It still could pass for that old town. Many of its nineteenth-century buildings still stand, including the Holloway Tavern, a stagecoach stop built by John Holloway about 1805. The town's first tavern featured six bays and a central chimney.

Of all Waynesville's history, the ghostly one intrigues me most. Although Dalton now lives in Lebanon, he knows every house and legend in Waynesville. He is one of those vanishing small-town characters, bigger than his reputation and perpetually in a good mood. But his biggest passion is history, particularly the folklore of ghosts. "Some people ask me why Waynesville has a lot of ghosts," he said. "I say it's because the town is built on or near a prehistoric area. You have two extreme cultures in one place."

As we walked along Main Street, passing benign-looking brick and wooden buildings painted in pastels, Dalton told the stories behind house after house, and I realized that Waynesville is at once a living town and a ghost town. Its past is superimposed on top of the present—slightly out of kilter, the way those old 3-D pictures looked before you put on flimsy cardboard glasses. Two towns exist, Dalton claimed, without each other's knowledge—sort of like two movies running simultaneously, side by side. In his world, Waynesville is a town of ghosts, one inhabited by the living but still dominated by the dead. "Oh, they're around," he said, glancing at the buildings. "I started this tour in 1987, right after I did the Haunted Hot Dog Roast in Springboro. It has grown every year."

I found exactly what I wanted at the Hammel House—a fish sandwich for lunch. The Hammel, a federal vernacular–style building at 121 South Main Street on Wabash Square, was an old stagecoach stop. Originally three stories but only two since 1934, the inn featured Flemish bond brick, limestone, and possibly the original wood frame. The building was started as a wooden tavern about 1800 and was expanded through the years. Some people claim the building is haunted. This is nothing new. Haunted buildings in Waynesville line up like tombstones in a country cemetery. This is why I brought along my favorite town crier, Dalton, to interpret more local history.

Built in 1822 and restored in 1987, the two-story Hammel House Inn has a wide front porch where people eat lunch on warm Saturday afternoons. Dalton's great aunt once owned the inn, so he is very familiar with the place. He knows every tale, rumor, and fact. According to lore,

Dennis Dalton explains the history of the haunted Hammel House in Waynesville. (Photo by Randy McNutt)

the innkeeper killed a traveling salesman in his bed in 1823, and the poor man's spirit still roams the building.

"I don't usually tell people which room it happened in," Dalton said with a grin.

I looked at him in disbelief.

"All right," he said. "I can't leave you in suspense." He escorted me around the Hammel, first through the restaurant and then up to the second floor, where he pointed to a room and stopped. He said, "Let me whisper this so I don't disturb the guests. This one is the haunted room."

Back in the lobby, we met Pam Bowman, who operates the inn's restaurant. When Dalton told her that we were searching for history and ghosts, she wasn't shy about talking.

"One of the young ladies who cleans here was working in a room on the second floor. Suddenly she came tearing down the steps. When I came around the corner, I saw her sitting at the bottom, all pale and shaking. She told me that she was standing on a bed in that upstairs room, dusting a ceiling fan, when a shadow approached her. It came out of the bathroom and passed in front of the ceiling fan and went around behind her. She jumped off the bed and ran downstairs. It unnerved her. Shadows don't usually move of their own free will. The same young woman also has seen a cat. But she knows it's not a flesh-and-blood animal. She said it steps onto one of the tables in the dining room when she passes by. Then he'll jump off and glide away. She also smells him."

"My Aunt Ollie had a cat," Dalton said, "and I have a picture of it sitting on a porch here."

"Maybe the cat we see here is her cat," Bowman said.

"Animals can return," he said.

"This is the oddest thing," Bowman said. "I was walking by the waitress station when I saw something—a young woman. It was like a flash of lightning, imprinted on my brain. Her hair was matted and dirty and she had on something like a muslin shirt with a white bodice and a burnt-orange apron. It was a real quick image—a flash. I didn't even look at her. It's just another ghostly thing we've seen in here."

"Now, where did the young woman see the shadow?" Dalton asked.

Bowman smiled. "Room 5."

"We know the story behind Room 5," Dalton said.

"I don't know if he's becoming more comfortable or the personalities here now are more receptive than before," Bowman said. "I think that to materialize or be obvious, they have to feel no fear. What's amazing is that before, I'd go into that waitress station and feel uncomfortable, kind of scared but for no reason. But now, I'm not afraid."

Dalton shook his head knowingly and said, "When this building was used for apartments years ago, the waitress station was a bathroom. A tenant once told me that she came home one day and opened the bathroom door and was overwhelmed. A man appeared to be floating above the floor. She described him well enough to be talking about somebody dressed in the manner of the early 1800s. His shoes were heavy and square-toed, and he had on knee socks. He wore knee britches and a homespun shirt. She couldn't get a look at his face. It scared her."

"Yes," Bowman said, "that's what I saw—like the person was floating. My ghost was like an imprint, too. Floating. We had one little boy, who was about eight to ten years old. He kept saying something cold was touching his face and neck in the dining room."

Dalton said, "Usually children are receptive because their minds aren't as cluttered as ours. Have you had anything move around in here?"

"Yes, I forgot to tell you!" Bowman said. "Everybody witnessed this during a wedding rehearsal dinner one evening. I went walking through the door with food and one of the knobs fell off the stove and bounced in front of me. My husband, a real skeptic, sat a sandwich under a light that keeps the food warm. It hangs with little chains. All of a sudden, the sandwich flew back and hit him. Six to eight people saw it happen. It couldn't have done that on its own. For him to say something about it, to be shocked, is a big deal.

"Something else bothers me. The lights in the basement go on and off for no apparent reason. Sometimes I'll say, 'Oh, give me a break!' When my daughter gets ready to go home for the night, she'll close the basement door and say, 'Goodnight.' Yes, it has been a lot of fun working in here, but scary at times. But anymore, I don't think about it."

Dalton recounted another story of the Hammel House Inn. He said, "Back in the 1800s, an itinerant 'spirit photographer' named William Mumler came here from New York. In those days, photographers like him used to go from town to town taking pictures of family members who were 'ghosts.' Actually, he was double exposing the image. So in 1870 he came back to Waynesville for a second time and set up his equipment in the Hammel. People came by to have their pictures taken with their ghostly relatives around them. He took a picture of an old man in town looking stoic. When Mumler developed the negatives, the old man actually had a hand on his shoulder. In fact, every picture Mumler took that day—and a friend of mine has one in his collection—had the same hand in it. Mumler left town completely dumbfounded. I think he was finally getting his comeuppance for exploiting the spirit world."

After saying good-bye to Bowman, we walked through town, listening to more of Dalton's stories.

Someone said, "Any community that's done a lot of living will be more haunted. It's only natural. The spirits are all over the place."

Dalton agreed. He said that Waynesville's strange occurrences aren't limited to the nineteenth century. "A more recent haunting occurred while the Art Guild was putting on a show at the museum—the Friends Boarding Home and old Quaker home, built in 1912. A young woman with light-brown hair came down the stairs, stood there for a moment, then walked back up halfway and disappeared into thin air. One artist got a good look at her and later painted her. The portrait matches the picture of a young teacher who taught at the school across the street. She used to eat her meals at the home. Maybe she never wanted to leave."

As a church bell on Harrison Square played "America the Beautiful," we walked south on Main Street, and we wondered.

16

Major Buxton, I Presume

> Etheric beings have a right to exist. Our minds, our emotional content have to be somewhere after death. . . . This basic idea has its foundation in physics. Matter and energy are neither created nor destroyed. They simply exist in different forms."
> —Peggy Little, psychic, at the Buxton Inn, 1979

As I drove down Broadway early one June night, the lights in Granville's business district went dark and sirens began to wail. I flinched as clouds turned inside out and a fierce wind thumped the car. At my destination, the historic Buxton Inn, I parked on the street and paused for a moment to find some notebooks on the back seat. Suddenly an ear-splitting crack—like a bullwhip, then an explosion—sent sparks spewing from a utility pole transformer and a big oak crashing to the street in front of me. As raindrops beat a rat-a-tat-tat on the car roof, floodlights flickered in the Buxton's front yard. I took a deep breath and dashed to the wooden front door.

Inside, candles lit a narrow hallway, as they did when the inn opened in the early nineteenth century. I saw a woman in period costume waving her arm at me, as if I were running in a relay race.

"Tornado!" she yelled, motioning for me to head to the cellar. "Coming right at us! Go!" I froze momentarily; she grabbed my arm and pulled me to the staircase. "Quickly now," she said, as I hurried to the tavern below.

I glanced around, took a seat at one of the few empty tables, and counted a dozen guests surrounded by thick gray walls of rough stone. I thought, If a tornado blows away the inn, the basement will surely survive. It's built like a castle. The cellar must have looked this way in stagecoach days, when the Buxton was a major stop on the Columbus–Newark route and coach drivers stayed the night there.

The other guests didn't bother to notice me. I nodded anyway. A man in his forties was telling Buxton ghost stories, even though a slim woman, about sixty years old, looked terrified. A younger woman, presumably her daughter, patted her hand reassuringly. I didn't think the older woman's problem was the weather.

"A young boy died down here back in the 1800s," the man went on. He received some unkind stares, so he changed direction. "Did you all know that stagecoach drivers used to cook over a big stone fireplace and sleep here on straw beds? I can't imagine what this place smelled like. A few years ago, one of the owners saw a mysterious figure lurking down here, and a bartender claimed he was touched on the shoulder by an invisible hand. Later, he discovered that overnight somebody had struck every match in ten matchboxes and then put each one neatly back into the boxes. Another time, somebody thought he heard an old-time moneybag dropping on the floor and coins rolling out."

The two women frowned and pretended to ignore him.

In the candlelit cellar tavern, we all sat for over an hour while the man regaled us with stories of strange occurrences at the inn. Every ten minutes he stopped for a moment to organize his thoughts, only to be greeted by silence. Assuming his truly captive audience expected more stories, he continued. "Did you know that some employees swear that they can hear their names being called softly in a dining room upstairs? Nobody's ever around, though. And in their rooms in the inn, some guests see visitors in the night—"

"No more!" snapped the older woman. She paused, obviously distressed. Then she added, "Please, sir. Can we talk about something else? We're staying here. We do want to sleep tonight."

"Yes. Anything else," added the younger woman.

"Oh, sure," he replied with a grin. "I just thought . . ."

The silence that followed was as thick as a Buxton brick.

Soon an inn employee came downstairs and told us that the danger had passed. She said the tornado had missed us by a mile, and now, at 8:30 P.M., our biggest problem would be finding a meal in a small town that was still experiencing a power outage. All of us good-humored but increasingly hungry guests gathered on the front porch (minus the storyteller, who stayed in the bar) to watch the light rain falling and to tell our personal stories. Innkeeper Orville Orr emerged on the porch briefly to apologize for the inconvenience. With a flashlight illuminating his face like a jack-o-lantern, he told us that other restaurants in town were also without power, but a pizza parlor a few blocks away was open. Six of us walked over to Elm Pizza, where gas-powered ovens didn't depend on electricity. That night we enjoyed pizza by candlelight. I soon forgot my longing for a salmon dinner.

When I finally came back to Room 9 later that night, I felt tired and satisfied. I didn't wake until morning.

After paying my bill the next morning, I walked onto the Buxton's stone front porch and took a breath of fresh air. The sun was shining through the trees. The Buxton, long a fixture at 313 East Broadway, looked every bit as much of a stagecoach stop as it did when Orin Granger bought the tavern in 1812 and expanded the place. It was colorful then, painted the same salmon color and trimmed in white.

In those days, the Buxton's reputation as an overnight house competed against that of another Licking County establishment, the Black Horse Tavern, a log house built in Newark in 1807 by John Cully. Historian N. N. Hill Jr. wrote in 1881: "It is hard to say what made the place popular, as it always appeared to be a tumble down rookery, and its outward appearance was anything but inviting, but Cully [became] a favorite with the traveling public and the place was well patronized."

But it was the Buxton that persevered. After Granger died in 1818, the inn had several different owners. For a time it went under the name the Dilley House. In 1829, owners added an east wing; in 1851, a two-story addition gave the inn a U shape. Now, the inn itself features only three guest rooms, several dining and meeting rooms, a gift shop, and a garden dining area.

Before I could explore the place on that sunny morning, a woman I'd never seen rushed up and asked, "Well, did you see her?"

She looked at me expectantly.

"See who?" I asked.

She looked disappointed. "The lady in blue, of course," she said. "Why, don't you know? You stayed in the haunted room!" She paused and frowned. "We wanted that room, but you got it first."

"Oh, I am so sorry to disappoint you," I said, backing away slightly. "I supposed I slept right through it—something—whatever."

She shook her head and walked away.

I decided to walk around downtown Granville, visiting its small shops, then return to the Buxton for lunch (the crab cakes). The genial Orville Orr greeted me. I explained to him what the woman had asked me, and he smiled knowingly.

"Well," he said softly, "she's one of those people who come here to see the supernatural." He chuckled as he looked around the restaurant. "That's what she meant when she asked if you saw her—the Lady in Blue, we call her."

"Do you talk about this stuff openly?" I asked.

"We do now. But for years we didn't mention it because we thought it might frighten the guests. Eventually, we realized that they want to know about it. They're intrigued. People call us 'America's Most Ghostly Country Inn.' Thirty-some years of renovations and all people want to talk about is ghosts."

In time, the Buxton started promoting its permanent residents. "People want to hear our ghost stories," said Orr, a former school official who bought the place in 1972 with his wife, Audrey. "Every fall, guests want to stay in Rooms 7, 8, and 9, but especially in 9. It seems to have more paranormal activity than any of them."

The rooms are in an addition that was built in the 1850s. In that area, and other more active ones, strange things have happened. In 1979, Gordon Kuster Jr., a photographer for the *Columbus Dispatch*, attested to this after stopping at the inn to take pictures for a story about the ghosts. "Kuster had repeated problems photographing areas of the inn where the spirits are reportedly more active," the *Dispatch Sunday Magazine* editor wrote at the end of the story by Mary Bilderback Abel published that June. "On his last trip, he joked about ghosts as he stood in the upstairs hallway. A pitcher on a nearby table flew into the air and went crashing to the floor. No one was visible near the table. You figure it out."

Years ago, Orr said, Room 9 was the apartment of the Lady in Blue—Newark, Ohio, native Ethel Houston "Bonnie" Bounell, a New York light opera star who returned to her native Licking County to live. She bought the inn in 1934 and resided there until her death in 1960. Ever since, what is believed to be her ghost occasionally projects itself in "living" color, adding whiffs of her favorite perfume.

"She loved the color blue and the smell of gardenias," Orr said. "She is always seen on the second floor. Maybe she has staked out her territory. Major Buxton usually is seen on the first floor. When I first bought the inn, she frightened a couple of young workers. They refused to finish their work unless I agreed to stand there with them. Since then, many guests have mentioned waking in the middle of the night and seeing a woman in their room. They ask me the next morning if we give keys to people. Of course, we don't. That wouldn't be a good idea. I believe they are seeing Bonnie. She wants to know if they're comfortable."

She has company—other permanent residents who've been staying here since the nineteenth century. Audrey Orr recalled the time she was painting in the pantry on the first floor. She hadn't owned the inn for long. "I could see a man to my right, in my peripheral vision," she said. "I went to get Orville, but he wasn't around. So I returned to the pantry and again saw the figure of a man in my side vision. I said, 'I don't know what's going on, but it scares me.' Apparently he left. Now I know that he was probably Major Horton Buxton, who lived here with his family for forty years—1865 to 1905. He might have been checking on the progress of our work."

Over the centuries, the inn has welcomed important guests, such as future presidents William Henry Harrison, Abraham Lincoln, and William McKinley; Henry Ford; famed march composer and conductor John Philip Sousa; Hoosier poet James Whitcomb Riley; and author Harriett Beecher Stowe and her famous brother Henry Ward Beecher.

Orr said proudly, "Legend has it that during the War of 1812, Harrison, a friend of Mr. Granger, rode up the main staircase on his horse to a ballroom on the second floor. I don't know how he rode back down. Just think of it—Mr. Harrison, Mr. Lincoln, and Mr. McKinley once stood right here in this inn, where we're standing. It makes me feel like I'm a small part of history. Anyhow, Mr. Ford came to Granville to see his niece, a student at our town's Denison University. He stayed at the inn several times. He liked it so much that he offered to buy it. He wanted to dismantle it and ship the pieces up to his Deerfield Village museum in Michigan. I assume he wanted to show the public what an old-time inn really looked like. Of course, owner Bonnie Bounell would have none of that business."

At lunch that afternoon, I jokingly asked a young waiter, "Seen any ghosts lately?"

He looked at me as if I had just caught him sampling the desserts. He looked around, possibly wondering who might hear him. Then he said softly, "As a matter of fact, I have. I saw a ghostly gray cat. We followed it to the second floor, where it suddenly disappeared in front of us. Bonnie Bounell owned a cat that fit the description. His name was the Major, named for Major Buxton. Another time, I was in the bathroom, cleaning up. A heavy wooden door suddenly swung open, then a cupboard door opened, and a chandelier nearby shook violently. There was no earthquake, so I guess it was the Major at play again."

Although Orville Orr, who has a degree in theology and was once a minister, admitted to being visited by the cat, he said he still isn't comfortable talking about the subject. Yet he can remember the terrified look on a guest's face when she told him that an invisible cat had played with strands of her long hair and walked on her during the night. She told him that she was so distraught that she didn't go to sleep until just before dawn, and shortly after that the cat returned to play with her hair again. "We've had many people report the presence of Major Buxton, the cat, and one of our people actually saw him running down the main staircase before disappearing into nothing."

In the narrow main hall, the Orrs keep a china cupboard filled with feline figurines—many of them gray. In front, the inn's sign features a gray cat—something like the Major.

Orr said, "Not long ago, a guest who was staying in Room 9, an Iraq veteran, felt a cat touch his hand as he lay on his bed. He told me that he was used to the touch of a cat, so he knew what had just rubbed against him. But he said nothing was there. I believe the man because so many people have reported feeling it or seeing it. One woman became so upset one night that the following morning she told me about feeling it touching her hair. I've felt the cat, too. Once, also in Room 9, I came in late and got into bed with Audrey, who was sleeping. I pulled the sheet over me and turned over. A short while later, I felt a cat crawl up my back. Now, I've had cats. So I know the feeling. I try not to talk about the ghost cat, though, because I think people will think I'm being silly." He paused and smiled. "Children are more likely to see the cat, which makes the thing all the more interesting."

Perhaps the Buxton's age has helped it acquire more ghosts than most buildings in town. Orr calls the Buxton "Ohio's oldest continuously operated inn in its original building," to distinguish it from Lebanon's Golden Lamb Inn, which he says is not in its original building. In the small lobby the Orrs keep the original innkeeper's desk, made of tiger maple and cherry.

While I was talking with Orville Orr in the office, I did recall seeing my room's doorknob turn several times early on the previous night. Before I opened the door, I wondered what I'd say: Ahh? Oh, no? Major Buxton, I presume? But when I quickly pulled it open, hoping to catch a peeping Buxton, the walkway in front of my room was empty. I forgot about the incident.

Orr shook his head and smiled at my paranoia. "Everyone wants to meet a ghost these days," he said. He learned this shortly after buying the Buxton in 1972, when he was writing drug education programs for the state and Audrey was teaching kindergarten. They dreamed of restoring the neglected inn, which they accomplished in time for Denison University's parents' weekend in September 1974. "We just knew we had to save this wonderful old building," he said. "It's such a big part of Granville's past."

I enjoyed walking along Granville's tree-lined streets, absorbing the soft illumination of living rooms with their wooden staircases and built-in bookcases. A blend of architectural styles from the late 1800s and early 1900s, the houses collectively represent the quintessential American home. Perhaps Granville looks different to southwest Ohio residents like me because New Englanders designed the kind of place they knew: white steeples, churches on the town square, two wide thoroughfares, and long front porches. The whole town is a piece of New England transplanted to the middle of Buckeye country. At Christmas, Broadway looks like something from an old-fashioned greeting card.

October remains one of the inn's busier times—for good reason. The inn sells a documentary DVD that chronicles its more spirited side. Sometimes the owners permit ghost hunters to visit.

"There's an increasing awareness of the paranormal," Orr said. "The ghosts used to aggravate me. I came from a conservative church background. You just didn't talk about this kind of thing. Nowadays, though, people want to talk about it. But it can be a little unnerving." He admitted that not every guest is dying to meet a ghost. "But it does help business," he said, "and it helps people express their feelings." He told me that several psychics have visited over the years, and some of them have claimed that the inn is inhabited by many spirits, including former owners and other people associated with the Buxton since its founding.

In the lobby, Orr pointed to three framed photographs on the walls—Horton Buxton, Bonnie Bounnel, and her gray cat, the Major. Posing next to Buxton's picture, Orr said, "People keep asking if I'm going to live here like Mr. Buxton when I die." He grinned. "Let me go on record right now: I do not intend to haunt this place!"

His joke reminded me of something that Thomas Freese, a Louisville writer and professional storyteller who has tracked ghosts in historic places, once told me: "You can expect public places to be haunted, rather than not. Spirits are attracted to people. Ghosts are everywhere." He believes the owners of historic inns and hotels seriously started promoting their ghosts, instead of denying them, after the terrorist attacks in 2001. Perhaps they did so because the economy and tourism had suffered, he said, or maybe it was an emotional release. "Or maybe they thought the time had come," he said.

Orville Orr laughed at the thought of his benign ghosts scaring anyone. Like him, he said, the Buxton's ghosts simply love the place, and his guests enjoy looking for the elusive ghosts. "It's more of a cultural development," he said of ghost watching. "If some people are afraid, we direct them to rooms that aren't so active. A medium visited years ago from Cincinnati. She said she 'saw' former owners walking down the hall with her. Her description of an elegantly dressed woman who liked hats and had been on the stage had to be Bonnie Bounell. When I asked how we could chase away the ghosts, the medium looked perplexed. She told me they provide the inn with energy and support. She said, 'Why would you want to get rid of them?' I guess she's right. There's room enough in this inn for the past and the present, the living guests and the invisible ones."

Vanishing Places

V

17

Ammo Towns

> The havoc wrought by sixteen tons of powder is dreadful. . . . The Peters Cartridge factory was burned to the ground and nothing but a mass of smoldering ruins remains to mark the spot where the building stood.
> —Columbus (Georgia) Enquirer Sun, *July 16, 1890*

Tiny Kings Station made the news on July 15, 1890, when a giant fireball consumed everything in its path along the banks of the Little Miami River in Warren County. Nowadays, drivers pass the site of the deadly tragedy and see only peaceful, beautiful land. Kings Station is one of a few towns in Ohio whose economy depended exclusively on the manufacturing of ammunition. It was founded on, by, and for the glory of firepower, and it died that way, too. What a way to go.

The Kings story began in 1878 on the big hill overlooking the Little Miami, where entrepreneur Joseph Warren King, a Connecticut native, built the village of Kings Mills for the workers of his King's Great Western Powder Company. He chose the river site because of the abundance of black willows, which he needed to make the charcoal used in the gunpowder manufacturing process. King produced ammunition for the military as well as for sport shooters.

In 1887, King helped his son-in-law, a Baptist minister named Gershon M. Peters, build the Peters Cartridge Company factory just across the river from Kings Mills. Their thinking was, if one of the factories ever blew up, the other wouldn't blow with it. Soon Peters became a big success, thanks in part to the founder's innovative shotgun-shell loading device, which could pack sixty shells per minute. The factory also produced other kinds of ammunition.

Naturally, a small town grew up around Peters's factory, too. It was called Kings Station, because a train station served the plant. The little community also consisted of workers' homes, warehouses, and a new train depot.

Well over a century after the heyday of the twin powder plants, Kings Station is gone, but Kings Mills does remain, as an off-the-path, old company town possibly destined for obscurity.

From 1878 through the 1940s, when the company plants closed, more than twenty big explosions rocked both communities. But the Kings Station blast of 1890 was the worst, always called "the Big One." Some people in Columbus—eighty miles away—reported hearing it. Locals knew those booming sounds all too well, and the sudden pain of fear that jabbed them in the stomach. Who will die today? One explosion shot a worker's body across the river.

To reach the place where Kings Station once stood, you have to drive through its older and larger neighbor, Kings Mills, which stands only one mile from Kings Island Amusement Park and not far from Interstate 71 and a sea of development. You take Grandin Road out of Kings Mills and into a wooded area, descending into a valley near the river.

On a warm day in early October, my friend Dick Swaim joined me when I went searching for the remnants of Kings Station. As we headed east, crossing the river, we passed more thick woods and reached the bottom of the ravine. His jaw dropped as we saw the old Peters factory with its shot tower and smokestack. The plant, composed of six buildings, was nearly empty. I remembered what Thomas D. Schiffer, who wrote a book about the Kings companies, had once said of the old plants, "They make a splendid corpse."

There might have been a watchman around somewhere, but we didn't see anyone as we pulled into the parking lot. Immediately Dick jumped out, camera in hand, and wandered away. I stood there staring up at the giant shot tower, half mesmerized by its height and trying to visualize workers dropping molten lead through a copper sieve at the top. As the lead drops fell, tension from air resistance helped mold them into little round spheres. When they finally hit a pool at the bottom of the tower, the spheres hardened into gunshot pellets. This was high-tech production in the 1880s.

The whole complex felt eerily quiet; the only other sounds were a million insects singing their autumnal dirge and an occasional breeze whistling through the factory's broken windows.

Dick walked toward me, yelling, "Hey, this old factory's on the National Register of Historic Places!" He added, "What are the odds of this place surviving all those years of making ammo?"

I told him that the original factory didn't survive. Most of it burned in the firestorm that summer day in 1890. Photographs taken days after the explosion show devastation that looks like a World War II bombing raid. Peters built the present factory on the site of the explosion.

In 1890, Kings Station was a busy little place built around its depot on the Little Miami Railroad. The community was located six miles southeast of Lebanon, the county seat. At 3:50 P.M. on July 15, a massive explosion rocked Kings Station and the Peters plant. Lebanon residents felt and heard the shock waves. Three more explosions, less audible, quickly followed, and a wide plume of smoke rose high into the sky. The disaster was caused by a runaway freight train that ignited 800 to 1,600 kegs of gunpowder. Days later, Lebanon's *Western Star* told the story in a stunning headline:

Terrible Explosion!
Blown to Atoms, Not One of a Dozen Houses Left Standing
Eleven Persons Killed,
Four of Whom Burned Beyond Recognition
Nearly 100 Wounded, Some Fatally
King's Station on the Little Miami Railroad

The fire and blast destroyed an office building, two three-story buildings, a warehouse, and eight to twelve company-owned homes. Three children were counted among the eleven dead bodies. The *Western Star* reported: "There were about forty persons employed in these buildings, most of whom were young girls from the neighboring towns. The girls worked next to the windows facing the river, and although temporary fire escapes of ropes hung within their reach, the flames spread so rapidly that the escape of the girls was miraculous. . . . The suffering of relatives and friends living on the surrounding hills was terrible and indescribable until they found out the fate of their loved ones."

Eyewitness Joseph Proctor told the *Western Star,* "The dense volumes of smoke came pouring from the doors and windows of the cartridge factory, and I saw men, women, and children tearing at each other in their frantic endeavors to escape."

Young Stephen McDowell was walking to school when the explosion occurred. In the 1930s, he still remembered seeing a man's body being hurtled across the river. "The explosion looked like the sun coming out of the hillside," he told a reporter. Another boy at the time, Timmy Dowdell, was playing under an apple tree with other children when the blast occurred. "After the explosion," he told the *Cincinnati Enquirer* in a 1970 interview, "everything got dark and all of the apples fell on top of us."

The fire consumed the railway station, the freight house, and adjacent buildings. "The explosion occurred on the south side and the destruction was enormous," the *Newark Daily Advocate* said on July 16, 1890. "The Peters Cartridge Factory was burned to the ground. A relief train was dispatched from Cincinnati to the scene of the disaster."

From my place by the side of the road near the big silent factory, I had trouble believing that so much grief and fire once blew across the spot where I was standing.

"Do you mean it happened right here?" Dick asked, shaking his head. "There must have been some incredible force from an explosion of that size, especially being down here in this valley. I can't imagine anybody living through that kind of nightmare."

When the days of local ammunition makers began to fade, Remington Arms bought Peters Cartridge in 1934. During World War II, the plant manufactured about 50 million rounds a month. In 1944, the company relocated the plant to Connecticut. Later, a section of the old Peters factory was used by Columbia Records to press records; Seagrams used another part as a whiskey warehouse. By the 1990s, however, the place was only the wistful dream of real estate developers.

Though the Kings company declined after World War II, Kings Mills survived. By the 1950s, the Kings Powder Company site was declining rapidly. In the early 1960s, most of its buildings were destroyed to eliminate any stray gunpowder residue. Nowadays, the only explosions come when Kings Island shoots fireworks into the summer night, illuminating the ghostly Peters cartridge factory along the river. Small, old-fashioned Kings Mills has become Warren County's antithesis: an

1880s town ignored by the modern county's trek to the suburbs. While development has boomed in Landen, Maineville, and Mason, it has purposely bypassed Kings Mills. A few years ago, a company planned to transform the empty Peters Cartridge Company factory into an office complex providing the area with 600 jobs. But it never happened, the jobs never came, and Kings Mills remained a town seemingly destined for obscurity in the twenty-first century.

Its population today is about 500. Gone are its three big hotels, a movie theater, rows of stores, and the powder workers who toiled in riverside bunkers that protected the factory. Its neatly mowed yards and attractive houses—once occupied by powder workers' families—now attract people who have a personal connection to the town, or who simply enjoy its historic homes.

"Our house used to rock," resident Charlotte Clark told me. "One time, five buildings blew up down at the powder company, and the entire town shook. Dad always left the house cussing. But somebody had to fight the fires."

Most of them occurred at the Kings factory, Thomas Schiffer said, because it used more highly explosive mixtures and "operated in flimsy wood buildings with metal roofs," all painted red.

Over the years there were many accidents. On August 21, 1917, the *Cincinnati Enquirer* reported "large clouds of white smoke rose from the valley [at Kings Mills]. Women and children from the town, whose husbands and brothers were employed in the powder mills, hurried to the place. Anxiously they awaited the announcement of the names of those men killed and injured."

On August 9, 1940, the *Western Star* published an interview with an unidentified worker who was driving to work when he heard two sharp blasts and then felt the big explosion from the powder factory. "I jumped from my car in time to see a cloud of debris shoot skyward hundreds of feet into the air. A large 12 x 12-inch [piece of timber] carried several hundred feet upward and then it seemed to be held as if suspended for several seconds. The particles spread, began to open like a parachute and descend[ed] to earth. I saw two bodies as they skyrocketed into space, and [it] seemed almost a minute before they fell to the ground."

Dayton and Cincinnati newspaper headlines told more horror stories in the 1940s: "Five Men Killed, 11 Hurt, As Blast Near Lebanon Rocks 30-Mile Area"; "Kings Mills Blast Takes the Life of Second Brother." After another blast, the *Cincinnati Times-Star* reported on

December 11, 1942: "When [Turner] Harrison and [Webb] Pancake heard the corning mill blow up, they started running . . . Harrison's clothing was set on fire but his life was saved when Pancake threw him in a tub of water."

Now, in the relative quiet of the morning, thousands of commuters drive near Kings Mills, many not knowing it even exists—or that explosions once shook it regularly. The town remains hidden by trees and the past. Its past is all but forgotten. Once, when I asked a county planning official about the potential of Kings Mills, he looked at me strangely and said, "The interstate isn't far away, but we're still not anticipating the kind of development that suburban areas have experienced." He paused. "We don't look for the town to expand into anything significant."

That sober assessment—"anything significant"—seems harsh when applied to anyone's hometown. Yet the town's past must seem odd to newcomers, who may have only a vague notion of where the town lies. If they drive from the interstate and into town, they will see houses from the late nineteenth century, most of them newly painted and lovingly attended. As I walked along the streets, hoping to talk with any townspeople, I thought it was unusual that some of them were sitting on their porches. Few people in the suburbs sit on their porches—if they even have porches.

"When my father-in-law came to this town in 1910," Frank Clark told me, "Kings Mills was booming. But it all fell off after World War II. After Kings Island opened in the early 1970s, the area around us expanded. We had to put sewers in here because people wanted to build fancy homes along the river. But Kings Mills itself will not change; it will always be old Kings Mills."

Harry Dalton, a Kings Mills resident since 1965, predicted the town will grow someday. He said its past purpose—supplying ammunition for the war efforts—was too significant for the town to just languish forever.

He looked down the street, at the gingerbread houses and quiet streets, and smiled, as if he knew something that I didn't know. Then he said, "I tell you this: Something's bound to happen here."

18

Phoneton Calling

> We are moving forward, if but slowly. This fact should move us to view the future in less cataclysmic terms—the future that will see man, in Faulkner's words, will "not only endure but prevail."
> —*Otto L. Bettmann*

In Miami County's Bethel Township, the traveler can't tell where Phoneton ends and development begins. The fading small town's southern flank is pressed by new subdivisions, businesses, and condominiums—all of them devouring everything in their collective path.

The same scenario is repeating itself all across Ohio, regardless of the economic situation. Too many small, historic towns are dying or being replaced by suburban communities and their vision of modern "towns"—rows of apartment buildings, subdivisions, shopping centers, and fast-food restaurants.

After annexing land in Bethel Township's southern end, the city of Huber Heights is colliding with Phoneton and threatening its rural identity. "Two thousand units will be built over the next fifteen years," township administrator Michael Gebhardt told me. "They will stand 400 to 450 yards diagonally from the town. Of course, this will change things."

As the future rolls north on State Route 202 like a shock wave, the old town—or what's left of it—is besieged by less invasive progress on its other three sides. A factory has opened to the west. If Phoneton had a sewer system, it would be an even more desirable town to suburban residents and business owners. No doubt sewers will be coming.

Ironically, Phoneton was created by the future—the telephone—in 1893, when the American Telephone and Telegraph Company established a small office with a lineman and his operator wife on the National Road in Miami County. The office grew, and five years later the company moved it into a house. In 1899, a post office opened in the growing town, now called Phoneton—the only town in Ohio named for the telephone. Noah Albaugh, a local nursery owner, had suggested the name, saying it would be more musical sounding than Phonetown. One newspaper described Phoneton as "the Ohio town that the telephone built."

As more AT&T employees arrived, the town continued to grow. When the company's transcontinental lines required a repeater station for amplifying long-distance calls, AT&T built a three-story brick building on the southwest corner of Route 202 at U.S. Route 40—the old National Road.

In the early days of the telephone, few people used the service. But the times were changing. It wasn't long before independent telephone companies began battling the majors—competitors Western Union and National Bell were among the larger ones—to service customers throughout Ohio and the nation. By 1910, the minors and majors occupied places in small and large communities. (In Chillicothe, one subscriber refused to pay his bill to the Home Telephone Company. Manager Harry Elliot climbed a pole to disconnect the subscriber's phone line. Not to be outdone, the subscriber started chopping down the pole—with Elliot still hanging at the top of it.)

Phoneton continued to grow. AT&T sent many people from the city to work there, with forty employees soon operating the Phoneton office. To serve them, a boardinghouse owner rebuilt his place as a thirty-two-room hotel. In the Grange hall, Sidney Eidemiller opened a grocery and general store. He benefited from the traffic on Route 40, which was busy in those pre-interstate years.

Bell benefited from its excellent long-distance network, which automatically became available to any of Bell's local subscribers. This forced the independents to remain local telephone companies. In the early twentieth century, AT&T, operating under the leadership of an Ohio native named Theodore Newton Vail, started buying out many local phone companies. Until 1913, Vail refused to give locals access to AT&T's long-distance lines.

In the middle of this national fight, Phoneton continued to expand with its AT&T station. The town became the first in the area to receive electric lights. Twenty new houses were built, and residents took classes in current events and landscaping. And when the wire services ran lines into town, company officials boasted, "Practically all the news of the world hums over the wires which pass through the Phoneton office." With access to the news wires, company employees got the news before anyone else in town. They knew who was getting elected, who had died, and who mattered that day, and they used their advance knowledge to impress the townspeople at the general store.

E. E. Aker, an AT&T worker, described the town this way: "The people take pride in their work and in their homes; know each other by their first names and know all the children's names; help each other clean the carbon and grind the valves. . . . The weather isn't greatly different from any other place—it is cold in winter and hot in summer, but Phoneton is home for us all, and I guess that's why we like it."

Mauveta Adams can see development coming. She first moved to Bethel Township in 1949, when it was mostly rural. She can remember the time when she could sit on the front porch of her old frame home in Phoneton and "see practically no traffic at all coming and going on Route 202. And now," she said, pausing and shaking her head in disgust, "it never stops."

Adams believes it is her duty to save scraps of township history—old newspaper stories, books, and photocopies of old photographs. One of them shows Jackson's general store in Phoneton in 1907. A picture triggered a memory of a dangerous snowstorm that stranded a traveling Ohio State basketball team and a pregnant woman in Phoneton. The whole town turned out to help shovel the woman's car out of a long lane, and she got to a doctor in time to give birth.

"Those times—the good and bad—are forgotten now," Adams said. "Phoneton is changing. Years ago, my brother owned a filling station in town, and some little cabins. He invested in them. But Interstate 70 came along years later, and it took a lot of the traveling business off Route 40. He lost his money."

Local traffic converges near Adams's house, at the intersection of 202 and 40. There, on Phoneton's southwest corner, stands a forgotten monument to fading technology—a brick building, painted white and weathered, that once housed the state's first AT&T exchange station. Adams showed me a dark image of the building from 1929. Striped awnings covered windows on three floors. She said the business employed many townspeople and inspired Phoneton's interesting name, although these days only a few people—residents and visitors alike—know when this happened and why. Clutching their cellular telephones, they'll say they don't even know the meaning of the term "exchange station"—a bank, perhaps?

Gebhardt said Phoneton gets the most attention from historians because of its interesting past. "But it's so small that motorists hardly realize they've passed it," he said. "They say, 'Why do they call it Phoneton?'"

Linda Moroney isn't quite sure either, and she owns the old telephone exchange building. It's her big storage locker now. "When you say 'Phoneton,' people immediately ask, 'Did you say Phonetown?'" she said. "You say, 'No, it's called Phoneton.' They look at you blankly, and you explain that the community was named for the telephone. Then they ask you if a telephone company's there now. And you have to say, 'No. All gone.'"

Her father, Vernard Paul Gardner, bought the old phone company building in the 1970s to house his small overhead crane manufacturing business. When rain damaged an upstairs apartment in the building, he removed the upper two floors, leaving only one story and about 800 square feet. He would regret the decision, she said, "Years ago, my father did some research and tried to get the building listed on the National Register of Historic Places, but he couldn't. He had already taken off the top." The building is now used for storage. "It's a car magnet," she said. "Cars run into it and bounce off of it."

A century ago, the first floor housed the power plant and the men's restroom. On the second floor, an all-female traffic department operated the long-distance switchboard with eight line operators and a chief operator. That floor also housed the women's restroom and a lounge that served as a library with a collection of 100 books for ladies. Banks of telegraph equipment and telephone test boards took up the third floor.

Three of AT&T's main long-distance lines—12,000 miles of wire—met in Phoneton: Chicago to West Virginia, Pittsburgh to St. Louis, and Detroit to Cincinnati.

But it was Phoneton's more general duties that impressed telephone users. People asked operators the most mundane questions: How do you spell _____? What's the date? How high are the rivers rising?

It was during the 1913 Great Miami River flood, in fact, that Phoneton got the most attention. If not for the little town, Dayton would have been isolated from the world during that disaster when its AT&T lines were knocked down and the power went out. Through it all, dry Phoneton persevered, providing Dayton with contact with the outside world.

"Little Phoneton saved the day," Adams said. "Now who will save Phoneton?"

19

Freezing on the Underground

Hunted, with the bloodhounds baying,
  Rushing in our dreary track,
And no voice of mercy, staying
  Those who fly to bring us back.
    —"The Fugitive Slave's Request" (1855)

The male caller didn't bother to identify himself. He simply said, "Do you want to visit John Thomas Wilson's house?"

I recognized the voice as Stephen Kelley's. "Thanks, but I've seen it before," I told him.

"No," he said with a soft laugh. "I'm talking about his house in the middle of renovation, with secret rooms exposed and owners ready to talk about them."

"When can we go?" I asked.

"Tomorrow," he said. "Dress for this cold weather. If the wind's whipping the way it usually does on that hilltop, we could get pretty cold."

On this trip to Tranquility, I wanted to experience the Underground Railroad, the network of antislavery activists who helped runaway slaves escape to Canada. By experiencing it, I mean the weather, the land, the buildings, the people—everything. By the early 1800s, the Underground Railroad had become an organized response to slavery. Until the Civil War years, it operated in a number of states and in both city and country. I tried to follow its hidden tracks for personal satisfaction: I wanted to stand in buildings that once boiled with tension and that offered hope and saved the lives of thousands of people who undertook a dangerous journey to freedom.

Neither slaves nor abolitionists cared how the job was done as long as the slaves eluded bounty hunters and slave catchers. Some people went to extremes. One story tells of a Cincinnati woman who saved a young black girl by finding a fancy dress for herself and another for the girl. She shaped rags into doll-like forms and placed them under blankets inside a baby carriage. A lace bonnet covered the "baby's" face as the women pretended to be on a stroll—a wealthy white woman and her nurse. Slave catchers walked right past them, never knowing the truth. Finally, the woman and the girl reached the home of an abolitionist, who helped the girl escape.

In Tranquility, John T. Wilson welcomed escaped slaves coming from the Ohio River and sent them north to Locust Grove and Sinking Springs in Highland County. No record exists of Wilson ever admitting to harboring slaves, which was against the law, but historians believe he did—and for years. Few Underground Railroad activists in Ohio ever acknowledged their participation. Until recently, in fact, scholars could only assume that Wilson worked with the Underground because he held strong abolitionist positions, lived deep in the country (where he could have carried out such a mission more easily), and never tried to correct the record when people claimed he hid slaves.

Fortunately for Wilson, though, his conduct was overshadowed by the blatantly abolitionist acts of Ripley's John Rankin. Rankin arrived in Ripley in 1822 to run the local Presbyterian Church and another church on rural Straight Creek. A Presbyterian minister, he operated his brick house on the Underground Railroad for forty years, despite a $2,500 bounty placed on his head by southern slave owners. In 1828, he built his famous house on Liberty Hill. It is estimated that its lights guided 2,000 slaves to safety. He lodged them in the house, the barn, and any other place he could find. His wife and nine sons and four daughters helped.

To just as many people in the old tobacco town, his views must have been considered incendiary, for many residents had family in neighboring Kentucky, a slave-holding state. No matter. He pursued the course that he considered right. In 1835, he organized the Ohio Anti-Slavery Society and wrote on the subject and lectured throughout southern Ohio. In 1845, Rankin founded the Free Presbyterian Church, which excluded slaveholders and actively opposed slavery. A sizable segment of Ripley's population must have appreciated him, for he lasted there until he retired from the church in 1866, a year after the Civil War ended.

In some ways, Wilson and Rankin are a study in opposites. Rankin is one of Ohio's most notable figures of the abolitionist movement; Wilson is one of the least recognized. An outspoken pastor from Tennessee, Rankin fathered thirteen children. He was not rich. Wilson, the quiet younger Buckeye State native, had only one son and a thriving business that made him Adams County's wealthiest man. Yet they shared a common, burning goal that bordered on the obsessive—the abolition of slavery.

"We keep coming back to Wilson's Ripley connections," Kelley said as we walked through the house. "Mostly they were financial connections, but with those came personal ones, I'm sure."

Perhaps the younger Wilson was inspired by Rankin's passion for freedom. No doubt Tranquility's first resident had heard the legend: Despite threats, Rankin and his wife, Mary Jean, once hid a dozen slaves in their small house—at one time. They also hid fugitives in haystacks, a barn, or in a neighbor's shed. Years later, Rankin's son, the Reverend S. G. W. Rankin, told a reporter that Harriet Beecher Stowe's Eliza character's walk across the icy Ohio River was true. Stowe had only added some dramatic effect to the story. He said Eliza traveled from rural Kentucky to Ripley three times over a period of years to escort her husband and children to freedom. He said his father helped the family escape. Eventually, they all settled in Canada.

I went to Ripley first, to climb the 100 steps that led to Rankin's story-and-a-half brick house. The solitude of Liberty Hill, with surrounding fields of tobacco and corn, is in stark contrast to busy Route 52 below. It was in this quiet atmosphere that Rankin toiled to end slavery. A century and a half has passed since then, but his reputation as a leader in the abolitionist movement lives on in the community of 3,500 people. I looked around the place and quickly realized why its position—on the Ohio River, and rural—made it a haven for runaways. "This house was an important part of the Underground Railroad," said Jane Zachman, a volunteer at the Rankin House, a state historic site. "There is a lot of feeling in this area for the house and for what it represents."

Rankin's abolitionist activities put him and his family in danger. Bounty hunters sometimes came to to his house with guns, looking for escaped slaves. That's one reason why Rankin left his home in the village and came to Liberty Hill, which was then about two miles from downtown Ripley. "It got too dangerous," Zachman told me. "Legend has it that he hung a lantern from his upstairs window at night for slaves to see from the other side of the river. He could see seven bends of the river from up here."

Stephen Kelley and I have a running joke that nowadays nearly every old building in Ohio has a supposed connection—no matter how tenuous—to the Underground Railroad. In truth, however, only a limited number of buildings are known stations used in the years before the Civil War. The Rankin home is one of them.

In Tranquility, we arrived at Wilson's house on a Sunday afternoon in December. A strong wind blew in my face. I wondered how so many poorly clad slaves ever survived the walk to this house in a time when the land and the weather were more treacherous. The radio weatherman had just reminded listeners that his prediction of fifteen degrees had already come true, with a wind-chill factor near zero. "There's no furnace in that house," Kelley warned as we walked toward it, wind in our faces. "Better grab your gloves."

In the early 1800s, Wilson's house must have been a surprising glimpse of settlement in an otherwise rugged landscape. The two-story brick house has a symmetrical east front with chimneys on the inside walls. A cellar, located under the east half of the building, is made of native rock and is accessible from the outside. It features a hidden stairway on the east side and false walls to create hidden spaces. Floor joists and rafters were cut by Wilson's own sawmill. Many of these hidden features were discovered in 2009, when the house was being renovated.

At the door, we met Ralph and Patricia Alexander of Batavia in Clermont County. They were standing in the front room with hammers in their hands. A fire burned in the stone fireplace. They've set out to remodel the 1830s house, using as few outside workers as possible to save money. The couple, who knew the magnitude of their task because they had restored houses before, began by stripping and polishing the oak and poplar floors and walnut window casings. "We had to stabilize the walls and fireplace by installing cables," Ralph said. "The brick walls were in decent shape; the bricks were fired on site. But we literally had to pull the house back together. It had been vacant for so many years that it was falling apart. Our next job is to install a geothermal heating system."

He paused, took a deep breath, and added: "We have to rebuild the fireplaces, mantels, and chimneys; rebuild the cellar; furnish the house in the 1840s period; raise the center corridor wall; sand and refinish all

The restored John T. Wilson house in Tranquility is now a bed and breakfast. (Photo by Randy McNutt)

Ralph and Patricia Alexander restored the John T. Wilson house in Tranquility as a bed and breakfast. (Photo by Randy McNutt)

floors; repair or replace all doors and interior ceilings and woodwork; install inside wall insulation and finishing; install underground electrical services and a septic tank. Whew!"

Patricia smiled slyly. "Oh, that should be fun."

He didn't mind her sarcasm, for he knew that she supported his plan to revive the fading piece of history. "After two of my former students told me about the old place, Patricia said, 'It would make a nice bed and breakfast.' Within two days, we had made our offer. That was in 2006. I must have driven past this place two hundred times in my younger years, and I never looked up here on the hill. We were lucky to get a federal grant to restore the house, but, until we actually finish the job, we won't see a penny. The interesting thing is, I came over here to Tranquility to buy a railroad caboose. I didn't like old houses. I didn't even know who John T. Wilson was. But suddenly I said to the real estate agent, 'How much do you want for this place?'" Ralph paused and smiled. "I believe something told me to do it. I'm being serious now. That something starts over in the cemetery [where Wilson's buried]."

Patricia also believes that something otherworldly drew them to the ramshackle house and its history. The house was a wreck. All but two windows were out. Ralph was lucky to find some old—but brittle—glass to replace them, thus qualifying for a historical restoration grant. She said finding information about Wilson's past was like hunting for architectural pieces for the house—hard to find but fascinating once discovered.

"Wilson was fifty years old when he joined the military," Stephen Kelley said. "He recruited men older than he was."

Ralph nodded. "Some were fifty, sixty years old—a lot of old Scotsmen. I can visualize Wilson and his group of fighters at Shiloh."

The former teacher has researched John T. Wilson's life so thoroughly that he feels that he knows him. Ralph gives detailed talks about the congressman to local groups. He said Wilson started his store in a log cabin that now stands against a side of the brick house. The 42-acre Wilson estate consisted of mostly woods. Between 1840 and 1844, Wilson built the brick house. As we walked around the main room on the first floor, Ralph explained that Wilson "was the richest man in Adams County, and he gave it all away. He paid off people's mortgages, helped colleges, and he helped the poor. He speculated on land, but he left money to the people."

His life seemed a sad story to me, despite his money. He married Hadassah G. Dryden in 1841, and the following year she gave birth to their only son, Spencer Wilson. On March 23, 1849, she died. Wilson sold his store in the 1850s; the new owner moved the business to another building in the Tranquility Valley. When the Civil War started in 1861, Wilson invested all his money in Union war bonds. His son died in the war on March 4, 1862. When he wasn't living in Washington or Columbus, he lived alone in the Tranquility house with the help of a housekeeper, Ellen Couser. He left her enough money to last her for her lifetime. She is buried with Wilson and his family.

"He created his own bank at Ripley in 1862," Ralph said. "It was the First National Bank—later renamed the Ripley National Bank. It exists today and was sold two or three years ago and operated under a new name."

Ralph tossed another log onto the fire. Sparks flew into the air. Then he walked over to the southwest wall on the first floor in the main room and, about three feet above the floor, pulled open a small, unnoticeable door. He peered into a dark, narrow space that led to a staircase leading to the second floor and said, "The last family to occupy this house left in 1962, and they didn't even know these stairs existed. Can you imagine a group of frightened slaves running down here from their upstairs hiding space and heading out the front door?"

He motioned for us to go up there to see the hiding place. First, we stopped in Wilson's bedroom, where Ralph exposed another hidden passageway that led to the attic above. We had to climb a ladder to get up there. Once we were all assembled in the attic, we stared toward the other end.

"This is where the slaves supposedly hid," Ralph said, squatting and running his fingers across some walnut, poplar, and white oak limbs that supported the roof. "This is where the slaves supposedly stayed." He smiled proudly. "Where can you find history like this? Just think, people actually stayed in here during their journey to freedom. You can imagine the stories that this space could tell. Of course, it was a very secret thing. People on the Underground Railroad went to great lengths to protect the slaves." He paused to glance around the room. "This is the last big thing of my life—the last thing I'll accomplish that really means something. It's something I care passionately about. Can you imagine those days? Every fireplace in the house roaring! Slaves in the attic! Wilson telling bounty hunters to get out of his house! The man had courage."

We walked downstairs and looked out the window. "There might have been an underground tunnel leading from the house," he said. "The bedrock would make a natural roof for any tunnel. I've heard tales of one from previous residents who claims they saw it filled in years ago. Such an escape route makes sense."

The Alexanders have no escape route from their venture. They've poured their money into the project with the hope that the history will appeal to travelers and people interested in the Civil War era. The couple plans to restore the house and open it as a bed and breakfast. "We won't make a fortune," Ralph said, "but we'll preserve history and allow people to see it up close. We'll make a mini-museum here on the Civil War, the Underground Railroad, and John T. Wilson's life. It was just one life, but it made a difference. He was a man of service and success. Without other men like him, the Union would have had a difficult time, and our nation's history might have changed."

20

Above the Fruited Bog

> Ohio's cranberry bogs link us to our past. They're living relics of the Ice Age, repositories of ancient pollens and boreal plants. Unfortunately, our cranberry bogs may not be around forever to appreciate.
> —*Ellen Gerl*

On the fringe of the Great Black Swamp in western Ohio, the pioneers found forests, wetlands, and fevers. Hardy English and German immigrants decided to drain the bogs, cut down the trees, and reclaim the land for farming. These days, trees stand in isolated clumps in Mercer County, looking as though some bored landscape architect decided to add them every few miles for effect.

Cranberry Prairie, a small community that lies one mile west of U.S Route 127, grew on the bogs. Every time I drive through the area, the town calls to me like a Siren. I drive over to see it. The place—the name—has fascinated me for years. I've watched it the way a child watches an ant farm. While visiting there one day in 2002, I saw something new—a state historical marker, one of those big bronze ones that look so impressive when seen from the car. I stopped to read it: "The Cranberry Prairie was created by centuries of peat accumulation in a late Ice Age lake that formed at the base of St. John's Moraine. Paleo-Indians or early archaic peoples probably killed the elk whose skeleton was dug up here in 1981. This elk was dated at approximately 7400 B.C."

To me, such a sign didn't seem to fit the community—a place so rural and agricultural that I've always imagined it to have no real history. After all, unincorporated Cranberry Prairie is a crossroads community with few buildings, people, and cars. It has managed to survive more than a century without much attention. Some people in Celina—the county seat, about eight miles to the north—haven't even heard of the place. "When we go into town," said Prairie native Frank Hemmelgarn, "and people ask us where we're from, most of us just say, 'Oh, we're from the central part of the county.' Then we'll add, 'By the way, you ever heard of a town called Cranberry Prairie?' The younger ones usually say no, because we're not on many maps."

Once, Ohio had many cranberry bogs; only a few of them have survived. Before statehood in 1803, 80,000 acres of peat bogs covered some of the land that would become Ohio. By the turn of the twenty-first century, however, only about 2 percent of Ohio's old peat bogs remained, mainly in the northeast, and their numbers were declining. The state's larger cranberry sites were the New Washington Bog in Crawford County and the Big Swamp in Licking County, east of Columbus. The nation's largest bogs produce edible cranberries in Wisconsin, Washington, Oregon, and a few other states. Ohio must remain content with boggy memories.

But a flicker of red remains at what Indians used to call the Big Swamp, where Cranberry Island—made of cranberries, not rooted in soil—floats off the north shore of Buckeye Lake. Settlers were afraid they'd sink into it, so they paid the Indians to harvest its cranberries. These days it is called the Cranberry Bog State Nature Preserve, where visitors—with a permit—can follow a wooden walkway around four cranberry meadows.

As the Ohio & Erie Canal was being built in the 1830s, workers dammed the Big Swamp area, resulting in the flooding of 4,300 acres for a canal feeder reservoir. In the process, the swamp's large bog mat sank—"except for a young, and thus particularly buoyant, fifty-five-acre section; it popped up like a cork," as feature writer Ellen Gerl put it.

The "island" has been floating ever since—and shrinking. In 1910, it was about 45 acres; by 1963, 20 acres. In earlier years, the force of lake wakes damaged the cranberry mat. It was dedicated as a state park in 1949, when it had more than 23 acres. When the site became a state nature preserve in 1973, Cranberry Island included only 19 acres. Since then, it has continued to decrease. As of this writing, it consists of about 10 acres, having declined over the years as the lake's alkaline oxygenated water has helped decompose the sphagnum moss. A state brochure says, "Just how much time the island has before it disappears is unknown."

In the days when Ohio's cranberries flourished, Native Americans harvested them to make dyes and calm upset stomachs. They mixed cranberries with maple syrup and sometimes added seeds and dried meat to create pemmican, which writer Gerl once described as "an early high-energy bar." She noted that Chief Pakimintzen of the Delawares served cranberries (*vaccinium macrocarpon*) at tribal dinners, as a peace offering. Impressed with the red berries, pioneers called them "craneberries," because their drooping white blossoms looked like cranes' beaks. Pioneers added sugar to the tart berries and made juices and jellies.

While other pioneer towns in Mercer County had promise and a feed mill, all Cranberry Prairie had going for it was that infernal muck. So when the erratic winds of commerce blew through the area in the mid-1800s, Cranberry Prairie didn't even notice. Its people were too busy trying to fashion homesteads out of the boggy soil to concern themselves with such arcane matters as business. Perhaps that's why banks and inns and the usual amenities of small-town Ohio never took root in their town. Cranberry Prairie was a place where only crops seemed to sprout. The soil on the west side of town consisted of the rich decay of the ages. For thousands of years, thick vegetation had grown and died until a 1,200-acre peat bog—the prairie part of Cranberry Prairie—remained.

A large settlement of mid-nineteenth-century German immigrants thought hard work could transform the swampy region into immaculate fields. By 1880, many of the once-busy towns of the county had already dwindled to obscurity, but Cranberry Prairie—always slow to start anything—kept on working at its own pace. Today, not much has changed. About 200 people, mainly descendants of the immigrants, are still locked in a perpetual motion of planting and harvesting on family farms.

The view and the hamlet remain uncluttered. About twenty-five houses cluster around the intersection of Cranberry Road and Recovery-Minster Road, with St. Francis Church, its rectory, and a couple of farm-related businesses in-between. Across the street, a former general store is now a center for migrant workers.

When Hemmelgarn's grandfather arrived from Germany about 1850, he immediately liked the quiet and the muddy topography. He was puzzled, however, by a crimson sea of wild cranberries that bloomed in the marshes. "Cranberries as far as you could see," Hemmelgarn said. "What a sight! Our people didn't believe they were edible, though, so they tore them out. Haven't had any cranberries here to this day. But the name stuck."

With prayers on their lips and pistols on their belts, the immigrants dug out the marshes. The work took years and ingenuity, and it was not done without sacrifice. Farmer Al Huwer said many men, including his uncle, reached down into the brush and came up screaming, rattlesnakes wrapped around their arms. "Not a pleasant way to die," he said. In time, the land was cleared. Farmers once burned batches of corn shocks and, to their amazement, saw the fire continue to smolder for years beneath the highly combustible peat bog.

Into this willful land came William Simison, a settler and hermit not known for his love of farming. He is discussed even to this day, a mystery to the people. They say he was afraid of neither man nor animal, and, considering that he lived alone in the prairie, they are probably correct. They like to tell their children of the time Simison borrowed a pair of pants because he had used his only pair to fill a crack in his log cabin to keep out wolves. To Hemmelgarn, Simison represented the wilderness, the roughness that was the early prairie.

"Old Bill had been in the army once, but he ran away," he said. "The army captured him and brought him to a point near the swamp on an express wagon, which was sort of a pickup with wagon wheels. But Bill was sly. He got loose and slipped out into the prairie. Well, nobody thought he'd survive out there. The army folks came to our house to ask where Bill was hiding, I'm told, but Grandpa refused to say anything. Bill lived the rest of his life out on the prairie. Now he's buried there."

With hard work, the settlers made the prairie into farmland. Obstinacy was as much their resource as flat land. Yet the land had only begun to show its potential. About 1906, a large supply of natural gas was discovered, and for a few years some fields near Cranberry Prairie helped fuel Dayton, Troy, Piqua, and other Ohio cities. But most farmers in Cranberry Prairie were too smart to lease their land for anything that did not grow.

The only thing they held more sacred than the land was the Roman Catholic Church. Sixty-five families organized St. Francis Parish in 1859; about the same number worship there today. Parish members are mostly German. They are new families with old names, displayed in large letters on shiny farm mailboxes: Huwer, Vonderharr, Langenkamp, Zahn.

As I drove around the outskirts of Cranberry Prairie, I saw a steeple on the horizon. I drove a mile west on Cranberry Road until I came to an old brick church. On the level terrain, the steeple glittered in the morning sun, like a little radio tower in the distance. The National Park

Service calls this area "the Land of the Cross-Tipped Churches" because so many small-town Catholic churches stand in the countryside. It's an achievement of German immigrants and Father Francis DeSales Brunner, a former Trappist monk and Benedictine who joined St. Gasper DeBufalo's Society of the Precious Blood and headed to Ohio.

In the mid-1800s, German immigrants arrived in northwest and west-central Ohio and bought land for farming. To meet their spiritual needs, the diocese in Cincinnati assigned Father Brunner to the area. At first, the farmers didn't appreciate his dedication to hard work and the word. But the Church appreciated his ability to speak German and cover wide stretches of territory. He could be harsh and demanding, but he was tireless.

Initial negative opinions did not deter Father Brunner's mission. He built a convent in a nearby community, St. John's Station, and called the order Maria Stein, in honor of the Benedictine Abbey in Switzerland. He set an impressive goal: build a church, school, convent, and rectory in every small town in west-central Ohio.

When he died in 1869, his dream was unrealized, but his followers continued the mission. St. John's Station, where the first church had been built, along with the convent, changed its name to Maria Stein. The local Catholics built thirty-four churches in the tradition of Father Brunner—all within a twenty-two-mile radius of the convent. The churches all have towering spires with crosses on top. They are in places named Montezuma, Coldwater, North Star, Russia, Houston, and New Breman.

In Cranberry Prairie, St. Francis Church and rectory still operates, even though the community has not grown much. I went there one day and found the front door unlocked. I walked into the empty sanctuary and found a dozen candles burning, radiating a peacefulness that I had not expected. The original church, now gone, was dedicated in 1860 to St. Francis Seraph, but its patron saint is Francis of Assisi. This brick church, with its tall spire, is the second church on the property, dedicated in 1906.

Just outside of town, the Stucke (pronounced *Stoo-key*) farmers, aided by their stubborn German blood, have taken an original sixty acres of prairie and expanded it to 1,400 acres of corn, beans, wheat, clover, and potatoes. Cranberry Prairie is a little gear in the big farm machine that helps feed the world, and Stucke Farms Inc. is a monument to perseverance. Henry Stucke founded it in 1934. Without a job, he bought a piece of undeveloped prairie and split the earth with a dream and a plow. When he died in 1968, the farm had established itself as one of the community's top producers.

"My Henry was a particular and intelligent man," Hilda Stucke said. "He built one of Ohio's top storage facilities. Our trucks are on the road seven days a week, shipping potatoes to Frito-Lay and other chip companies. But all this didn't grow up overnight. When Henry first bought a farm on the prairie, I couldn't believe it. I remember saying, 'What do you want with a water hole, Henry?'" Waving her hands over neat green rows of potatoes, she said, "See, we've got the prairie out there. That helps. But we just don't grow potatoes. We store them until they sweat. That's the secret to good taste."

A breeze blew gently on Hilda Stucke's face as she looked dreamily up Cranberry Road, toward John Huwer's farm and her past.

"Perfect," she whispered.

21

Camp Sherman of the Mounds

> Across southern Ohio, industrial and residential developments gobble up the giant earthworks, many of which stretch over hundreds of acres; mechanized plows pound surviving mounds into oblivion.
> —Heather Pringle, In Search of Ancient North America

At a highway rest stop one overcast September day, I met a man who was sowing tree seeds. In the last month, he said, he and other volunteers had sown an estimated 500,000 seeds in the fields and woods near Interstate 71. He hoped that 10 percent of them would grow. He said he continues to sow because he can leave something behind. He gave me a seed packet and a map of Native American towns. He didn't know I had been driving around Ohio in search of those missing towns and along the way finding forgotten places of all kinds.

In Ross County, I found Camp Sherman—a military ghost town that was built over ancient Hopewell mounds. The Hopewell were American Indians who lived 2,200–1,500 years ago. Many of their larger mounds were built near the present-day city of Chillicothe, Ohio's first capital in 1803. During World War I, the army built the massive training camp—a city unto itself—on land called Mound City, primarily a ceremonial center for the Indian dead. What an odd image it conjures up: all those citizen-soldiers marching past big mounds, watching silent movies in camp theaters in their spare time, and learning how to kill in a place where death was celebrated 2,000 years ago.

As America's participation in the war grew, Camp Sherman continued to expand over more mound tracts that were sold to the government. Many mounds were leveled, when necessary, but by then farmers had already plowed over dozens of others. With the war on, survival—not preservation—was the government's priority. Thanks to the efforts of Henry Shetrone and other members of the Ohio State Archaeological Society, the army agreed to stop destroying the Central Mound.

When Camp Sherman was razed in the early 1920s, it became a ghost town on top of a burial ground. Most of its 2,000 buildings were torn down before federal archaeologists started restoring the site, which is now a national park.

Perhaps the Hopewell would be pleased to learn that their handiwork has outlasted a U.S. Army base and two world wars.

When the pioneers arrived in the Ohio Country in the late 1700s, they saw hundreds of mounds and earth enclosure walls. (Ohio contains more of these mounds than any other state.) The Shawnee could offer no explanations. Many people concluded that the builders must have been a lost race that vanished before the Indians arrived. For the next seventy years, American scientists could not imagine any Indian people advanced enough to build the mounds. In the 1840s, Edwin Davis, a Chillicothe physician, and Ephraim Squier, a local newspaper editor, drew maps of the mounds and wrote about what had been found inside them. In 1848, the Smithsonian Institution published their work as *Ancient Monuments of the Mississippi Valley*.

I came to Chillicothe looking for both Camp Sherman and the mounds. I wondered whether the spirits of ancient Indians chase those of dead doughboys through the woods on moonlit nights. It was an unusual juxtaposition of times, places, and people.

Immediately I felt time passing more slowly here. You can almost sense that life is slowing down when you arrive in Chillicothe and see its historic architecture. But the real time lag hits when you arrive at Mound City. Although I read about the Indian lineage—ten centuries—on a sign near the park, I found the idea too incredible to comprehend. After all, the tribes explain the term "Native American." (When Stonehenge was being built, 2000–1,800 BC, Ohio's Hopewell were building their mounds.)

Eventually, the Hopewell absorbed the Adena, who farmed in Ohio, Indiana, Kentucky, Pennsylvania, and West Virginia. The Adena name, which is Greek, came from Ohio governor Thomas Worthington's

An early Indian mound in the park system at Chillicothe. (Photo by Randy McNutt)

Chillicothe estate, a rich mound site. The Adena came to Ohio about 800 BC, when Pharaohs controlled Egypt and Homer sang of the Trojan War. The Adena liked flat heads. They deformed their children's heads early by tying infants to boards so their skulls would grow high and flat in back. In time, the Adena civilization vanished, possibly merging with the mound-building Hopewell, whose legacy also remains in the earth and stone Fort Ancient in Warren County.

The Hopewell were a more advanced people who probably borrowed from the Adena culture. Some archaeologists wonder whether the Hopewell were a tribe or a culture, considering their vast religious and trading network. When they disappeared, about 600 AD, the less sophisticated Fort Ancients arrived. The Hopewell were named for Captain Mordecai Hopewell, on whose Ross County farm a large earthwork was excavated in 1891.

Starting as early as 300 BC, the Hopewell fashioned earspools, headdresses, breastplates, and ornaments from Lake Superior copper; developed more efficient agricultural techniques; established an elaborate social order; and mapped far-flung trade routes. They cremated high priests and officials, leaving with the ashes intricately carved stone ornaments, grizzly bear teeth from the Rockies, shells from the Gulf of Mexico, and quartz and mica from the Blue Ridge Mountains. In death, Hopewell art, craft, and religion glorified their Cult of the Dead. Priests operated charnel houses, where they dismembered heads, legs, and arms before burning the body parts in crematories and burying the ashes in pits or mounds. Before starting a mound, they placed their dead—usually tribe officers—in the center, lowered his lodge on top, and then set it afire. They covered ashes with dirt until the mound was finished. When burning wasn't required, they laid bodies in a fetal position because less dirt was needed to cover them.

The whole concept of mound building intrigued me. The Hopewell must have made the work a priority, for they had to remove thousands of basket loads of earth to build the mounds. "Every burial needed to be a public project," said Bill Kerrigan, of the Archaeology Conservancy. "How else could you get people to carry dirt—it's so heavy—to the mound?"

So much Indian history made me understand the brevity of our own nation's history. I wondered how the government could arbitrarily demolish such an important part of our past for something as temporary as an army training camp.

Camp Sherman—named for Ohio's other larger-than-life Civil War general, William Tecumseh Sherman of Lancaster—opened on September 7, 1917. During construction, a new building went up every twenty minutes. The army built a septic tank that measured 53 feet wide by 127 feet long by 10 feet deep and enclosed it with 13-inch concrete walls. At its peak, the $4 million camp held 60,000 soldiers (four divisions) and workers as well as 12,000 horses and mules. (In those days, even Ohio's medium-sized cities weren't that populous.) The camp operated its own railway system, multiple libraries, eleven YMCA buildings, a hospital campus consisting of fifty interconnected buildings, several movie theaters, a 3,500-seat YMCA auditorium, 2,000 barracks, a large Salvation Army building, a DAR lodge, music groups, worship places for nearly every religion and Christian denomination, and many post exchanges where soldiers could watch movies, see vaudeville plays, and buy candy. When the war ended in 1919, the government used the camp to help decommission the huge army.

The whole camp came to life for me when I stumbled on the Camp Sherman Room at the Ross County Heritage Center. Museum guide Lissa Wittrup volunteered to show me the exhibits, which included uniforms, German and American helmets, rare German paper sandbags (cloth was scarce), bayonets, and other historic items from the collection. As we browsed, she noted that 600 German prisoners of war were held at Camp Sherman. The survivors of a captured ship and a sunken submarine tended the camp's massive vegetable gardens.

"It was tedious work—boring," she explained. "Six months after the war ended, they were still being held. They saw no release coming. So they dug a tunnel and escaped. Two of them ended up in Baltimore, where they tried to get jobs but couldn't because of the language barrier. Lacking food and alternatives, they decided to return to Camp Sherman. When they arrived in Chillicothe, they asked a policeman to arrest them. He said, 'Sorry, fellows, but you're not in my jurisdiction. Besides, the war's over.'"

In the fall of 1918, the worldwide influenza epidemic struck the camp and Chillicothe. Headlines in the *Camp Sherman News* read: "Death Grip of Epidemic Broken, Following Toll of 483 Dead and 1438 Serious" and finally "Epidemic Claims 926 Here." To stop the spread of the so-called Spanish flu, camp officers ended all public meetings and ordered soldiers to gargle twice daily. They watered dirt roads to keep down the dust (which was believed to transmit the illness) and told soldiers to sleep with their faces away from one another. Floors were scrubbed with lye water daily, and beds and barracks were aired. As the number of dead soldiers and civilians mounted, undertakers from Chillicothe and other towns were unable to cope. So many soldiers died that the Majestic Theater and other buildings in town had to be used as makeshift morgues. (The alley behind the movie house is still nicknamed Blood Alley.) On their way to Chillicothe's railroad depot, army bands played while they marched behind wagons stacked with the dead bodies.

Soldiers who didn't contract the flu or pneumonia faced challenges of fate. One nineteen-year-old soldier took a walk and got lost just outside the base. He stopped at an inn and asked the owner how to get back to Camp Chase. The owner, who wanted to collect a $50 reward for turning in a deserter, suggested that the soldier stay the night and return to camp the next morning. He agreed. When they both arrived at the camp the next day, however, the owner claimed he had caught a deserter and was turning him in to camp authorities. He received the $50. Within hours, the soldier was executed by a firing squad. It was only later that the camp commander learned the truth.

Punishment for lesser offenses was also often swift and severe. For cursing at an officer, a private was sentenced to fifteen years of hard labor. Another private refused an order to report to the medical department for duty and was sentenced to twenty years of hard labor at Fort Leavenworth, Kansas. In contrast, a private who said he wanted to "fight for the Kaiser but . . . [not] for the United States," received a sentence of only five years at Leavenworth.

As I looked around at the exhibits, Wittrup recited the titles printed above each one: "Women in the Service," "Over There," "Making Doughboys," and "Great War Small Arms." She smiled proudly, knowing the effort that has been put into the room.

"The camp was a boon to the city's business," she said, pointing to a black-and-white photo of the city in 1918. "And the red-light district, down on Mulberry Street, boomed, too. For years it had been fading with the decline of the Ohio & Erie Canal. Then all those soldiers came into town."

As I started to walk to the other side of the room, she asked, "Would you like to see our silent movie? In 1918, the War Department produced this movie as a propaganda film for theaters." I stepped back to watch dark images of soldiers learning to shoot rifles, throw hand grenades, and march in rhythmic time. A screen title proclaimed: "No fear of Fritz Gas." Next, I watched a mortar crew load and fire thirty-five rounds a minute (and missing the national record by only two shots). The soldier who loaded the mortar appeared to be working in fast motion, but he was not. How did he manage to pull his hand away before the weapon discharged?

Stepping away from the screen, Wittrup said, "Over here you'll see some photographs taken at the camp's parade grounds. The one in the middle, taken in 1918, is the most fascinating. Twenty-one thousand soldiers posed for six hours to re-create the image of President Wilson's head. The photographer who took the picture built a tower so that he could shoot down on the men. You can see barracks in the top of the picture. His problem was perspective; he was shooting toward them. Some people say the picture looks like Wilson is made of flowers. The soldiers wore light and dark shirts for effect. I think the detail is amazing. Even the ear is realistic."

The photograph was a success in more ways than one. Shortly after the picture was taken, a Ross County deputy sheriff named George

Hamm studied it with a magnifying glass and found a man who had escaped from a prison in Michigan and whose "Wanted" poster hung in the sheriff's office. The photo's subject was also impressed, Wittrup said. "The photograph was so detailed that President Wilson requested one for himself."

At Hopewell Culture National Historic Park, three miles north of Chillicothe on State Route 104, I walked to the edge of a large grass-covered field. A park ranger told me that the information office and museum would close in an hour, but I was welcome to stay in the ceremonial center until dark. I decided to visit the small museum, and there I saw ancient artifacts that might as well have come from Mars—a clay pot reassembled from shards found in a local mound, a mound replica made of iron ore, crystal quartz arrowheads, and shell bead necklaces. Many of the pieces were made of materials found far from Chillicothe, including metals from the Great Lakes and shark teeth from the Atlantic.

I've seen mounds all over southern Ohio—Miamisburg, Newark, Adams County, to name a few. They all seem a little different. In the Ross County area, however, the mounds are more prevalent. "What's so spooky," according to archaeologist Mark Lynott, "is how many of these things existed at one time." Early researcher Caleb Atwater must have felt the same way when he arrived at some mounds to the east of Mound City in the early 1800s. He wrote, "What surprised me is the exact manner in which they had laid down their circle and square; so that after every effort, by the most careful survey, to detect some error in measurement, we found that it was impossible."

On the west side of the national park, I saw the gray and imposing Ross County Correctional Facility with its barbed-wire fences and, just to the south, the Chillicothe Correctional Institution. They looked like fortresses and carried a negative energy. The green patch of woods and grasses that is now the park is only a fraction of the size it was in the early 1800s.

Above me, dark clouds were overtaking the few blue patches. As thick white balls rolled across the gray sky overhead, a sudden and strong wind scattered brown leaves across the tops of twenty-three mounds of varying heights that are surrounded by a low earthen embankment. Mounds cover the remains of ceremonial buildings. The mounds were named for things found in each one—Mound of the Pipes, Death Mask

Mound, Elliptical Mound, Mound of the Pottery, and Mound of the Fossils. Most fascinating to me was the Death Mask Mound, once measured at 17.5 feet high and 90 feet in diameter. There, archaeologists discovered a sunken room with a crematory basin with thirteen burials. The Ohio State Museum "put together the fragments of one of the skulls and found that they were the upper part of a mask possibly worn by a shaman to personify Death." In the Mound of the Fossils, archaeologists found fragments of mastodon and mammoth tusks—burial offerings.

There was something meaningful in all of this—an odd conjunction of the ancient mounds, Camp Sherman and its prison successors, old Chillicothe and its pioneers, the faded canal, and the Scioto River. I realized that Mound City is a timeless place, the home of a hundred generations. I wondered why its people left, and when, and whether my own civilization's monuments will last 2,000 years. I tried to imagine the unusual ceremonies that were conducted here, those of the Adena, Hopewell, Fort Ancient, and Shawnee.

Now, the old tribes have scattered like the autumn leaves and subdivisions lurk only a few miles away. One day they will surround this ancient place, becoming extensions of the first Indian villages. Suburban golfers will putt atop unrecognizable history. In time, man's reservoirs will dry up and his highways will crumble. The few remaining remnants of Camp Sherman will deteriorate and crumble to dust.

Only the mounds will survive.

Ghost Town: The Naming of Ohio

> To discover our true address, we will have to stay off the interstates, avoid the friendly franchises, climb out of our cars, hunt up guides who have lived heedfully in place, and we will have to walk around with eyes and ears open to the neighborhood.
> —*Scott Russell Sanders*

Traveling the Ohio countryside for twenty years, interviewing and researching for my *Lost Ohio* books, I discovered many nearly forgotten ghost towns and neighborhoods that didn't deserve their own chapters. But their names and stories intrigued me, so I have included them here. I don't recommend that you visit them—most of them no longer exist—but collectively they tell one more story of Lost Ohio.

Afton

For various reasons, Afton and some other towns used pseudonyms. Many times the reason stemmed from wanting a post office but being denied the name because another town was already using it. Instead of changing the town's original name, residents simply applied for a post office under a new name. Years passed and the local post offices closed, but the towns still had their original names. Unincorporated Afton, on Old State Route 32 in Clermont County's Williamsburg Township, was named by Sarah Lytle, daughter of county founder William Lytle. Apparently she enjoyed a popular song of the 1850s, "Sweet Afton," and applied the name to the new town. Interestingly, in 1849 the town had a post office named California. Today, Afton is still not much of a community. The post office is gone, but nearby stands a former Ford parts plant, built in the early 1980s.

Arena

The momentum has finally stopped for Paulding County towns named Arena, Canal Port, Hipp's Lock, Smiley, Sophia, Sunnyside, and Timberville. Now they are nothing but forgotten names on old maps. These towns depended on the Miami & Erie Canal, the timber industry, or both. Timber was, in fact, what built the county. As late as 1880, thirty-four factories operated in Paulding County making staves for wooden barrels. At the time, timberland sold for $5 an acre, but then settlers arrived, systematically cut down the trees, and thus destroyed the county's financial base. When the trees were finally cleared, in about 1900, farming became feasible. During the timber boom years, 1840–1900, the county's population increased from 1,035 to 27,528, still an all-time high. From 1830 to about 1860, canal towns opened to accommodate the lumber towns. Workers loaded logs onto canal packets and sent them to Cincinnati and other port cities.

"When forestry was no longer a viable industry, and the canal business went under, people left the county to find other work," county commissioner Elaine Harp told me. "New Rochester, the biggest village in the county in the 1830s, used to be the county seat. When the village of Charloe took the seat in 1840 by offering a two-story courthouse, New Rochester started downhill. Both towns depended on the canal traffic. Now New Rochester is gone and Charloe is nearly gone. These towns were founded on businesses that declined. We had a lot of towns like them. My mother used to own eighty acres in a town called Holcombsville, but it disappeared when the Cincinnati Northern Railroad went out."

Buckingham

Buckingham had a royal name, but the place was anything but regal. The Perry County community was a Sunday Creek Coal Company town. Its men worked at Sunday Creek Mine 19. Originally a farm owned by Benjamin Sanders, Buckingham became a town in 1879 when Sanders and a partner decided to go into business. Coal was a booming industry then, so the entrepreneurs decided to build a town to accommodate the miners. It was only several years before the government opened a town post office, named Comley. When the Toledo & Ohio Central Railroad Company arrived in the county in the 1880s, Buckingham became another local coal town with access to faraway markets. Sanders also founded Hemlock, another mining town. Today, all that remains of Buckingham is a one-room schoolhouse. The town once stood on a site across from the football field at Miller High School.

The Bottoms

The Bottoms is a Cincinnati ghost neighborhood, a town within a town that peaked in the early 1900s with theaters, homes, businesses, and dreams. Today, only a historical plaque identifies the east-central downtown area as the Bottoms. Most people don't even know that it had a name; many of its old buildings have been torn down. Despite its downtown setting, the Bottoms today is a quiet place with apartment buildings, museums, and Lytle Park. Once, it was the home of Irish ward boss Mike Miller, who had direct connections to city hall. Roy Rogers was born and reared there. The neighborhood had three theaters—the Lyric, the Bijou, and the Star. An important neighborhood landmark, the American Book Company building, still stands, but much of the older architecture does not. In the heyday of the Bottoms, a life-size statue of Christopher Columbus stood at Sixth and Broadway.

Brimstone Corners

Too bad Brimstone Corners wasn't listed on the map next to a town named Fire. What a combination! As it was, Brimstone was part myth, part reality. Early travelers laughed at the name, and stories began to circulate about it. Most of the travelers came by stagecoach or the Ohio & Erie Canal, which ran through neighboring Canal Fulton. Some people claimed that Brimstone, in Stark County, was a part of Canal Fulton; others insisted that it was its own village. Located at the intersection of Routes 21 and 93, the town was a meeting place for farmers, canal deck hands, and miners. Native Burton P. Porter once wrote that the town's name came from the fact that liquor was sold on each of its four corners. On Saturday nights, he said, people gathered to watch "grudge fights" on the town square. Anyone could participate in the fisticuff festival, but most often fights were between men who carried grudges. In the mid-1800s, the town started to decline as a canal stop, and residents moved to Cleveland, Akron, Canton, and Massillon. By World War II, Brimstone Corners had become legend. As Porter wrote in 1942, "Today numerous great double-headers, mile-long coal trains, thunder their way northward through the quiet village to the industrial centers and Lake Erie ports." The day of the grudge match had passed.

Buckeye City

There is no better name for an Ohio town than Buckeye City. Unfortunately, the Knox County community didn't last. In 1880, insurance agent J. C. Tilton laid out the town and his hope for the future. Before long, a feed mill and a Brethren Church opened and people moved to town. In 1882, a post office opened. The economy prospered, and more than 200 homes were built. By the turn of the twentieth century and the arrival of the railroads, however, interest in Buckeye City had declined. The post office closed in 1924. Meanwhile, the community depot, named Danville, continued to grow, and it became the dominant area town. In 1928, Danville merged with Buckeye City, which lost its name and identity.

Cliptown

In Hamilton County's Colerain Township, Cliptown died by the late 1800s. But its legend lives. Cliptown was the home of several businesses. A brick school operated there from 1857 to the early 1900s, at Colerain and Miami River Roads, near the Venice Bridge. One graduate was Murat Halstead, who would become a nationally known newspaper editor and writer from Cincinnati. Officially, Cliptown was known as the Village of Colerain, but most people preferred the name Cliptown. It had several businesses—sawmills, woolen mills, grain mills, and others—powered by the Great Miami River. The name came from people referring to the mills' clips of wool.

Democracy

Once, Democracy thrived in Knox County's Pike Township. It grew in the early years of Ohio's life, and by 1834 it had established a post office. Surprisingly, Democracy didn't have many competitors for the patriotic name. There were Freedom and Union and all manner of others, but Democracy was an original. Its post office lasted until early 1924, when the town started to decline and the mail was sent to Mt. Vernon. Today, Democracy is a part of Amity. I drove through that town on State Route 3 one Sunday afternoon and didn't even know I'd passed through what was once Democracy.

Dreamsville

To soldiers during World War II, the train depot at Dennison, 80 miles south of Cleveland, was known as Dreamsville. The name caught on, and soon people were referring to the area as Dreamsville. The name originated with soldiers who thought they must be dreaming when their trains pulled up at the station. Regardless of the time of arrival, local women would be standing there wearing white dresses and holding trays of fruit, cookies, and sandwiches for soldiers. Usually, troop trains didn't stop while they were traveling to cities on the coasts, but they stopped at Dennison for fuel. When the Salvation Army opened a canteen in the depot, at least ten volunteers from the community served there twenty-four hours a day; 4,000 volunteers from eight counties helped distribute food. From 1942 to 1946, Dreamsville served 1.3 million soldiers, who consumed two million sandwiches, 1.3 million cups of coffee, and happily received 500,000 magazines. The women volunteers were called Dream Girls by the soldiers heading overseas. According to an old story, big band leader Glenn Miller was one of the soldiers who passed through town. Based on his experience, he composed "Dreamsville." These days, the depot is a museum, renovated by vocational students in the 1980s. Trains don't stop there anymore.

Equity

In the early 1830s, a group of economic and social reformers from Cincinnati, including Josiah Warren, purchased 400 acres in Tuscarawas County to start a communal town that allowed private ownership of property. Like others in this vein, the village was named Equity. Some new residents came from Spring Hill, another communal town. But in a short time the founders learned that the land was malarial, causing low fever, ague, and constant sickness. By then, a sawmill and several houses had been built. Residents decided not to invite more people to join them in the sick town. Within two years, they had moved away, leaving Equity abandoned. They lost their investments.

Fort Ancient

Most people know Fort Ancient as one of the better Indian mound sites in the nation, but it is also the name of a ghost town in Warren County's Washington Township that reached its peak in 1850–80, when Little Miami River floods and disease finally drove residents away. The town first started attracting people in the early 1820s, when Henry and Parthenia Evans Hizar bought the Crossed Keys Tavern, just across the Little Miami River from Fort Ancient. Pioneers moved near the inn, which was built about 1802.

The Crossed Keys was used as a Lebanon man's summer residence when *Cincinnati Enquirer* reporter Jim Rohrer discovered it in 1972. Built at a primary ford on the Little Miami River by former Revolutionary War captain Benjamin Rue, the tavern—called "the hotel" by locals—was a stop for stagecoaches if they were running late or in trouble. "The old stagecoach trail led by the tavern," Rohrer wrote, "and meandered up the steep hill that the state road now tumbles down." Local schoolboys used to go to the tavern to hear ghost stories told by an older inn resident. The building housed a large kitchen and tavern on the first floor, two sleeping rooms on the second, and a half-story dormitory on top. When Rohrer saw the tavern, its two-story barn was also in good condition. After the town was platted in 1849, Fort Ancient became the home of a railroad depot, a hotel, and a post office. In the late 1800s, archaeologists descended on the Fort Ancient area to examine the great mounds. Today, a park there celebrates the ancients with a Native American museum.

Fulton

Lewistown and several neighboring towns started growing on the Ohio River in the early 1800s. They united as the town of Fulton, a crescent-shaped village that bordered Cincinnati. Fulton was named for Robert Fulton, inventor of the steamboat. Its seal featured an escutcheon and the legend, "Town of Fulton, Hamilton County," and the figure of a steamship—Fulton's main product. By 1839, the town boasted 1,500–2,000 residents, many of whom had arrived in the last year. The town supported many small businesses, two schools, two major lumberyards that sold to Cincinnati and St. Louis, three steam sawmills, and four boatyards. A decade later, Fulton's businessmen were operating eight boat-building yards. Then, in 1847, the Cincinnati Marine Railway and Dock Company opened in Fulton. Its presence would change the way business was conducted in the town, for the big company drove away the competing boat builders. Built in Fulton were the *Natchez* (which in 1870 would race the *Robert E. Lee*), the *Mississippi, Missouri, Lady Gay, Queen City, Guiding Star,* and *Golden Rule*. Based at the foot of Litherbury Street, Cincinnati Marine accepted larger boats from the whole river system.

The *Cincinnati Enquirer* described the town in a 1968 Sunday magazine feature story: "This was still the golden day. By 1851 a businessman could say, 'we are not building and finishing as many steamboats as in former years.' The trade and its adjacent activities would continue, however, to be the mainstay of the Fulton area for the next half century." Fulton's end came on August 1, 1854, when its mayor recommended that the town council accept Cincinnati's offer of annexation. On January 1, 1855, Fulton became the Seventeenth Ward of Cincinnati. A century and a half later, few people know anything of Fulton.

Gandertown

In researching my book *Ghosts*, I tried to find Goose Haven in Morrow County and failed. So imagine my excitement when I stumbled on a proposed community named Gandertown near Butler County's Ross, Morgan, Reily, and Hanover townships. I imagine it would have been an interesting but awful place, with hundreds of geese squawking constantly and chasing small children around with their heads and beaks outstretched. An early historian wrote: "This village was never platted. It took the . . . [name] because, when the first citizens lived here, there were a great many geese raised, and it is said that, like Bunker Hill [another old town], a furious quarrel took place over some wild gander, who strayed from one farmhouse to the other and disturbed the docility of the average goose." Today, Auburn stands where Gandertown should have been.

Georgetown and Laura

Georgetown and Laura, two villages in western Miami County, were founded about 1840—Laura on hilly ground, Georgetown on flat. Laura had one school and two churches. "Although its population is superior to that of Georgetown's," a local historian wrote in 1880, "being some 200 residents, its trade is not as great. It, however, enjoys one great advantage or blessing not possessed by many villages. It has no liquor den, because the inhabitants will not tolerate one. The proximity of these to villages to Milton, and their want of a railroad, will necessarily prevent them from receiving that growth, which would follow were they more favorably situated." Today, Laura is a small community that pops up on Rand McNally maps. Georgetown does not.

Griffithsburg

In 1833, General James A. Griffith had an idea: create a town in a small, but growing, Cuyahoga County community called Pleasant Hill. Two miles southwest of Chagrin Falls, Griffithsburg promised growth and development, but that never happened. Most of the growth went to Solon, which had a rail connection. Griffithsburg, on the Chagrin River, did have a cheese factory and a post office. These days, however, most of the ghost town is in the Quarry Rock Picnic Area of the South Chagrin Reservation. The foundation of a storage barn was still there in the early 1990s. Visitors used it as a bench.

Jefferson

By 1883, Jefferson in Fairfield County was "a mere collection of houses" on the once-important military road to Virginia. Laid out before the War of 1812 by George Hoshor, Jefferson, named for the president, had sixty-four lots. It soon blossomed into a busy small town, with a hotel and other businesses, but the coming of the canals and later the railroads took away its business. Jefferson has fallen from the maps these days.

Manhattan Junction

Manhattan Junction sounds part urban, part rural, but really it was a small community that grew up in the late 1800s around a train station not far from Toledo, north of the Maumee River in Lucas County. By the early 1900s, the place was declining. Atlases didn't even list the population in 1895, although they did mention the town. This small place and its wooden, two-story train tower were owned by the Pennsylvania Railroad and operated by the Nickel Plate Railroad. Manhattan Junction was served by rail, of course, but it had neither a post office nor an express office. By the early 1980s, the weathered train tower was used only sporadically. It looked like something from a ghost town.

Mungen

This Wood County oil field town was surveyed in 1888 for merchant Philander McCrory, who was serving as postmaster. (Now there's a first name you don't see these days!) Just as Mungen started to boom, "the great fire of October 27, 1895" broke out. A historian once wrote that the blaze burned a strip nearly a mile wide, extending two miles northeast from Mungen. The loss was estimated at $150,000—a fortune in those days. The Sun Oil Company lost nine derricks, four tanks, and a boiler house. The Palmer Company lost twelve derricks, several tanks, and other property. The Ralf Brothers lost several derricks and buildings. When I went to Wood County some years ago, I couldn't find any trace of most of the local oil towns.

Outville

I found Outville while driving from Hamilton to Granville one summer afternoon. I saw a green sign with white letters that read, "Welcome . . . You're in Outville." This ghost town in Licking County's Harrison Township was named for its location, being "out there"—about three miles north of Kirkersville, population 349, in 1880. It was officially named Kirkersville Station, but the post office was called Outville. It grew in the 1880s and owed its existence to Kirkersville's need for a link to the railroad line.

The area around Kirkersville Station was once known for its big squirrel hunts. To protect their corn crop, farmers held massive annual hunts in which they divided into two groups and set out to kill as many squirrels as they could in one day. On a "good" day, farmers would kill thousands of squirrels. The men scalped the animals and stuck the tops of their little heads (and ears) into bags. At the end of the day, the

Above: A local man erected this sign in Outville to let people know that the community once existed in Licking County. (Photo by Randy McNutt)

Right: A red-and-white-checkered wall on a store in Outville in Licking County. (Photo by Randy McNutt)

farmers compared their killings. The team that killed the most squirrels was treated to dinner. The day ended in a "grand carouse, which was continued into the small hours of the night."

Pink and Polkadotte

The first time I saw Pink listed on an old Rand McNally map, I was intrigued. Tom Adkins, a genealogical researcher at the Portsmouth public library, said he had never heard of the place, but he wanted some time to inquire about the town. Later, he called and told me not to bother looking for Pink. "There's nothing there anyway," he said. "The town had a post office in 1890, but it closed in 1906. The place is no longer a community." Pink is listed on some county maps, as a dot on the far western side of Scioto County, at State Route 125 and Upper Twin Creek Road in Brush Creek Township. That dot will have to be enough for ghost town hunters. I haven't given up on learning how Pink was named, however.

When you drive deep into Ohio's Appalachia, in rural Lawrence County, you hear a different pronunciation. I passed a town named Polkadotte, but pronounced Pokey-Dot. It's one of a dozen ghost towns that died when the jobs left in the early part of the twentieth century. Polkadotte once had a broom factory, but now all it has is a couple of rusting cars and a mobile home. Too bad historians can't determine how the town was named. In its heyday in the 1890s, Polkadotte had an undertaker and a baloney factory. Then the post office left, and Polkadotte vanished as quickly as it had come to life. Too bad the two towns couldn't merge as Pink Polkadotte.

Renollet

On Palm Sunday, March 28, 1920, a tornado ripped through northwestern Ohio, destroying Renollet in Paulding County and killing five people. From there, the storm roared over to Brunersburg in Defiance County, leveling many buildings and knocking down the Brunersburg Bridge, reportedly one of the world's larger single spans of the early twentieth century. "Brunersburg was once a big town—bigger than its neighbor, Defiance," researcher Richard Helwig told me in 1995, "but now it's just a bedroom community and a good example of a town that has almost lost its identity. After the tornado, it couldn't seem to pick itself back up and get on with life. On the same afternoon, the tornado ravaged the town of Gerald and parts of Swanton and, finally, Raab's Corners. In all, the tornado killed twenty people, injured hundreds, and caused millions of dollars in damage." Renollet and Raab never did come back. Today, you wouldn't even know some of the towns existed unless you read about them; the tornado became nature's eraser. In the *Fort Wayne News-Sentinel* the next day, a headline read: "Six Are Dead at Renollet: Town Eight Miles West of Defiance Is Wiped Out of Existence." The newspaper reported that "the twister came from the southwest, apparently from the direction of Indiana. . . . Practically every house was leveled to the ground."

Shattersburg

Shattersburg is one of the more interesting town names that I ran across during my travels. I went looking for it, but I couldn't find it. That's because it is now the village of Mount Holly in Warren County's Wayne Township, on U.S. 42. This qualifies Shattersburg for ghost town status. I'm not sure how it got its name, or when. In 1833, a man named Jacob

Pearson laid the town out with twenty-five lots. By then it already was the home of the Black Bear Tavern. Twenty years later, the Pence House, another tavern, operated there. At some point people dropped the name Shattersburg and started calling the place Mount Holly.

Slabtown

In Wood County's Henry Township, a new hamlet was founded just before the turn of the twentieth century. Apparently the oil workers and other roughnecks who lived in the area didn't have much time to ponder their new town's name. So they called it Slabtown. The name brings to mind a row of shotgun houses built on slabs. No wonder this place is nearly forgotten. Other towns in the township were Lawrence, a railroad station; Eberly, an oil town; Hammansburg, a sawmill and stave manufacturing town; and Denver, another oil town. All are ghost towns now and listed on a map of the Wood County oil field. But Slabtown is not. It is too obscure for obscurity.

Squeal

Although Ankeytown was named in honor of blacksmith George Ankey, the Knox County community started as a mill owned by Aaron Bull. As the town grew, it absorbed neighboring Shaler's Mill. A post office opened in town in 1848. In 1850, the town changed its name back to Shaler's Mills. From 1884 to 1938, the community was called Ankeytown. At its peak, it had a hotel, sawmill, school, and stores. Richard Helwig, an Ohio ghost town researcher, once wrote that the locals called their town Squeal because nineteenth-century locomotives squealed when they pulled into town. And Squeal became the dominant but unofficial name for years. Resident German immigrants were so upset with the noise that they ripped up parts of the railroad tracks to stop the trains. But the railroad won the war. The squealing continued.

Steam Corners

This Morrow County town was named for the steam-powered sawmill that operated nearby. For a brief time in the mid-1800s, Steam Corners grew, and by 1864 a post office opened. It closed the next year and then reopened in 1870, closing again in 1901. At its peak at the turn of the last century, Steam Corners had a general store, school, Methodist-Episcopal Church, baseball field, and recreation lake. In 1911, the population reached 100. In the years before World War I, however, the town died when its citizens lost interest in living there.

Transylvania

Transylvania took a small bite out of the stagecoach business in the early 1800s. Heading south out of Xenia, stagecoaches would stop at a tavern in Transylvania for supplies and continue on to Waynesville in Warren County. Some people believe that Transylvania became Spring Valley, a small town in Greene County, but others insist that Transylvania was only close to Spring Valley. Regardless, Transylvania is no more.

Bibliography

Abel, Mary Bilderback. "Ghostly Guests Linger at an Inn in Granville." *Columbus Dispatch Sunday Magazine,* June 24, 1979.

"Abraham Lincoln at Fort Laurens?" *Tree of Liberty* (Spring 1997).

Andrew, Roy. *A History of the Coal Mines of the United States.* Westport, CT: Greenwood Press, 1970.

Barmann, Floyd A., and J. Martin West. *St. Clair's Defeat.* Fort Recovery, OH: Fort Recovery Bicentennial Commission, 1991.

Bauer, Cheryl, and Rob Portman. *Wisdom's Paradise: The Forgotten Shakers of Union Village.* Wilmington, OH: Orange Frazer Press, 2004.

Bettmann, Otto. *The Good Old Days—They Were Terrible!* New York: Random House, 1974.

Blount, Jim. "Father, Son Among Fort Hamilton Soldiers." *Hamilton Journal-News,* May 5, 2004.

———. *Fort Hamilton Diary.* Shandon, OH: Books in Shandon, 2006.

Bradley, Eric. "Peters Cartridge Armed the Frontier." *Cincinnati Enquirer,* October 4, 2010.

Broadstone, M. A. *History of Green County, Ohio.* Indianapolis: B. F. Bowden, 1918.

Burress, Marjorie. *Whitewater, Ohio: Village of Shakers.* Cincinnati: Friends of White Water Shaker Village, 2003.

Cayton, Andrew R. L. *Ohio: The History of a People.* Columbus: Ohio State University Press, 2002.

Compton, Fred. *The Golden Lamb: Tales from the Innside.* Wilmington, OH: Orange Frazer Press, 2009.

Cranberry Bog State Nature Preserve. Columbus: Ohio Department of Natural Resources, n.d.

Denny, Ebeneezer. *Delaware and Shawnee Vocabularies.* N.p.: n.d.

"Dunlap Occupies Site of Village of Colerain." *Cincinnati Enquirer,* n.d.

Eckert, Allan W. *Blue Jacket: War Chief of the Shawnees*. Boston: Little, Brown, 1969.

Eilers, Richard G. "Resort Loses Its Attraction: Desolate Hotels Reflect Poor Health of Economy for Magnetic Springs." *Cleveland Plain Dealer*, November 3, 1976.

Elliot, Geneva, and Lowell M. Duffey. "Tranquility: Quiet, Calm, Undisturbed." *Ohio Southland*, Summer 1989.

Farkas, Karen. "Bustling Little Town Was Lost in Time." *Cleveland Plain Dealer*, August 16, 1992.

Frazier, Ida Hedrick. *Fort Recovery: A Historical Sketch Depicting Its Role in the History of the Old Northwest*. Columbus: Ohio State Archaeological and Historical Society, 1948.

Freeman, Douglas Southall. *Washington*. New York: Collier Books, 1998.

"Fulton." *Cincinnati Pictorial Enquirer*, February 18, 1968.

Gerl, Ellen. "Relishing the Cranberry." *Ohio Magazine*, December/January 1998.

Hagedorn, Ann. *Beyond the River: The Untold Story of the Heroes of the Underground Railroad*. New York: Simon & Schuster, 2002.

Hannah, James. "Helping Preserve Black History." *Cincinnati Post*, January 7, 2003.

Heiss, Willard. *Memoir of Esther Whinery Wattles*. Waynesville, OH: Mary L. Cook Public Library, 1995.

Helwig, Richard M., and Richard H. Helwig. *Ohio Ghost Towns No. 34, Morrow County*. Galena: Center for Ghost Town Research in Ohio, 1991.

———. *Ohio Ghost Towns No. 35, Knox County*. Sunbury: Center for Ghost Town Research in Ohio, 1995.

Herzog, Brad. *Small World: A Microcosmic Journey*. New York: Pocket Books, 2004. http:www.cliftonmill.com.

Hill, N. N. *A History of Licking County, Ohio*. Newark, OH: A. A. Graham, 1881.

History of Perry County, Ohio. Somerset: Perry County Historical Society, 1980.

"Home of Labor Movement Quiet on Workers' Day." *Cleveland Plain Dealer*, September 3, 1984.

Jackson, Helen. *A Century of Dishonor*. Boston: Roberts Brothers, 1885.

Jacobs, Charles M. *Wayne's Trace: Fort Deposit to Fort Industry*. Chicago: Arcadia, 2003.

John, Peter. "'Dark Error's Night Will Soon Be Gone!' Dynamics of Participation in New Harmony, 1824–1827." *Communal Studies* 28, no. 2 (2008).

Journal of Captain Daniel Bradley. Greenville, OH: Frank Jakes, 1935.

Kelley, Stephen. "The Haunting of the Wickerham Tavern." *Ohio Southland*, Winter 1992.

Kemme, Steve. "Volunteers Work to Restore White Water Shaker Village." *Cincinnati Enquirer*, May 16, 2010.

King, Rufus. *Ohio: First Fruits of the Ordinance of 1787.* Boston: Houghton, Mifflin, 1888.

Knepp, Gary L. *Freedom's Struggle: A Reponse to Slavery from the Ohio Borderlands.* Milford, OH: Little Miami, 2008.

Knopf, Richard C. *Indians of the Ohio Country.* Columbus: Modern Methods, 1959.

"Land of the Cross-Tipped Churches." www.Grandlake.net.

"Laurens Called 'Conservative Revolutionary.'" *Tree of Liberty* (Summer 2003).

"Longtime Church Bell Ringer Looking to Step Down." *Hamilton Journal-News,* June 25, 2003.

Madden, Lois. "From the Shaker Chair." *The HistoricaLog* (July–September 2010).

Magnetic Springs Centennial Cookbook, 1883–1983. Magnetic Springs, OH: SOS, 1983.

Martzolff, Clement L. *Fifty Stories from Ohio History.* Columbus: Ohio Teachers, 1918.

McBride, James. *Pioneer Biography: Sketches of the Lives of Some of the Early Settlers of Butler County, Ohio.* Cincinnati: Robert Clarke, 1869.

McNutt, Randy. "Kings Mills: Boom Ended with World War II." *Cincinnati Enquirer,* January 25, 1993.

———. "The Old Way Stagecoach Line Is New Attraction." *Cincinnati Enquirer,* August 5, 2000.

———. *Lost Ohio: More Travels into Haunted Landscapes, Ghost Towns, and Forgotten Places.* Kent, OH: Kent State University Press, 2006.

———. *Ghosts: Ohio's Haunted Landscapes, Lost Arts, and Forgotten Places.* Milford, OH: Little Miami, 2008.

McNutt, Randy, and Cheryl Bauer. *Ohio Civil War Tales.* Milford, OH: Little Miami, 2009.

"Moccasins, Muskets, and More." In *The Restoration of Fort Laurens.* Milford, OH: Friends of Fort Laurens, 1999.

Morris, James M. "Communes and Cooperatives: Cincinnati's Early Experiments in Social Reform." *Cincinnati Historical Society Bulletin* (Spring 1975).

Mound City Group. Reprint. Washington, DC: Government Printing Office, 1972.

Niquette, Mark. "Tiny Towns May Be an Endangered Species." *Bloomberg Businessweek,* June 2, 2011.

North Union Village: Summary of the 2000 Archaeology Survey. Shaker Heights, OH: City of Shaker Heights, 2000.

Oehler, Charles. *Turpin Indians.* Cincinnati: Cincinnati Museum of Natural History, 1973.

Ohio Underground Railroad Association. *Freedom Seekers: Ohio and the Underground Railroad.* Columbus: Friends of Freedom Press, 2004.

Pelzer, John, and Linda Pelzer. "Hijack! Confederates on Lake Erie." *Civil War Times Illustrated*, September 1983.

"Perry County Widow Digs Crazy Cellar." *Cleveland Plain Dealer*, December 15, 1956.

Pieper, Thomas I., and James B. Gidney. *Fort Laurens, 1778–1779: The Revolutionary War in Ohio*. Kent, OH: Kent State University Press, 1976.

Pringle, Heather. *In Search of Ancient North America: An Archaeological Journey to Forgotten Cultures*. New York: John Wiley, 1996.

Rohr, Martha E. *Historical Sketch of Fort Recovery*. Fort Recovery, OH: Fort Recovery Historical Society, n.d.

Rohrer, Jim. "Stagecoach Stop Awaits Restoration." *Cincinnati Enquirer*, September 11, 1972.

Roosevelt, Theodore. *Anthony Wayne's Expedition into the Northwest*. Fort Wayne, IN: Public Library of Fort Wayne and Allen County, 1957.

Shooner, Greg. "Discover the Shaker Pottery Found at Union Village." *The HistoricaLog* (July–September, 2010).

Schiffer, Thomas D. *Peters and King: The Birth and Evolution of the Peters Cartridge Co. and the King Powder Co*. Iola, WI: Krause, 2002.

Scott, Linda. "Fort Ancient's History Recounted." *JournalNews*, September 13, 2010).

Seewer, John. "Depot Was 'Dreamsville' for Soldiers." Associated Press dispatch, June 3, 1994.

Shooner, Greg. "Discover the Shaker Pottery Found at Union Village." *The HistoricaLog* (July–September 2010).

Shriver, Phillip R. "Little Turtle and the Miami Nation." *Passport to History Series*. Book 1. Celina, OH: Mercer County Historical Society, 1989.

Simmons, David A. *The Forts of Anthony Wayne*. Fort Wayne, IN: Fort Wayne Historical Society, 1977.

Slocum, Charles Elihu. *The Ohio Country: Between the Years 1783 and 1815*. New York: G. P. Putnam's Sons, 1910.

Smith, Thomas H., ed. *An Ohio Reader: 1750 to the Civil War*. Grand Rapids, MI: William B. Eerdmans, 1975.

St. Clair's Defeat 1791. Fort Wayne, IN: Public Library of Fort Wayne and Allen County, 1954.

Stille, Samuel Harden. *Ohio Builds a Nation: A Memorial to the Pioneers and the Celebrated Sons of the "Buckeye" State*. New York: Arlendale Book House, 1939.

Tebbel, John, and Keith Jennison. *The American Indian Wars*. Edison, NJ: Castle Books, 2003.

Thay, Edrick. *Ghost Stories of Ohio*. Edmonton, Canada: Ghost House, 2001.

Thom, James Alexander. *Panther in the Sky*. New York: Ballantine Books, 1989.

Tribe, Ivan M. *Little Cities of Black Diamonds: Urban Development in the Hocking Coal Region, 1870–1900.* Athens, OH: Athens Ancestree, 1986.

———. *Sprinkled with Coal Dust: Life and Work in the Hocking Coal Region, 1870–1900.* Athens: Athens County Historical Society and Museum, 1989.

"Village Takes Steps to Dissolve: Magnetic Springs Can't Cure Its Woes." *Cincinnati Enquirer,* October 8, 2005.

Wells, Ruth. *Colerain Township Revisited.* Cincinnati: Privately published, 1994.

Wilcox, Frank. *Ohio Indian Trails.* Kent, OH: Kent State University Press, 1970.

Williams, Gary S. *The Forts of Ohio: A Guide to Military Stockades.* Caldwell, OH: Buckeye Book Press, 2003.

Winnenberg, John. *The Little Cities of Black Diamond of Southern Perry County, Ohio: The Story of Our Community.* Shawnee, OH: Sunday Creek, 1999.

Young, Calvin M. *Little Turtle: The Great Chief of the Miami Indian Nation.* Cincinnati: Privately published, 1917.

Zimcus, John J. "No Brandy or Parade for Charles Dickens." *Western Star,* May 8, 2002.

Index

1st American Regiment, 93, 94, 99
54th Massachusetts Regiment, 116–17

Abel, Mary Bilderback, 191
abolitionism, 129, 183, 210, 211, 212; and John Randolph, 119; and John Rankin, 211, 212; and John T. Wilson, 128–29, 211, 212; and Quakers, 111; and Ripley (Brown County), 113; and Robert Gould Shaw, 116; and Waynesville (Warren County), 183
Accommodation Line, 174, 181, 182
Adams, Mauveta, 207, 209
Adams County, 125, 126; Civil War and, 130, 131; Civil War veterans of, 132, 133; Confederates' raid through, 165; creation of wildlife preserve in, 124; freed slaves in, 112; historic inns of, 162, 163, 164, Underground Railroad in, 129; Zane's Trace and, 167
Adeyemon, Oloye, 114
African American ghost towns. *See* Gist Settlements; Payne's Crossing; Randolph Settlement
Afton (Clermont County), 232
Aker, E. E., 207
Albaugh, Noah, 206
Alexander, Patricia, 213, 214, 215
Alexander, Ralph, 213, 214, 215, 216
American Book Company, 234
American Federation of Labor, 58

American Notes (Dickens), 177
American Pad and Textile Company, 138
Ancient Monuments of the Mississippi Valley (Squier & Davis), 225
Andres, Adah, 181
Andres, Ed, 181
Andrews, Edward Deming, 37
Angfang, Peter, 143
Arena (Paulding County), 233
Argosy (ship), 131
Athens County, 56, 60
Auburn (Butler County), 238
Auglaize County, 118

Bailey, De-De, 176, 179, 180
Balch, Ensign William, 96
Baldwin, Sam, 129
Ballard Inn, 27, 33, 34
Battle of Bloody Run. *See* St. Clair's Defeat
Battle of Fort Donelson, 149
Battle of Fort Henry, 149
Battle of Fallen Timbers, 88, 89, 94
Battle of Fort Recovery, 89, 96
Battle of Tippecanoe, 89
Battle of the Wabash. *See* St. Clair's Defeat
Baughman, Robert, 25, 34
Beall, Captain John Yates, 155
Beecher, Henry Ward, 192
Believers. *See* Shakers

250

Bell, Aunt Ida, 120
Benton, U.S. Senator Thomas, 168
Berne, Joseph, 45
Bethany Hall (the Shaker Center House), 39, 40. *See also* Union Village (Warren County)
Bevis (Hamilton County), 170, 171
Bevis, Jesse, 170
Bhines, Ensign Maxwell, 96
Big Swamp, 219. *See also* Cranberry Bog State Nature Preserve
Black Hoof, 89
Blackstone, Benjamin, 129
Blue Jacket, 85, 88, 89
Blue Jacket: War Chief of the Shawnees (Eckert), 81
Bodman Road Settlement, 113
Boice, Martha, 42, 44
Bolender, Frannie, 124
Bolivar (Tuscarawas County), 100
Boone, Daniel, 104
Bottoms, the (Hamilton County), 234
Bounell, Ethel Houston "Bonnie" ("The Lady in Blue"), 191, 192, 193, 194, 195. *See also* ghosts
Bowman, Pam, 185, 186, 187
Boyd, Lieutenant Samuel, 96
Brake, Sherri, 145, 146, 147
Branshaw, Robert, 74, 75, 76, 80, 81
Brimstone Corners (Stark County), 234, 235
Brown, Mary Ann, 120
Brown County, 110, 111, 112, 113, 129, 161
Brunersburg (Defiance County), 242
Buckeye City (Knox County), 235
Buckeye Lake, 219
Buckingham (Perry County), 233, 234
Bull, Epaproditas, 150
Burbeck, Major Henry, 87
Burnside, General Ambrose, 178; and General Order No. 38, 155
Bush, David, 149
Butler, Captain Edward, 78
Butler, Major General Richard, 72, 73, 74, 78, 79, 80, 81, 82, 84, 86, 90, 96
Butler, Major Thomas, 78, 79
Butler County, 45, 85, 156, 178, 181
Buxton, Major Horton, 191, 192, 193, 194, 195. *See also* ghosts

Camp Chase (Columbus), 154, 228
Camp Sherman, 224, 225, 227, 228, 229, 231
Camp Sherman News, 228
Canal Fulton (Stark County), 234
Caniff, Milton, 140
Cannon, Edward, 129
Chagrin River, 239
Charloe (Paulding County), 233
Chidester, Samuel, 142
Chief Pakimintzen, 220
Chillicothe (Ross County), 162, 224, 225, 226, 228, 230, 231
Chippewa–Rogues' Hollow Nature Preserve and Historical Park, 141
Cincinnati Enquirer, 172, 202, 203, 237, 238
Cincinnati Gazette, 118
Cincinnati Marine Railway and Dock Company, 238
Cincinnati Phalanx, 13. *See also* Clermont Phalanx
Cincinnati Times-Star, 203
Civil War, 35, 43, 69, 109, 122, 125, 130, 131. *See also specific battles*
Clark County, 181
Clay, Henry, 117, 165, 168, 182
Clermont County, 12, 14, 22, 232
Clermont Phalanx, 13, 15, 16
Cliptown (Hamilton County), 235
Cockerill, Colonel Joseph, 130, 131, 133
Cockerill, John A., 133
Cole, Captain Charles H., 154
Colerain Turnpike, 172
Collier, Walter "Turp," 142
Columbiana County, 178
Columbus Dispatch, 191
Columbus Hotel, 27
Compton, Fred, 177
Confederates, 148, 149, 150, 152, 156, 165
Conrad Hotel and Sanitarium. *See under* Magnetic Springs (Union County)
Conrad, Jesse T., 27, 29, 30, 31, 32, 33
Conrad, J. F., 27
Continental Congress, 71, 101
Copperheads, 148, 154, 155, 156, 178
Corwin, Ichabod, 174
Coshocton Trail, 163
Cranberry Bog State Nature Preserve, 219
Cranberry Island, 219

Index   251

Cranberry Prairie, 218, 219, 220, 221, 222
Crawford, Richard, 22
Crawford, William, 104
Crawford County, 219
Crosby, Dr., 143
Crouder, Paul, 116
Cry Baby Bridges, 146
Cully, John, 190
Cummings, Charlie, 141
Cumming, Dr. F., 162–63

Dalton, Dennis, 181, 182, 184, 185, 186, 187
Danville (Knox County), 235
Day, Isaac, 122
Dayton and Lancaster Lines, 176
Delaware and Magnetic Springs Railway, 29
Democracy (Knox County), 235, 236
Dennison (Tuscarawas County), 236
Denny, Major Ebenezer, 76, 78, 81, 82, 92
DeSales, Father Francis, 222
Dickens, Charles, 162, 176, 177, 182
Donges, George, 156, 157
Dowdell, Timmy, 202
Doylestown News (newspaper), 142
Drake, Colonel, 78
Dreamsville (Tuscarawas County), 236
Dunbar, James, 164
Dunlap (Hamilton County), 170–73
Dunlavy, Francis, 41

E. L. McClain Manufacturing, 138
Eckert, Allan, 81, 89
Edgington, Ashael, 168, 169
Eidemiller, Sidney, 206
Elliot, Harry, 206
Ellis, William J., 130
Emlen Institute, 118
Equity (Tuscarawas County), 236, 237
Erie County, 112
Evans, Jack, 63
Excelsior (Clermont County), 17; flooding of, 18, 19. *See also* Utopia (Clermont County)
Ezekiel, Sir Moses, 152

Fincastle (Brown County), 111, 112, 113
Fisher, Scott, 104, 105
Fleming, Colonel William, 103

Fleming, John, 60, 61
Ford, Henry, 192
Fort Ancient (Warren County), 237
Fort Greene Ville, 87, 88
Fort Hamilton, 70, 73, 85
Fort Jefferson, 78, 80, 81, 86
Fort Laurens, 100, 101, 102, 103, 104, 105
Fort Recovery: battles at, 84, 88, 89, 95, 96, 97, 98; historic fort of, 87, 88, 89, 92, 93; memorial of, 95, 96, 97; State Memorial, 85, 92, 95, 96; village of, 84, 85, 87, 88, 90, 91, 92, 93, 95, 97, 98
Fort Washington, 70–74, 85
Fort Wayne, Indiana, 73
Fourier, Charles, 12, 13, 14
Fourierite Association of Clermont County, 13, 15
Freed Gist Slave Settlement Foundation, 114
Freese, Thomas, 195
Frey, Russell W., 142, 143, 145
Friends of White Water Shaker Village, 45
Fulton (Hamilton County), 237, 238
Fulton, Robert, 237, 238

Gales, Seth, 129
Gallipolis (Gallia County), 129
Gandertown (Butler County), 238
Gano, Captain John S., 85, 86
Gardner, Vernard Paul, 208
Gebhardt, Michael, 205, 208
Georgetown (Brown County), 113
Georgetown (Miami County), 239
Gerl, Ellen, 219–20
ghosts, 195; at the Buxton Inn, 189, 190, 191, 192–93, 194, 195; in Dunlap, 172, 173; at Fort Laurens, 100; at the Golden Lamb, 179, 180, 181, 182; at Johnson's Island, 151; at Rogues' Hollow, 144, 145, 146, 147; in Utopia (Clermont County), 22; in Waynesville (Warren County), 183, 184, 185, 186, 187; at Wickerham Inn, 166, 167, 168
Gibson, Lieutenant Colonel George, 76
Gillespie, Rebecca, 144
Gilmore, Helen, 116
Girty, Simon, 78, 104
Gist, Samuel, 110, 111, 112, 114
Gist Cemetery, 122

Gist Settlements, 110, 111, 112, 114, 121, 123
Golden Lamb: Tales from the Innside (Compton), 177
Good, Nelson, 122
Grand Lake St. Marys, 119
Granger, Orin, 190, 192
Grant, U. S., 178
Granville (Licking County), 188, 191, 194
Great Black Swamp, 218
Great Depression, 64
Great Miami River, 47, 72, 115; 1913 flood, 208, 209; and Fort Hamilton, 70, 73; towns and villages on, 48, 49, 50, 235
Great Serpent Mound, 126, 128
Greene County, 181
Greenfield (Highland County), 136, 137, 138, 139, 162
Griffith, General James A., 239
Griffithsburgh (Cuyahoga County), 239
Gwinnett, Button, 102

Hall, Anthony, 32
Halstead, Murat, 235
Hamilton (Butler County): neighborhood of Lindenwald, 2, 3, 6
Hamilton County, 181; Madisonville site, 50
Hamilton True Telegraph (newspaper), 156
Hanktown (Miami County), 119
Harmar, General Josiah, 72, 76
Harper, R. Kevin, 181, 183
Harris, F. R., 138
Harrison, William Henry, 85, 89, 90, 192
Hartman, Cindy, 53, 54
Hatfield, Pioneer, 143
Haymarket Riot, 58
Heighway, Samuel, 183
Heilman, James, 48, 49, 50, 51
Helwig, Richard, 242, 243
Herwick, Frank, 144
Highland County, 112, 134, 162, 211
Hill, N. N., Jr., 190

History of the Coal Miners of the United States, A, 56
History of Warren County, A, 41
Hocking County, 60, 109
Hodgdon, Quartermaster General Samuel, 71

Holloway, David, 182
Hopewell, Captain Mordecai, 226
Hopewell Culture National Historic Park, 230, 231
Hopewell mounds, 224, 225, 226, 227, 230, 231. *See also* Native Americans; Native American tribes
Horner, Mickey, 36, 37, 38, 39
Hornung, Vernon, 170, 172, 173
Hoshor, George, 239
Hughes, Arthur, 137
Humphrey, James P., 119
Hunt, Judge Samuel F., 133

Ibos, Robert, 149, 150
Incor Hotel, 33
Indians. *See* Native Americans; Native American tribes
Innis, Jim, 45
inns, historic: Bevis Hotel, 170, 171; Black Horse Tavern, 190; Bradford Hotel, 164; Bradley House, 174, 177; Buxton Inn, 188, 189, 190, 191, 192, 193, 194, 195; Central House, 178; Columbian House, 178; Crossed Keys Tavern, 237; Dilley House, 190; Glen Airy House, 172; Golden Lamb, 174, 175, 176, 178, 179, 180, 181, 193; Halfway House, 181, 182; Hammel House Inn, 184, 185, 186, 187; Holloway Tavern, 182; Horn's Hotel, 164; Kilpatrick Tavern, 165; Lebanon House, 174, 178; Madison House, 175; Malabar Inn, 177; the National Hotel, 181; the Old Worthington Inn, 177; the Red Brick Tavern, 176; the Rider Inn, 176; the Six Mile House, 172; the Stone House, 164; Symmes Tavern, 177; Travellers Rest, 162; Treber Inn, 168, 169; the Twenty-Mile House, 177; Wickerham Inn, 165, 166
Jackson, Andrew, 117, 162, 165, 168
Jackson, W. Sherman, 111
Jackson (African) Cemetery, 116, 121
Jefferson (Fairfield County), 239
Johnson, Earl, 112
Johnson, Leonard B., 150, 155
Johnson, Major General "Allegheny" Ed, 148
Johnson, Richard, 90

Johnson's Island: Confederate cemetery on, 152, 156; monument to Southern soldiers at, 153; Museum, 149; Pleasure Resort on, 151; Preservation Association of, 149, 156; prison on, 148, 149, 150, 151, 154, 155, 156, 157
Jones, Robert H., 176
Juneteenth, 110

Kekionga, 73
Kelley, Stephen, 163–66, 167–68, 169, 210, 212, 213
Kelleys Island, 155
Kenton, Simon, 104
Kerrigan, Bill, 227
Kindness, Thomas, 121
King, Joseph Warren, 199
King's Great Western Powder Company, 199, 202, 203
Kings Mills (Warren County), 199, 200, 202, 203, 204
Kings Station (Warren County), 199, 200, 201, 202
Kirker, George, 129
Kirkersville (Licking County), 240
Kitchell, Ashbel, 37
Knights of Labor, 55, 54, 56, 57, 58
Knights of Pythias, 58
Knowles, William, 115
Knox, Henry, 71, 72, 82
Knox County, 233, 235, 243
Kregenhofer, Peter, 156
Kuster, Gordon, Jr., 191

Lacyburg (Shelby County), 120
Lafayette (Allen County), 176
Lake County, 38
Lake Erie, 148, 149
LaMarr, Earl "Frenchy," 33
Laura (Miami County), 239
Laurens, Henry, 101, 102
Lebanon (Warren County), 174–78, 193, 201
Lee, Ann ("Mother Ann"), 36. See also Shakers
LeFevre, Helen, 95
Lick Fork, 164, 169
Licking County, 190, 219
Lilly, John, 60

Lincoln, Abraham, 120, 148, 178, 192
Lindenwald, 2, 3, 6
Linter, C. W., 142
Little Cities of Black Diamonds, 54
Little Cities of Black Diamonds (organization), 61
Little Cities of Black Diamonds (Tribe), 61
Little Cities of Black Diamonds: The Story of Our Community (Winnenberg), 56
Little Miami Railroad, 201
Little Miami River: floods of, 237; villages and towns on, 50, 183, 199
Little Turtle, Chief, 69, 74–77, 80, 85, 88, 89, 92, 93
Lockyear, Jesse, 116
Locust Grove (Highland County), 164, 165
Logan, Joe, 129
Logan County, 16
London, Judge D. C. W., 133
Lucas County, 88
Lytle, Sarah, 232
Lytle, William, 232

Macdonald, A. J., 14, 15
Mackey, Tammi, 101, 104
Madden, Lois, 40
Magnet, The (newspaper), 28
Magnetic Reporter (newspaper), 28
Magnetic Springs (Union County), 24, 25, 26, 30, 32; and Conrad Hotel and Sanitarium, 30, 33; decline of, 33; founding of, 27, 28; and Maple Dell, 27, 28; and Park Hotel, 27, 29, 32, 33; popularity of, 29; properties of the water in, 33; Sager Hotel, 29; treatment of, 31
Magnetic Springs Foundation, 33
Mahanes, Oren D., 134, 135
Manchester (Adams County), 164
Manhattan Junction (Lucas County), 239–40
Maple Dell. *See under* Magnetic Springs (Union County)
Marble Hall, 40
Marblehead (Ottawa County), 148, 149, 151
Maria Stein (Mercer County), 222
Marshall Town (Miami County), 119
McAndrew, Dr. William, 139

McBride, James, 86
McClain, Edward Lee, 136, 138, 139, 140
McClain, Lulu, 137, 140
McClain High School, 136, 137, 138, 139
McCreight, John, 128, 133
McCrory, Philander, 240
McCullough, Sanford A., 125
McDowell, Stephen, 202
McElwee, John, 148, 156, 157
McFerran, John W., 130
McGate, John, 164
McIntosh, General Lachlan, 101, 102, 103
McKeek, Alexander, 104
McKinley, William, 60–61, 178, 192
McKnight, Albert, 120
McMahon, Major, 97
McNemar, Richard, 37, 42
Meece, Pam, 20, 21–22
Mercer County, 69, 86, 118, 218, 220
Metz, Charles, 50
Miami County, 115, 119, 120, 205, 206
Miami and Erie Canal, 233
Miami Whitewater Forest park, 44
Miller, Mike, 234
Millfield (Athens County), 56
Molder, William G., 140
Montgomery County, 51
Mooskingum River. *See* Tuscarawas River
Morgan, Blinky, 145
Morgan's Raiders, 164, 165
Moroney, Linda, 208
Morrison, Delbert, 124, 125
Mound City, 224, 225, 230, 231
Mulford, Robert, 172
Mumler, William, 187
Mungen (Wood County), 240

National Register of Historic Places, 65, 121, 162, 168, 181, 201, 208
National Underground Railroad Freedom Center, 114
Native Americans: confederation of Native American tribes, 69, 72, 74, 81, 87, 88, 89; mounds of, 224, 225, 226, 227, 230, 231
Native American tribes: Adena, 225, 226, 231; Delaware, 87, 220; Fort Ancient, 49–50, 51, 226; Hopewell, 224, 225, 226, 227, 230, 231; Miami, 72, 73, 87, 88, 92; Ojibwa, 88; Ottawa, 88; Piankeshaw, 72; Potawatomi, 87; Shawnee, 72, 87, 89, 92, 168, 225, 231; Tuscarora, 101; Wea, 72
Nelsonville (Athens County), 60
New Bremen (Auglaize County), 118
New Harmony, Indiana, 12, 13, 15
New Rochester (Paulding County), 233
New Straitsville (Perry County), 60, 109
New Vienna (Highland County), 121
New Washington Bog, 219
Newhouse, John E., 26, 27, 28, 33
Nichols, Lewis, 120
North Union (Cuyahoga County), 35, 37, 38, 39. *See also* Shaker Heights (Cuyahoga County); Union Village (Warren County); White Water Village (Hamilton County)
Northwest Conspiracy, 154, 155
Northwest Territory, 71, 77, 82, 85, 90, 91, 94

O'Driscoll, Mary, 6
Ohio Anti-Slavery Society, 211
Ohio Country, 51, 71, 72, 93, 225
Ohio Department of Natural Resources, 134
Ohio Division of Wildlife, 134
Ohio & Erie Canal, 103, 219, 229, 234
Ohio Historical Society, 101
Ohio River, 11, 13, 70–72, 94, 129, 131, 164, 211, 212, 237
Ohio Stage Company, 175
Oneida, New York, 14
Orr, Audrey, 192, 193, 194
Orr, Orville, 190, 191, 192, 193, 194, 195
Outville (Licking County), 240, 241
Owen, Robert, 12, 15

Painesville (Lake County), 176
Park Hotel. *See under* Magnetic Springs (Union County)
Parrott, Bob, 26
Paulding County, 233
Payne's Cemetery, 109
Payne's Crossing, 109
Peaceful Revolutionist, The (Warren), 13

Index   255

Pearl, Harrison, 122
People's Advocate (Shawnee newspaper), 60, 64
Perry County, 53, 54, 57, 59, 60, 64, 109, 141
Peters, Gershon M., 199
Peters Cartridge Company, 199, 200, 201, 202, 203
Philo Parsons (ship), 154–55
Phoneton (Miami County), 205–9
Pierce, Charles, 150
Pierson, William, 152
Pink (Scioto County), 241
Piqua (Miami County), 115
Polkadotte (Lawrence County), 241–42
Portage County, 145
Portman, U.S. Senator Rob, 176
Portsmouth (Scioto County), 129
Powderly, Terrence, 57, 58
Prescott, Daniel, 15
Proctor, Joseph, 201
Pugh, Issac C., 131

Quakers, 111, 112, 183

Radcliffe, Dr. J., 13
Randolph, John, 110, 117, 118, 119, 121
Randolph plantation, 119
Randolph Settlement, 110, 115, 116, 117, 119, 120
Rankin, Reverend John, 113, 129, 211, 212
Rankin, Reverend S. G. W., 212
Rankin House, 212, 213
Rankins, Elizabeth, 120
Ravenna (Portage County), 145
Reagan, President Ronald, 121
Reily, John, 85
Renollet (Paulding County), 242
Revolutionary War, 101, 102, 104, 105
Rial, Jimmy "Jeems," 120
Rial, Thompson, 121
Rial, York, 121
Richmond, Assistant Adjutant General Lewis, 156
Riley, James Whitcomb, 192
Ripley, George, 12
Ripley (Brown County), 113, 129, 211, 212, 216

Rittman Press (newspaper), 142
Road to Health, The (Conrad), 30
Robinson, Sue, 27, 28
Rogers, Roy, 234
Rogues' Hollow (Wayne County), 141–47
Rogues' Hollow: History and Legends (Frey), 142
Rogues' Hollow Historical Society, 141, 142
Rohrer, Jim, 237
Ross County, 162, 224, 226, 229, 230
Rossville (Miami County), 115, 116, 119, 121
Rossville-Springcreek Historical Society, 116
Rue, Benjamin, 237
Rumley (Shelby County), 116
Russell, Ralph, 37

Sager, E. T., 29
Sager, Ora, 29
Sager Hotel. *See under* Magnetic Springs (Union County)
St. Clair, General Arthur, 72, 90, 97; army of, 70–74, 76, 78, 79, 81, 85, 95, 96; as governor of the Northwest Territory, 71, 72, 77, 82; as president of the Continental Congress, 71
St. Clair's Defeat, 69, 70, 71, 74, 75–82, 85, 86, 87, 89, 91, 94–98
St. Clair's Shame. *See* St. Clair's Defeat
St. John's Station. *See* Maria Stein (Mercer County)
Sample, George, 164
Sanders, Benjamin, 233, 234
Sandusky Bay, 148
Sargent, Winthrop, 71, 73, 76, 79
Satterthwaite, John, 181, 182
Save Our Springs Committee, 33
Scheider, David, 34
Schiffer, Thomas D., 200, 203
Scioto County, 129
Scioto River, 231
Scranton, S. S., 98
Shaker Heights (Cuyahoga County), 35, 36, 38, 39. *See also* North Union (Cuyahoga County)
Shaker Historical Society, 35

Shakers: architecture of, 39, 40; beliefs of, 36, 37, 38, 41, 42; decline of, 37, 38, 43, 45, 46; North Union Shakers, 35. *See also* North Union (Cuyahoga County); Union Village (Warren County); White Water Village (Hamilton County)
Share, Henry, 174
Shattersburg (Warren County), 242–43
Shaw, Robert Gould, 116
Shawnee (Perry County), 53, 54, 55, 56, 58, 59, 60, 61, 62, 63, 64, 65
Shelby County, 116, 119, 120
Sherman, William T., 131, 227, 228
Shetrone, Henry, 225
Shield's Hollow, 60
Sidney (Shelby County), 119, 120
Simison, William, 221
Sinking Springs (Highland County), 211
Slabtown (Wood County), 243
Sousa, John Philip, 192
Spence, Richard, 44, 45
Spring Valley (Greene County), 181, 244
Squeal (Knox County), 243
Steam Corners (Morrow County), 243–44
Stephens, Uriah S., 56
Stephenson, Jeremy, 19, 20, 21, 22
Stovall, Tina, 34
Stowe, Harriet Beecher, 192, 212
Strain, Dan, 137, 138, 140
Struble, George, 172
Stucke, Henry, 222, 223
Stucke, Hilda, 223
Sunday Creek Coal Company, 54, 233
SunWatch (Montgomery County), 47, 48, 49, 50–51
SunWatch Indian Village/Archaeological Park, 47, 48
Swaim, Dick, 200–202
Symmes, John Cleves, 183

Taylor, Major Richard, 104
Taylor, Zachary, 104
Tecumseh, 89, 90
Thom, James Alexander, 89, 90
Thompson, Jacob, 154
Tilton, J. C., 235
Toler, James Peter, 113
Tomb of the Unknown Soldier of the American Revolution, 103, 104, 105

Tranquility (Adams County), 126, 127, 210; and abolitionism, 130, 211, 212; cemetery of, 132, 133, 134; decline of, 125; and the John T. Wilson house, 214; naming of, 128; and the Underground Railroad, 125; as wildlife preserve, 124, 134
Transylvania (Greene County), 244
Treaty of Greenville, 84, 88, 89, 93
Treber, John, 168
Tribe, Ivan, 61, 62, 63
Trimble, Major General Isaac, 148
Troy (Miami County), 119
Turner, Henry, 122, 123
Turner, Paul, 122
Tuscarawas County, 15
Tuscarawas River, 100, 101
Twain, Mark, 176

Underground Railroad, 110, 211; and the Gist Settlements, 112; and the John Satterthwaite House, 182; and Ripley (Brown County), 113, 129; and Tranquility (Adams County), 125, 210, 212, 216, 217; and Utopia (Clermont County), 21–22; and Waynesville (Warren County), 183; and the Wickerham Inn, 165
Union County, 24
Union Village (Warren County), 36, 37, 40, 41, 42, 43, 44. *See also* North Union (Cuyahoga County); White Water Village (Hamilton County)
United Mine Workers, 58
United Society of Believers in Christ's Second Appearing, 36. *See also* Shakers
U.S. Colored Troops, 109, 116
USS *Michigan,* 154, 155
Utopia (Clermont County), 11, 12, 17, 22–23; established, 16; flooding of, 18, 19; ghosts in, 21–22; renamed as Excelsior, 17; underground church in, 20. *See also* Excelsior

Vail, Theodore Newton, 206
Vallandigham, Clement, 156, 178, 179, 180
Van Sweringen, Mantis James, 38, 39
Van Sweringen, Oris Paxton, 38, 39

Wabash River, 69, 73, 74, 80, 83, 84, 86, 95–96
Walsh, Mike, 143
Warner, Mary Lou, 40
Warner, Peggy Mills, 111, 112, 113, 114, 115
Warren, Josiah, 13, 14, 15, 16, 236
Warren, Lieutenant Winslow, 96
Warren County, 39, 142, 178, 181, 184, 199, 202, 226
Washington, George, 71, 72, 74, 81, 82, 86, 102
Wattles, Augustus, 118
Wattles, Esther (neé Whinery), 16, 17, 18
Wattles, John O., 16, 17, 18, 19, 22
Wayne, Anthony, 85, 86, 87, 88, 90, 92, 93, 94, 95
Wayne County, 141
Wayne National Forest, 61, 109
Waynesville (Warren County), 181, 182, 183, 184, 185, 187
Wells, William, 77
Werden, Colonel Billy, 181
West, Reverend Landon, 126
West Milton (Miami County), 119
West Union (Adams County), 126, 132, 164
Western Pioneer (newspaper), 164
Western Shaker Study Group, 40, 42, 43
Western Stage, 175

Western Star (newspaper), 177, 201
Wetzel, Lewis, 104
Whippoorwill Hollow (Perry County), 60
White, Shadrach Meshach Abed-nego ("Buddie Shang"), 120
White Water Village (Hamilton County), 44, 45. *See also* North Union (Cuyahoga County); Union Village (Warren County)
Wickerham, Peter, 129, 165, 166, 167
Wilkinson, General James, 85, 86
Wilcox, Frank, 85
Williams, W. D., 122
Willis, Governor Frank B., 105
Wilson, John Thomas, 126, 128, 130, 131–32, 134, 215; and abolitionism, 129, 211, 212; house of, 125, 129, 210, 213, 214, 215, 216; statue of, 133; tomb of, 133, 134
Wilson Soldiers Monument, 132
Winnenberg, John, 56
Worley, Malcomb, 36, 42
Worthington, Thomas, 225–26

Young, Katie, 147

Zane, Ebenezer, 163
Zane's Trace, 163, 164, 165, 168